POPULAR PARTICIPATION IN PLANNING FOR BASIC NEEDS

The World Employment Programme (WEP) was launched by the International Labour Organisation in 1969, as the ILO's main contribution to the International Development Strategy for the Second United Nations Development Decade.

The means of action adopted by the WEP have included the following:
- short-term high-level advisory missions;
- long-term national or regional employment teams; and
- a wide-ranging research programme.

Through these activities the ILO has been able to help national decision-makers to reshape their policies and plans with the aim of eradicating mass poverty and unemployment.

A landmark in the development of the WEP was the World Employment Conference of 1976, which proclaimed inter alia that 'strategies and national development plans should include as a priority objective the promotion of employment and the satisfaction of the basic needs of each country's population'. The Declaration of Principles and Programme of Action adopted by the Conference will remain the cornerstone of WEP technical assistance and research activities during the 1980s.

This publication is the outcome of a WEP project.

POPULAR PARTICIPATION IN PLANNING FOR BASIC NEEDS

Concepts, Methods and Practices

Edited by
Franklyn Lisk

A study prepared for the International Labour Office within the framework of the World Employment Programme

St. Martin's Press   New York

338.9
P831

Printed in Great Britain
First published in the United States of America in 1985.

The responsibility for opinions expressed in studies and other contributions rests solely with their authors, and publication does not constitute an endorsement by the International Labour Office of the opinions expressed in them.

The designations employed and the presentation of material does not imply the expression of any opinion whatsoever on the part of the International Labour Office concerning legal status of any country, area or territory or of its authorities, or concerning the delimitation of its frontiers.

87-2925

Library of Congress Cataloging-in-Publication Data
Main entry under title:

Popular participation in planning for basic needs.

    Includes Index.
    Contents: The role of participation in basic needs-oriented development planning / Frank Lisk — Popular participation in decision making with reference to development planning / Jean Majeres — Alternative forms and levels of popular participation / Arnold Hughes — (etc.)
    1. Basic needs — Developing countries — Planning — Citizen participation — Addresses, essays, lectures.
I. Lisk, Franklyn.
HC59.72.B38P66   1985   338.9'009172'4   85-18436
ISBN 0-312-63060-3

Contents

Preface

One of the key features of development planning that has emerged from the wider conceptualisation of development since the mid-1970s is the notion of *popular participation*, both as an important condition for achieving sustained economic growth and social progress and as a fundamental goal of development in its own right. According to this conceptualisation, popular participation is generally associated with the active involvement of the broad mass of the population, but especially hitherto disadvantaged groups, in the formulation, implementation and monitoring of policies, programmes and specific projects aimed at the attainment of clearly-defined objectives and targets of development.

With specific reference to ILO's concerns, effective broad-based participation in the development process is regarded as a prerequisite for the attainment of employment and income objectives in the context of strategies to reduce poverty and to bring about significant improvements in the conditions under which people live and work. In this connection, both the *Programme of Action* of the ILO World Employment Conference (1976) and the *Resolution Concerning the Follow-up of the World Employment Conference*, adopted by the International Labour Conference in 1979, were quite explicit in their recognition of popular participation as an important means of meeting basic needs. Similarly, various resolutions and declarations adopted in recent years by major conferences of the UN system and other agencies concerned with development have emphasised and reaffirmed the vital role of popular participation in the overall development process.

But, while there is universal agreement about the important role of popular participation in promoting economic development and social progress, the concept of people's participation in the development process lends itself to a plethora of definitions and interpretations which reflect the variety of participatory practices and experiences in the real world situation today. This is not surprising since differences in cultural and socio-economic settings, stages of development and political structures and styles are bound to influence both the degree and the nature of popular participation in the development process. Effective popular participation in development can be realised through a range of practices and institutional arrangements of both a formal and informal nature.

The purpose of this volume, which is a product of research undertaken within the framework of the ILO's World Employment Programme (WEP), is therefore modest. To begin with, it does not claim to cover anywhere near the entire range of participatory practices that today characterise the development process in the Third World societies. Nor is it intended primarily to assess and compare the various participatory experiences reported and analysed in the different cases studied from the standpoint of efficacy or with a view to identifying the most suitable practice or practices for attaining the objectives of basic needs-oriented development. The aim, instead, is to shed light on important conceptual and practical issues involved in translating the notion of popular participation in the development process into reality. This, it is hoped, would provide a better understanding of the positive linkages between participatory development and the objectives of employment promotion, poverty alleviation and basic needs satisfaction.

The focus of the present volume is limited essentially, though not exclusively, to the practice of participation as it is and can be pursued within the framework of the formal planning process. Without wishing to enter into controversial discussions concerning the aims and patterns of development, the analytical framework within which the various studies which make up this volume are presented is closely linked to the basic needs approach which was popularised by the World Employment Conference. The basic needs approach corresponds to a broader and more meaningful conceptualisation of development in terms of its emphasis on poverty alleviation and reduction in income and asset inequalities. It is precisely in this regard that the notion of popular participation takes on its full meaning, in terms of popular influence on decisions affecting human well-being and mass involvement in the mobilisation and channelling of resources into the production of needs-satisfying goods and services for the benefit of the vast majority of the population.

Given, on the one hand, the controversy that surrounds the concept and practice of participation in the development process, and, on the other hand, increasing recognition by planners and practitioners of the importance of participatory development for improving living standards, the present volume has been prepared in response to the need for information on the mechanics and critical issues involved in attempting to translate the notion of popular participation into reality. Through the exploration of conceptual issues and the examination of actual participatory practices from different socio-economic settings in Africa, Asia and Latin America, this volume provides useful insights into the vital role of popular participation in the development process, and, in particular, the important contribution that broad-based participation in decision making and planning at all levels can make to the fulfilment of basic needs-oriented objectives of development. More importantly, it examines how and under what conditions effective participation in development can be realised, what are the constraints, and what are the dangers to guard against.

J.P. Martin
Chief
Employment and Development Department
International Labour Organisation

Editor's Introduction

MAIN THEME AND FOCUS OF THE VOLUME

This volume brings together the findings of conceptual and investigative research on the role of popular participation in the development process, with special reference to the fulfilment of basic needs-oriented goals and objectives. The basic needs approach to development (BNA), as endorsed by the ILO World Employment Conference (Geneva, 1976), assigns a key role to popular participation as a means of action for meeting basic needs, in addition to being a fundamental goal of development in its own right. Of importance then for making operational the BNA are the ways and means of promoting and sustaining popular participation in the development process in general, and the mechanisms through which such participation can be made to have an impact on levels of basic needs satisfaction in particular.

The various studies which make up this volume seek, through different perspectives, to shed light on important conceptual and practical issues that underlie possibilities for (a) translating the notion of popular participation into reality and (b) making use of broad-based participation in development to achieve basic needs satisfaction especially among poorer groups in society. In essence, the volume addresses itself to the fundamental issue of how the participation of people in the making and implementation of key decisions which affect their livelihood can be realised in order to achieve significant improvements in human well-being.

1

The concept of participation is subject to numerous definitions and quite different arrangements may be adopted for making the concept operational within the context of the development process, making it impossible to cover the subject anywhere near adequately within the confines of a single volume. Examination of the role of popular participation in the development process in this volume is limited mainly to the contribution of broad-based participation in decision making to the satisfaction of basic needs. The operational framework within which this relationship is investigated and analysed has been restricted, more or less, to that of the *formal* planning process or system – which, admittedly, is not the only means through which development is or can be pursued. Furthermore, popular participation in the development process can be realised as effectively through informal arrangements outside the structure of formal planning. This, as such, raises the question of how relevant is the operational framework, within which the various studies in this volume are cast, for examining the relationship between popular participation and basic needs satisfaction.

The focus on the formal planning system to examine this relationship could, however, be defended at least on one important ground, especially from the standpoint of the purpose of this volume. In most developing countries the formal planning process is the main means through which key policy decisions about development and related programmes and projects are formulated and implemented. As a consequence, in terms of total expenditure on development programmes and projects that have potential impact on basic needs satisfaction by far the largest proportion is budgeted and spent within the context of the formal plan – be it at the national, regional, district or local level. Therefore, if popular participation in the development process is to make an impact on levels of basic needs satisfaction it should have links with the operational framework of the formal planning process. It is through popular influence on key decisions taken and implemented within this framework that popular participation could, perhaps, achieve its full potential as an agent of basic needs-oriented development.

In addition, from a practical point of view, the planning system in general is not exclusive of the activities of informal organisations. In the context of most developing countries it is hard to perceive the existence of a very rigid division between development activities undertaken within the state apparatus and those carried out outside it. Often there tend to be significant overlaps due to the dominating role of government on all matters of development even when planning, organisation and implementation of programmes are undertaken outside the state structures. On the other hand, certain forms of participation, though practised essentially outside the formal planning system, can have an impact on decision making within the formal planning process; this seems to be so for

2

informal self-help groups or movements which in certain developing countries have, through their activities, been able to influence official policy on local-level development. It should also be stressed that even when popular participation is practised through organisations and institutions within the formal planning system this often involves a dynamic process that transcends established organisational norms and rules, giving rise to the possibility of changes or modifications to the practice of participation along less formal lines or the creation of new and more appropriate organisations that may fall outside the state structures. For these reasons, our examination of popular participation in development with reference to the formal planning system is carried out in the context of an operational framework that takes into account the interaction between formal and informal participatory organisations and institutions.

ORGANISATION AND OUTLINE OF THE VOLUME

This volume is divided into three parts, roughly according to the types of issues and aspects of popular participation examined in relation to the main concern of the volume – i.e. the contribution of participation to basic needs satisfaction. Broadly speaking, Part I deals with relevant issues of definition, concept and typology; Part II looks at specific country experiences of efforts to incorporate popular participation in the making and implementation of decisions into the overall planning system; and finally Part III examines certain local-level experiences of attempts to translate the concept into practice, focusing on the participation of disadvantaged groups in concrete development programmes and projects as a means of improving their well-being.

The first three chapters, which constitute Part I, generally present and analyse the mechanics of different forms and levels of participation in the development process in relation to the fulfilment of basic needs-oriented goals and objectives. In Chapter 1 (Lisk) an attempt is made at an operational definition of the concept of participation in terms of how it can contribute to development goals and objectives. Four main directions are distinguished through which participation could facilitate basic needs-oriented development planning. These then may be regarded as yardsticks for assessing in a specific setting the effectiveness of different forms and levels of participation for meeting basic needs.

The next chapter (Majeres) is particularly relevant to the development planning focus of this volume, in so far as it draws attention to the importance of an appropriate institutional framework for ensuring broad-based participation in public decision making within the planning process. The guide-lines and general framework for institutional development, as presented and elaborated upon with illustrative examples, represent not only a firm basis for working out feasible arrangements to promote mass participation in development planning but also, and perhaps more importantly, provide some indications of how state institutions can be made more amenable to participatory or people-centred development strategies. In this latter context, this chapter sheds much light on the important and often controversial issue of the role of the state in local-level development planning by emphasising the need to build and maintain the right types of institutions in order to reduce conflicts in decision making between government and the people. The nature of the interaction between government and the people in development planning is particularly important in the context of the wider development process in terms of bringing about desirable structural changes in the socio-economic system as a whole.

Chapter 3 (Hughes) is a general survey of different forms and levels of participation that are relevant to the main theme of the volume. The scope of the survey clearly indicates the wide variety of interpretations and arrangements that are associated with the concept. Furthermore, the assessment of the different forms of participation in terms of actual and potential contribution to successful basic needs-oriented development planning strongly supports the view that the translation of the concept into practice in a meaningful way may not be dependent so much on any one pattern or style of development. Instead it depends on the existence of appropriate institutional arrangements and administrative structures within a given political and socio-economic context.

In common, the three case studies of national experiences of participatory development which are reviewed in Part II focus attention on institutions and administrative structures within the formal planning system in relation to their relevance for promoting popular participation in the development process. The analytical framework adopted in each case is more or less based on the definitions, concepts and typology explored in Part I, thereby providing a coherent approach for evaluating different types of participatory institutions, organisations and practices that characterise the systems or models examined. Taken together, the results of these three case studies offer an opportunity to identify strengths and weaknesses of quite different institutional arrangements and administrative structures for promoting popular participation in the development process, as well as more appropriate directions for policy and action programmes for meeting basic needs.

For example, the historical experience of China which is presented in Chapter 4 (Ng) illustrates the scope that exists for the coexistence of centralised and local-level decision making within the overall planning framework. While one should not ignore the somewhat special circumstance of the Chinese model – being that of a major change in political orientation and socio-economic organisation following the take-over by

4

the Communist regime – this chapter, nevertheless, holds important lessons for contemporary developing countries seeking to involve the broad mass of their population more meaningfully in the development process. In this regard an important lesson that emerges from the Chinese experience concerns the internal mobilisation of locally available human and material resources to implement development programmes that enhance basic needs satisfaction.

Chapter 5 (Freedman) looks at the more recent experience of the United Republic of Tanzania in the process of that country's transformation to socialism since independence. This case study is particularly useful for assessing the prospect for replicating the Chinese model, or important aspects of it, in the context of present-day developing countries. What comes out most strikingly from the Tanzanian case study is that endogenous factors such as level of economic development, social structures and people's attitude to externally imposed changes to their life styles may be more crucial to the successful implementation of participatory development strategies than the creation of centralised political institutions and decentralised administrative structures and production units based on the Chinese model.

Providing some contrast – particularly in terms of a different political framework – to the Tanzanian experiment is the Kenyan case study in Chapter 6 (Oyugi) which highlights the well-known government-sponsored *Harambee* (self-help) movement as a major feature of participatory development planning since independence. This study, which examines a wide variety of participatory organisations throughout the country, shows that conflicts, and hence setbacks, have appeared in the pursuit of participatory-oriented development mainly as a result of inconsistencies between the wider political system, on the one hand, and the administrative and institutional structures of the planning system on the other. Cast within a looser and more flexible framework of political decision making than the Tanzanian system, the modalities of popular participation are nevertheless based on fairly rigid administrative and institutional arrangements that effectively impede the decentralisation of planning responsibilities, decision making powers and resources to the local level – contrary to the declared policy of government.

In Part III attention is focused more narrowly on the practice of participation at the local or grass-roots level. The experiences presented and analysed do not fall exclusively within the state apparatus (although there are links with the formal planning system), but are related more to efforts by local people or disadvantaged groups to influence the pattern of development and the distribution of benefits therefrom in their favour through organisations of their own choice, be it with or without external support from the state or elsewhere. Here the emphasis is on how the concept is translated into reality in terms of achieving or ensuring popular involvement in the planning and implementation of concrete development programmes and projects with a view to raising the living standards of the 'participants'. The limelight is therefore on such groups as rural workers, peasants and women who as a result of greater awareness and consciousness about their disadvantaged situation vis-à-vis the rest of society, accordingly, take action to redress the balance. Their aim in general is to participate more effectively in the making and implementation of decisions that affect their well-being.

Chapter 7 (Huizer) reviews in historical perspective the varied experience of attempts by the peasantry in Latin America over the last half-century to organise its members for effective participation in their own development. The examples cited give much support to the protagonists of 'conflict resolution' type of development strategies in their claim that such strategies (which generally advocate major structural changes in the wider politico-socio-economic system) are a prerequisite for the promotion of genuine popular participation in the development process. The argument in this regard is that, given the existence of inequalities and distortions in the development process which inevitably contribute to conflicts between socio-economic groups and classes, participation of poorer and weaker groups cannot be realised without first resolving existing societal conflicts. In the absence of an appropriate conflict resolution strategy, the Latin American experience shows overall that the desire and demand for participation by disadvantaged and oppressed groups could unfortunately be expressed eventually in rather violent forms, especially when confronted with fierce opposition by the elites or privileged groups which dominate decision making.

While peasants and similarly disadvantaged groups have long been identified as targets for greater participation in the development process, the situation of women who in many cases have equally been excluded from effective participation in decision making has received little attention, at least until quite recently. In Chapter 8 (Croll), China is used as a case study to shed light on the problems and prospects of increasing the participation of women in the development process for the benefit of their sex in an often male-dominated society. The choice of China seems appropriate in this regard since the special problems of women were a major concern of the new regime soon after liberation – clearly putting the Chinese at least some two decades ahead of even most developed countries in terms of perceiving and defining a positive role for women in society. Yet it is clear from this study that even with official support for their cause, women in China had to struggle to overcome various discriminations based on traditional biases and prescriptive behavioural norms in order to defend their newly endowed rights which would give them equality with their menfolk. What the Chinese experience goes to show above all is that even with a favourable legal and institutional climate the full participation of women may not come about until women as a group first gain confidence in their own ability and effectively organise themselves to bring about desirable changes in attitudes both outside and within their own gender-specific groups.

Finally, in Chapter 9 (Alamgir) the role of popular participation in the development process is examined in the specific context of the planning and actual implementation of a communal self-help canal digging project in rural Bangladesh. The majority of the participants who provided labour as a vital resource input for the execution of the project was drawn from the poorer segments of the local population – landless labourers, casual workers and smallholders – who had in the past been excluded from participation in decision making pertaining to their well-being. As a consequence, they had benefited least from whatever development had taken place in the local community. This study, in a way, throws some light on the important question of whether or not the self-help approach to development holds out any promise as an alternative strategy for improving living conditions of such disadvantaged groups. The popular assumption is that the approach provides greater opportunity for broad-based participation in the decision-making process; yet the controversy that surrounds the notion of self-help development is derived mainly from scepticism about the extent to which the masses can actually influence key decisions concerning the choice, organisation and implementation of self-help projects. The Bangladesh experience clearly shows that without a significant degree of popular influence on decision making it becomes extremely difficult to motivate the poor to take an interest in such projects: indeed, this danger threatened the early phase of the project before changes were introduced in the organisational structure to allow for further decentralisation of decision making right down to the village level and, hence, closer to the people. The case study also highlights the important and often controversial issue of the distribution of benefits from self-help projects between different socio-economic groups in the community: as to be expected, it was observed that the poor and hitherto disadvantaged groups were motivated and willing to participate in this state-sponsored project only or mainly because they perceived certain tangible benefits from their involvement – access to land and some wage employment opportunities. Equally important in this respect was the 'formula' adopted for the distribution of work tasks among the different groups in the community which somehow took into account equity consideration by relating work load proportionately to expected benefits. Lastly, the study provides useful insights and relevant lessons about the nature and extent of state support for local self-help projects: the Bangladesh experience shows that by taking decisions in consultation with the local people the State can indeed play a positive role in local-level development, without jeopardising the fulfilment of genuine popular participation in the development process and the prospect for greater self-reliance.

SALIENT ISSUES FROM THE FINDINGS OF THE STUDIES

The Nature of Popular Participation in the Development Process

The nature of popular participation in the development process gives rise to much controversy regarding its definition and the modalities for giving it practical significance in relation to the fulfilment of basic needs-oriented goals and objectives. The various studies in this volume clearly show that the interpretation of popular participation in a practical context varies considerably from one country setting to another, and may even vary between different regions within the same national entity. Broadly speaking, it may range from the token involvement of people, indirectly, in the formal decision-making process to autonomous decision making by popular organisations at the local level. It can include co-operation between decision makers and those affected by their actions, without any formal surrender of power to participants, although these may be allowed to modify decisions in order to retain their co-operation. In another form, participation can concede to participants a share of formal power varying from the right to impose temporary or permanent vetoes, to rights to joint or sole decision making. Furthermore, effective participation may be obtained by negotiation between power-holders and representative groups within society. Because of these differences in interpretations and practices, the concept could, perhaps, best be examined in a location-specific context in relation to existing political and socio-economic structures as well as cultural characteristics, all of which combine to determine the nature and scope of participation as an agent of development.

The role of popular participation in the development process is closely related to possibilities for the broad mass of the population to influence decision making in favour of popular needs and aspirations. In terms of national development, such possibilities may contribute to the attainment of more balanced and equitable patterns of development, given the opportunities provided for a wide variety of interests to be reflected in public decision making. The underlying assumption is that popular influence on decision making would result in the adoption of development policy options and programmes that can bring about a fairer distribution of the benefits of development. Yet this assumption is valid only in a context wherein participation in decision making, as a basic need in its own right, is enjoyed as well by especially disadvantaged groups in society – i.e. those who hitherto have been bypassed by past development efforts precisely because of their non-participation or inadequate representation in decision-making bodies. This is the main criterion used to assess the effectiveness of popular participation in the development process in the various case studies examined in this volume. One general conclusion reached on the basis of the investigations undertaken, is the need for institutions within the planning system that make it possible for the poorer segments of the population to participate fully and effectively in the decision-making process at all levels. Only then can popular participation realise its full potential in terms of impact on development objectives oriented towards basic needs satisfaction.

Popular Participation and Development Planning

While today an often stated concern of development planning in the Third World is the participation of people in the decision-making process, in many cases the nature of popular participation in the planning process is generally limited in its jurisdictional scope and restricted in its application. As is evident from some of the studies in this volume, participation in development planning is being pursued through arrangements and modalities that are hardly consistent with the aim to achieve popular influence or control over the making and implementation of key decisions that affect the well-being of the majority of the population. The gulf that often exists between official statements of intent and what actually obtain in practice as regards broad-based participation in the planning process has been found to be related more to weaknesses in the institutional framework of administrative planning and the overall socio-economic structure than to conscious efforts by the authorities to exclude the majority from having a say in their own development.

Now that the focus of development planning in most Third World countries has shifted from purely growth objectives to more welfare-oriented goals and objectives, the absence of popular participation in the planning process can have more serious implications in terms of distorting planned development. If indeed development planning is to serve as a viable mechanism for attaining a fairer distribution of the benefits of development within the economy as a whole, thereby reducing poverty and meeting basic needs, it should be characterised by popular influence on decisions pertaining to the allocation of resources, the selection and prioritisation of development projects, the implementation and monitoring of such projects, and so on. Put in another way, popular participation in the formal planning process can play a vital role in achieving desirable redistribution of productive assets between socio-economic groups; shifts in investment resources between sectors and regions; efficient mobilisation and utilisation of local resources; and re-orientation of production towards needs-satisfying goods and services.

To give practical significance to the concept of popular participation in decision making as a fundamental aspect of development planning would, therefore, require changes in institutional arrangements within the planning system itself, in addition to certain structural changes in the overall socio-economic system as may be necessary on an individual country basis. This general conclusion is aptly supported by the findings of several of the studies in this volume. With reference to planning for basic needs satisfaction, it becomes clear from the investigations carried out that institutional and structural reforms should aim at creating conditions that facilitate the full integration of particularly disadvantaged groups – whose basic needs are far from being met – into the decision-making process mainly through equalisation of socio-economic opportunities.

Conditions for Promoting Popular Participation in the Development Process

By examining the role of popular participation in the development process through a wide variety of socio-economic and political contexts and administrative structures, as depicted by the various studies in this volume, it has been possible to draw conclusions that have wide applicability regarding the more important conditions that are necessary for promoting and sustaining effective popular participation in the development process. With reference to the formal planning system, these include the decentralisation of decision-making powers and resources to local-level planning authorities; the two-way flow of information between central and local-level authorities; adequate representation of diverse interests in local and higher-level decision-making bodies; and the creation of institutions amenable to broad-based participation in decision making.

However, it was found that the decentralisation of planning responsibilities to the local level by itself is not a sufficient condition to guarantee effective popular participation in the development process. This needs to be complemented by the existence of committed and capable leadership of popular organisations at the grass-roots level to ensure the effective mobilisation and efficient use of local resources for development purposes. Capable leadership at the local level is also necessary for the creation of consciousness among people about development problems and possibilities for improving their situation. This condition is not only important in terms of facilitating the participation of disadvantaged groups in the development process through their collective action and initiatives, but, perhaps more significantly, it provides the basis of a dynamic process aimed at the establishment of a more equitable and just society.

Another important condition that emerged from the various studies

10

relates to the need for consistency between the modalities adopted for promoting popular participation in the formal planning process and broad societal values of the potential participants in terms of existing socio-economic structures, deeply entrenched organisational norms, tradition and culture. The shortcomings of some of the experiences reported in the volume clearly suggest that problems, conflicts and disillusionment have arisen mainly as a result of insufficient awareness by the authorities of prevailing socio-cultural identities and values in a given context. Thus efforts to build and sustain participatory institutions or to decentralise decision-making powers to the local level end up being merely symbolic or even counterproductive because of incompatibility between the modalities adopted for promoting popular participation, on the one hand, and people's ties and commitments to long established values and traditions that affect their well-being. The important lesson in this connection is the need for an appropriate balance between desirable changes and people's own perceptions of needs in particular and overall development in general.

The need for self-reliance in local-level development was also found to be complementary to the promotion of popular participation. The adoption of more self-reliant attitudes in matters of development at the local level contributes to the creation of confidence among people in their own ability to take action in defence of their interests. This in turn puts them in a better position to influence public decision making in their favour. However, the relationship between self-reliance and popular participation tends to be often misunderstood. Within a national planning framework, or the development process itself for that matter, it is certainly misleading and even dangerous to conceptualise local self-reliance in terms of isolation from the mainstream of national development efforts. Recent experience from at least one of the countries investigated points to the danger that could emerge: central authorities might be inclined to neglect development needs in rural areas by evoking the doctrine of local self-reliance to justify lack of official attention and public resources as required for meeting basic needs and achieving a more balanced pattern of national development. The relationship between self-reliance and popular participation should in fact be seen as mutually reinforcing. While self-reliance implies greater initiative on the part of the people to mobilise local resources effectively for their own benefits, the prospects of this happening in many cases will depend, to some extent, on the provision of external support such as from the state apparatus.

In the case of self-help projects, it was observed that this support might be related to the need for requisite financial and technical assistance; but perhaps equally as important is the support that the state could give through the provision of the right type of political and institutional climate that will make it possible for local people to take initiatives on matters of

11

their own development without undue intervention or interference from outsiders. The view that state involvement in local-level development is not incompatible with the goal of self-reliance is supported by the findings of some of the country case studies. The extent of state involvement or any other form of external support should, however, be carefully monitored in order to avoid two sets of possible dangers: first, there is the possibility that such support could lead to the take-over of local development by outsiders whose interests might not coincide with those of local people; and secondly outside assistance provided over a long period of time and at a very high level of support could be detrimental to the goal of self-reliance in that it might stifle local initiatives and capacity to take and implement decisions on essentially local matters of development and human well-being.

Finally, the various studies collectively have contributed to a better understanding of the more common obstacles and constraints to the promotion of effective popular participation in the development process. The insights thus provided from investigation of a wide variety of experiences should be useful for identifying more appropriate directions for policy changes as well as institutional and structural reforms that may be required for making development planning more responsive and relevant to the felt needs and aspirations of the broad mass of the population.

PART I

DEFINITIONS, CONCEPTS AND TYPOLOGY

1 The Role of Popular Participation in Basic Needs-Oriented Development Planning*

Franklyn Lisk

POPULAR PARTICIPATION AND BASIC NEEDS SATISFACTION: DEFINITIONS AND CONCEPTS

A wide variety of interpretation is associated with the idea or concept of popular participation; therefore, it would be useful to attempt some relevant operational definition as the point of departure for this essay. Popular participation in development should be broadly understood as the active involvement of people in the making and implementation of decisions at all levels and forms of political and socio-economic activities. More specifically, in the context of the formal planning process, the concept relates to the involvement of the broad mass of the population in the choice, execution and evaluation of programmes and projects designed to bring about a significant upward movement in levels of living.

When planning is aimed at the attainment of basic needs-oriented goals and objectives, the concept of popular participation should be interpreted even more broadly with reference to the economic, social and cultural requirements of human well-being, as well as to certain concerns of an intangible nature that are nevertheless requisite to the satisfaction of basic needs. In this latter context, a wider interpretation of popular participation should include its contribution to the satisfaction of important non-material needs of human well-being such as equity, social justice, basic

* An earlier version of this paper was published in *Labour and Society* (Geneva, International Institute for Labour Studies), vol.6, no.1, Jan.-Mar. 1981, pp.3–14.

human rights and related freedoms. If participation is thus broadly defined, the application of the concept to an operational basic needs planning framework would have certain important implications.

First it implies popular influence on policy decisions pertaining to the allocation and utilisation of productive resources. A second inference concerns the need for popular involvement in the planning and implementation of activities that create socio-economic opportunities for raising productive employment and income levels and for enhancing human well-being. Third, there is also the implication that participation should serve as a means of improving access of the poor to key productive assets, on the one hand, and to essential public services and facilities, on the other. Collectively, these three goals of participation underline the relevance of the concept for meeting basic needs. However, from the point of view of the overall development process, the political dimension of popular participation is equally important for facilitating the attainment of socio-economic objectives. More specifically, popular participation in the political system may be necessary to bring about an adequate decentralisation of administrative powers and resources to the local level as required to ensure that popular decisions can be taken and acted upon by people themselves according to their felt needs and aspirations.

It is now, more or less, widely accepted that effective broad-based participation in decision making can best be realised when it is pursued within a socio-political climate that is favourably disposed to the idea of people freely organising themselves into action groups for the articulation of what they themselves perceive to be their fundamental needs and interests. Given initially the absence of such a climate, the concept may achieve practical significance through the recognition and resolution of societal conflicts and contradictions in ways consistent with the interests of the mass of the population. The critical point then will be that level of people's participation required to achieve popular influence over the making and implementation of key decisions. In the context of planning, the important decisions mainly concern policy formulation, the allocation of resources, project selection and implementation and the distribution of benefits. Therefore, unless people are involved in this decision-making process participation will not take on its full significance from a practical standpoint.

The concept of popular participation should also be defined in relation to the notion of *self-reliance*. This consideration is derived from the observation that in order to sustain broad-based local participation at a satisfactory level, a substantial degree of self-reliance must characterise the attitudes, aspirations and activities of those involved.[1] Self-reliance is, indeed, an important instrument for raising consciousness and increasing confidence of local people in their own ability to participate effectively in matters and activities relating to their own development. Self-reliance also supports the requirement that the desire to participate should ideally be voluntary and originate from people themselves. Again, from a practical point of view, this condition constitutes a safeguard against 'paternalistic' or 'authoritarian' forms of mass mobilisation or participation which may well work against the interests of the majority.

Nevertheless, there are instances when the initiation of action by the people themselves might require the assistance of 'outside' forces to stimulate the requisite levels of consciousness and awareness for taking action; this is particularly so in the case of especially disadvantaged groups who have hitherto been alienated from all forms of collective and public decision making of relevance to their well-being. Ideally, the role of an outside force in the process of mass mobilisation and organisation should be restricted to that of an 'enlightened catalyst', working in consultation with the people in defining their felt needs and formulating appropriate strategies and programmes for meeting these needs.

The *raison d'être* of broad-based participation in basic needs-oriented development planning stems largely from the belief that mass involvement in the development process is an effective means of mobilising and channelling available, and often underutilised, local resources into the production of needs-satisfying goods and services. In this regard, effective participation can best be achieved when people are motivated, and motivation itself is more likely to be created if people perceive and expect concrete benefits from their involvement in development. Indeed the inherent strength of effective participation is related to its potential to articulate the actual or felt needs of deprived groups in society and the motivation to satisfy those needs mainly through local initiatives and efforts. Hence, the relevance of popular participation for meeting basic needs is derived from its impact on economic and social conditions to bring about improvements in human well-being, in addition to the political dimension implicit in the need to provide more appropriate alternatives to existing forms of decision making. Popular participation is therefore an end goal of development as well as a means of attaining more equitable development.

The main purpose of this chapter is to explore ways and means through which popular participation can contribute to the satisfaction of basic needs. The formal planning system is taken as the basic framework for the analysis. This approach is adopted in view of the fact that in most developing countries today, policies and action programmes that are relevant to the achievement of economic development and social progress – i.e. in terms of impact on both individual and collective well-being – are usually embodied in the formal plan document. The *development plan* – whether national, regional or sectoral in coverage; short, medium or long-term in duration – has come to occupy a position of paramount importance in the development process, especially with reference to the making and implementation of decisions that are crucial to the attainment of a wide range of development objectives, be they growth, anti-poverty, welfare or basic needs-oriented. This is besides the question of whether or not the plan itself could be effectively implemented. Therefore, if people's participation is to play a vital role in the development process, through popular influence on key decisions, the locus of operation should be the planning system. Indeed, this is where the impact of popular participation on the pace and pattern of development is potentially greatest.

Before proceeding to show how popular participation can contribute to the successful implementation of a basic needs-oriented development strategy, it seems desirable first to sketch out an operational framework that may be regarded as appropriate to planning for basic needs fulfilment. In this context, attention is drawn to certain characteristics, or more precisely requirements, of popular participation that stand to give the concept practical significance within the framework of the formal planning system. The aim is to provide a useful background for understanding better the linkages between popular participation and the attainment of basic needs-oriented goals and objectives.

BASIC NEEDS SATISFACTION IN THE CONTEXT OF ECONOMY-WIDE PLANNING

Main Feature of an Operational Framework

By definition, planning for basic needs satisfaction involves the formulation and implementation of policies, programmes and projects that are aimed especially at the fulfilment of private (i.e. household) and essential public consumption requirements. Conceptually, the basic needs approach to development focuses sharply on human well-being in so far as its ultimate objective is to achieve significant improvements in levels of living, particularly with reference to disadvantaged and deprived households and socio-economic groups within a country's population. Furthermore, planning for basic needs satisfaction should be regarded as a continuous process of economic development and social progress, in view of the dynamic nature of the basic needs approach to development which aims at both absolute and relative improvement in standard of living.

From the foregoing, it is clear that basic needs-oriented planning calls for a broader operational framework than that required for, say, planning models that emphasise purely growth-related objectives. For example, a basic needs planning framework should not be concerned merely with monitoring changes in the rate of economic growth but should be broad enough to include parameters that relate as well to changes in the pattern and distribution of growth. Specifically, such a framework should stress changes in levels of living of individuals and households in different socio-economic situations, consequent upon shifts in consumption levels and effective demand, and changes in the structure of production and the pattern and distribution of needs-satisfying output.

As far as the satisfaction of private consumption basic needs is concerned, the planning framework should relate to such key deter-minants of economic well-being (at the household level) as ownership and control of productive assets and the levels of productive employment among different socio-economic groups – on the demand side, and the levels and distribution of basic needs output – on the supply side. With regard to the provision of essential public services, the planning framework should be concerned with the important issues of access and usage as they relate to different socio-economic groups and geographical locations within a country. Yet, the satisfaction of both private and public consumption needs of the mass of the population can hardly be accomplished at a satisfactory or tolerable level without the active involvement of the people in decision making at all levels. Planning decisions are often of a nature which affects the lives and well-being of people, individually and collectively. Therefore, popular participation has been identified as a major feature of the basic needs approach to development.[2]

Popular Participation as an Important Feature of Basic Needs-Oriented Planning

In several ways, as will be shown later, effective broad-based partici-pation in the development process, especially at the local level, can contribute to the attainment of employment and income objectives. In turn, this may serve to articulate and raise effective demand for basic needs goods and services as well as improve supply management with reference to the production and distribution of those goods and services. However, for this to happen, it may be necessary to decentralise the planning system to local levels.

Decentralised Planning

Clearly a strong case can be made for the decentralisation of planning in support of promoting popular participation and engendering broad-based interest in development efforts at the local level. In fact, the notion of 'decentralised participatory planning' is not new, as is evident from the planning system in a number of developing countries. Usually, this is made operational through organisational structures and institutional arrangements that allow for varying degrees of control over decision making and resources by local-level administrative bodies and popular organisations. As discussed elsewhere in this volume, variations of decentralised planning have been adopted in countries with different political systems as the United Republic of Tanzania and Kenya, and different levels of development as China and Bangladesh. Leaving aside ideological considerations which commit governments to a decentralised approach to planning, an underlying motive or reason for decentralisation common to radical and reformist regimes in the Third World is the realisation that the generation of poverty and inequality is, among other things, a function of the concentration of power and monopolisation of productive resources by the few who control decision making. Decentralisation of planning is therefore a prerequisite for effective popular participation if for no other reason but to meet the requirement of more equitable redistribution of decision-making powers and resources within society.

However, the issue of decentralisation is one that readily evokes the idea of a 'power struggle' between the *centre* and the *periphery*, and also one that is sometimes viewed with suspicion by central and higher-level authorities. Under what circumstances and to what extent will the central government introduce genuine decentralisation of planning and tolerate the establishment of effective participatory institutions and organisations which are intended to redistribute power and resources to the weaker and disadvantaged groups or communities in society?

Without wishing to play down the importance of political and related considerations involved in adopting a decentralised system of planning, it can be argued, on the basis of the experience of some countries, that decentralisation of economic and political power and resources is not incompatible with the principles and aims of comprehensive or economy-wide planning. Far from replacing comprehensive planning or competing for resources with national development programmes, decentralised participatory planning can complement and even increase the effectiveness of comprehensive planning. This is done through a more rational choice of sectoral and local projects and their judicious integration into national development programmes. Decentralisation of decision-making power and resources could in fact be a relatively efficient and economical way of actually promoting development at the local level, according to the felt needs and aspirations of the intended beneficiaries. Decentralisation of planning, it can then be argued, is a recognition of the need to define overall national policy and priorities in the interest of society as a whole; to reconcile diverse local interests; and to ensure some degree of equity in the distribution of benefits from development.

It is not possible to generalise about the conditions required to make operational the decentralisation of planning in similar systems let alone in the context of diverse systems globally. However, it may be stated, on the basis of the experience of the more successful attempts, that the nature and degree of decentralisation required for planning purposes should be determined through an objective assessment of local and national capacities and constraints in relation to desired goals and objectives of development.

The above condition has certain economic and political implications that are inherent in the operational definition of popular participation outlined in the preceding section. Viewed in terms of the distribution of economic power, decentralisation of planning is crucially concerned with the issue of ownership and control of key productive assets. In a decentralised system of planning, local-level participatory institutions and organisations should have influence over the allocation and use of productive resources in order to ensure that development efforts are directed towards satisfying the basic needs of 'participants'. How this is achieved will depend on the prevailing socio-political structure in a given context. Theoretically, the possibilities range from liberal through reformist to radical options. As regards the decentralisation of political power to the local level, this is inextricably linked with the role of the State in the development process. Here again, the ideological bias of the government as well as its political will or commitment to introduce appropriate changes and reforms will no doubt influence the extent and effectiveness of popular participation in decision making at the local level.

Popular Influence on Decision Making

Closely related to the requirement of decentralised planning is the need for popular influence on decision making pertaining to the planning of development and the distribution of benefits therefrom. As implied in the basic needs approach, the thrust of development efforts should be on meeting the consumption requirements of the population but especially disadvantaged and deprived socio-economic groups with the aim of reducing existing levels of poverty and inequality. The persistence of the twin problems of poverty and inequality in many developing countries today has been found to be strongly correlated with the virtual absence of low levels of effective mass participation in decision making within the development process.[3] As a result of lack of popular influence on decision making, the fuller utilisation of a country's physical and human resources may be stifled. In such a situation, the opportunities for the poor to find productive and adequately remunerative employment are severely curtailed. Low purchasing power or effective demand among the poor – who usually constitute the majority of consumers – is itself the result of lack of popular influence over the structure of production and the composition of output. The picture then is one of a distorted pattern of demand reinforcing a structure of production that is heavily biased in favour of the needs of the affluent few, as against the elemental needs of poorer segments of society. Furthermore, in such a situation, there is a strong tendency for production to shy away from the adoption of labour-intensive technologies and the mobilisation and utilisation of local resources which are nevertheless required for the rapid generation of productive employment opportunities and incomes. It becomes clear then that viable solutions may lie mainly in changes in the structure of the production system and in the pattern of effective demand. Popular influence over the allocation and utilisation of productive resources represents an important tool for bringing about requisite structural changes in support of employment and basic needs objectives.

From the foregoing analysis, it can be argued that broad-based participation, in particular – but not exclusively – at the local level, has an important role to play in the successful implementation of a basic needs strategy. The validity of this argument hinges mainly on the potential of popular participation to contribute both to the generation and articulation of effective demand for mass consumption goods and essential services on a sustainable basis and to the operation of an efficient system of supply-management (i.e. the production and delivery of basic needs goods and services).

POPULAR PARTICIPATION AND THE SUCCESSFUL IMPLEMENTATION OF A BASIC NEEDS STRATEGY

In this section an attempt is made to show how effective popular participation can contribute to the successful implementation of a basic needs strategy. Broadly speaking, one can distinguish four main directions through which broad-based participation in development can enhance the fulfilment of basic needs.[4] These are by:

1 playing a part in the definition of basic needs in a particular context;
2 enhancing the generation of resources required to achieve basic-needs output targets;
3 improving the distribution and access to essential goods and services; and
4 satisfying the psychological desire of people to influence decisions which affect their conditions of work and life.

The Definition or Identification of Basic Needs

One of the fundamental decisions involved in planning for basic needs satisfaction concerns the identification of desirable items of human needs

22

in a given context. In this regard, there are certain points that must be borne in mind from the onset. First, definitions of what constitutes basic needs are generally country specific; more precisely, core basic needs are likely to vary between regions or communities within the same country. Second, the composition of a recognised 'basket' of basic needs goods and services may change over time, reflecting, for example, changing levels of income and consumption preferences among and within households; thus current needs, if and when satisfied, may be replaced by higher order and even different types of needs. Sustained popular participation in decision making is therefore required to guarantee the permanent satisfaction of basic needs, even if and when the composition of output changes over time. The specifications of basic needs goods and services cannot therefore be carried out in isolation from normative value judgements.

Ideally, core basic needs must be endogenously determined through some process of collective decision making at the local level.[5] Put in another way, the definition of basic needs in a given context should be based on extensive familiarity with local conditions, which somehow implies the participation of intended beneficiaries in identifying their most fundamental needs. This is to ensure that, in a specific situation, a recognised set of basic needs targets is in line with what the people themselves perceive to be their felt needs.

Besides the need to reduce the scope for manipulation of consumption patterns and behaviour by both internal and outside forces and influences or powerful vested interests, experiences from a number of countries – some of which are recounted elsewhere in this volume – have shown that the involvement of people in the identification of local needs (for example communal projects) leads to a more rational choice between different alternatives. This can be achieved, for example, by consultation and candid dialogue between representative local-level bodies and higher-level decision-making authorities responsible for development planning. But as already noted, the existing institutional arrangements and administrative structures have to be amenable to the practice of popular participation in decision making. It is, perhaps, only in such a situation that different and often divergent interests can be satisfactorily reconciled.

Vertically, meaningful consultations between national, regional and local-level authorities would contribute much to the identification of the right type of local development projects as well as to their integration in a coherent manner into comprehensive planning. Horizontally, there is an acute need for communication between neighbouring communities as regards the identification of basic needs, particularly in cases where needs and interests might coincide. The importance of such a horizontal flow of information lies mainly in opportunities to co-ordinate development efforts with implications for saving of scarce development resources. In addition, this should also be seen as a means of fostering popular participation beyond the basic community level.

Mention has already been made of the importance of popular influence over the structure of production as a means of reorienting output towards the fundamental needs of the poor. This is particularly relevant in view of the possibility that the fulfilment of basic needs (at a satisfactory level and within a tolerable period) might well be determined, to a large extent, by the degree and extent of popular involvement in the making of decisions about the allocation and use of productive resources. From an institutional standpoint, popular influence over the making of decisions pertaining to the identification of basic needs (for example, the choice of infrastructural projects to be implemented in a particular locality) would require that organisations and bodies through which people participate in public decision making are truly representative of diverse local interests and that decisions taken adequately reflect the needs and priorities of the broad mass of the population. Here again one may recall the need to decentralise economic and political power and financial resources if, at all, participation is to be genuine and effective rather than merely symbolic. It is widely claimed that the Chinese system of collectivisation has been instrumental in improving the living standards of the rural population in that country mainly as a result of the partial decentralisation of decision-making power to local communes where broad-based local participation plays a role in the definition and satisfaction of communal needs.[6]

The Generation of Resources for Meeting Basic Needs

In many developing countries, the quantum of human and material resources required for meeting basic needs on a sustainable basis will be substantial and certainly in excess of current levels. Such a situation clearly points to the need to increase the mobilisation of locally available resources as well as for a more efficient use of those resources. The critical problem of resource constraint in relation to meeting basic needs can be minimised through the adoption of appropriate measures that seek to optimise the rates of accumulation of scarce capital and the use of underemployed labour as is typical of many developing countries. Popular participation in development can play a decisive role in generating internally some of the resources required to satisfy basic needs. For example, through people's participation in local development projects it should be possible to create capital out of otherwise underemployed and unutilised labour.

This is most evident in the context of the provision of essential public services and infrastructural facilities such as health, education, water supply and roads. In this connection, the mobilisation of local resources can be significantly enhanced by the adoption of 'self-help' and community development schemes that are operated on the basis of popular participation. In addition, self-help and community development projects provide the foundation for encouraging more self-reliant forms of local development, in the sense that they help to create confidence among people in their own ability to perceive their problems and accordingly to take appropriate action in terms of solutions.

Thus, local self-reliance implies that the people themselves, as a reaction to deprivation of certain felt needs, take the initiative to mobilise and channel local resources into activities that contribute to the satisfaction of those needs. In a manner, the mobilisation of human creativity is enhanced through popular participation in development. At the national level, the concept of collective self-reliance advocates increased mutual economic co-operation between developing countries, mainly by facilitating intra-regional trade (for example, in the framework of a regional common market), the exchange of technological information, and the development and sharing of certain common services like transportation where appropriate. According to the doctrine of collective self-reliance, neighbouring countries should co-ordinate production and distribution of essential goods, thereby minimising the wastage of scarce resources due to unnecessary and costly duplications of development efforts. Thus, through local and collective self-reliance, it should be possible for developing countries to increase substantially output of basic needs goods and services from their own resources.

The implementation of public works projects at the local level also offers much scope for realising the potential of popular participation with respect to efficient resource mobilisation. For example, the high level of local participation that characterised the ILO/World Bank Rural Access Roads Programme in Kenya is known to have been instrumental in contributing to savings in construction and maintenance costs as well as to higher implementation rates. The active involvement of the local population in all stages of individual road projects (from the choice of route to maintenance) somehow created a feeling of 'ownership' among local people, who, as a result, were willing in many cases to donate freely portions of their land for project roads. It was estimated at one time that the amount thus saved by voluntary renouncement of compensation for right of road was equivalent to the cost of constructing about 150 km of additional roads at 1976 prices.[7] Active local involvement in the planning and implementation of this particular programme has also been given some credit for the relatively high implementation rates that characterised many of the individual projects.[8] Through broad-based local participation in the programme, it was also possible to take advantage of local knowledge of participants about the economic realities and physical and social conditions pertaining to implementation, a factor which undoubtedly contributed to high levels of labour productivity. Perhaps most important in this Kenyan example is the fact that participation made it possible to ensure that the opportunities for employment provided by the roads programme benefited mainly the local unemployed and underemployed through the recruitment of on-site labour in consultation with local leaders. Further evidence of how popular participation in the implementation of public works projects has actually contributed to the mobilisation and efficient utilisation of resources for meeting basic needs is provided by the case study of a self-help canal-digging project in Bangladesh in this volume.[9]

Given the importance of land as a productive asset in most developing countries, popular participation can be and has in fact been crucial to the successful implementation of agrarian reform programmes designed to improve access of the poor to arable land. Elsewhere in this volume, examples from Latin America (particularly Mexico and Cuba) are provided which show conclusively that the organisation of peasants into participatory organisations has been instrumental to both the successful implementation of land reform programmes and the consolidation of ownership rights thereafter. It is also well known in the case of India that some peasant organisations have consolidated and secured their right to land through higher levels of income derived mainly from the establishment and running of co-operative ventures involving the sharing of farm equipment, labour inputs and managerial skills.

Improved Access and Efficient Distribution of Basic Needs Goods and Services

Popular influence over the allocation and use of productive resources may help to ensure that priority is given to the needs of the majority in the production system, yet this on its own is not sufficient to guarantee increase in the levels of real consumption by the household. It may further require the operation of an efficient distributive network for the purpose of ensuring *access* to basic needs in terms of both availability and user-cost. Broad-based local participation can play a decisive role in the organisation and operation of efficient 'delivery' systems.

As far as access to private consumption goods is concerned, the satisfaction of basic needs will be closely linked to the level of household income. In order to raise levels of household incomes of the poor for the purpose of satisfying basic needs, a satisfactory level of popular influence and control over ownership of productive assets will be required since it is the prevailing pattern of ownership of assets that, to a large extent, determines the overall distribution of income. Furthermore, given that the distribution of income influences the level and pattern of effective demand, the ownership of assets will also be relevant to changes in the

26

composition of output in the direction of mass consumption goods.

With regard to the provision of essential public services like education, health, sanitation and water supply, the problems of access relate more to availability, where and when required, than to income levels *per se*. The adequate provision of essential services does not depend only, or even mainly, on narrowly financial and economic considerations, but more on desirable changes in the way resources are allocated in relation to the production and delivery systems. In this regard, the involvement of popular organisations at the local level in the planning and operation of delivery systems has been identified as an effective mechanism for ensuring reasonable access of local people to health and other basic services.[10] The efficient management of services ministering to the needs of the poor requires ingenuity from the standpoint of adapting existing organisational structures to the demands of efficient delivery systems. One could, for example, use popular organisations such as producer co-operatives and peasant organisations as contact and delivery points for reaching especially deprived and disadvantaged groups.

Evidence exists to show that popular participation in the operation of delivery systems increases overall efficiency significantly. In the Ivory Coast, for example, the use of local community organisations as contact and delivery points for the provision of nutritional advisory services and medical facilities has led to a wider coverage among hitherto dis-advantaged groups. In Kenya, local *Harambee* self-help organisations are sometimes used by the authorities as important links with the villagers for the distribution of certain essential inputs and services such as fertilisers and health care facilities.

The need to build appropriate mechanisms into the planning system so as to ensure that the benefits of development reach the poor can hardly be over-emphasised. In order to satisfy the basic needs of the vast majority of a country's population within a reasonable time frame, the planning system must also include the means by which policies and programmes that are designed to benefit target poverty groups can be effectively implemented. Indeed, this has been a major weakness of some anti-poverty strategies in the sense that the bridge between production and consumption (i.e. the delivery system) has been left virtually unspecified in the context of planning. As a consequence, the effectiveness of even well-intentioned anti-poverty programmes can be substantially reduced: often, the benefits intended for the poor are 'hijacked' by the richer segments of society.

The related issues of distribution and access warrant special attention in the formulation and implementation of a basic needs strategy. Essentially, one should be concerned with seeking the best means of ensuring that the benefits of development are distributed in ways that are consistent with the objective of satisfying the basic needs of the mass of the population. Given that the main problems involved in planning for basic needs satisfaction are not conceptual but operational, the formulation of appropriate solutions to problems of distribution and access calls for a pragmatic approach. In this respect, the collective efforts and ideas of local people regarding matters that directly concern them hold out a great potential for increasing the efficiency of delivery systems requisite to the satisfaction of basic needs.

Psychological Satisfaction and Motivation

There is the view that the participation of people in the making of decisions which affect them is a basic human need in its own right. Thus, in addition to being a means of satisfying material needs, popular participation may be regarded also as an end in itself.[11] It is in this respect that participation is associated with the fulfilment of intangible requirements of well-being or even welfare, such as human rights, social justice, equality, self-confidence, dignity, and so on. Control or influence by the individual over institutions which take key decisions pertaining to his or her well-being and social existence affords greater scope for human development and self-enrichment.

Yet, the idea of participation as an *end* in itself – i.e. something that provides the individual with innate satisfaction – cannot be entirely isolated from the possibility that the psychological satisfaction derived from participation is linked to the satisfaction of individuals from actually having a say in key decisions relating to their *material* well-being. Hence, the distinction between participation as an end in itself and participation as a means to development ought not to be too rigidly applied. The two need to co-exist in order to fulfil basic needs satisfaction.

Another dimension of the psychological satisfaction associated with participation in decision making relates to motivation. It is widely believed that genuine participation increases confidence of individuals or groups in their own ability to initiate actions in defence of their interests. If this is so, popular participation may then be regarded as a psychological stimulant towards greater efforts and, hence, higher levels of productivity under normal circumstances. Thus, motivation is regarded as necessary for the successful implementation of local self-help and similar community level projects. However, one should not lose sight of the simple fact that motivation is more likely to emerge when people themselves perceive direct or indirect benefits in relation to their inputs to communal development activities.

CONCLUSION

The role of popular participation in a basic needs strategy relates mainly to its potential for shifting production in favour of the felt needs of the poor and for increasing the efficiency of supply-management. These are key requirements for meeting basic needs through formal planning. Considered together, they underlie the importance of necessary structural changes to support the implementation of a basic needs strategy. Yet, such structural changes are not likely to be achieved unless there is popular control or influence over the allocation and use of productive resources. On the basis of this reasoning, we can conclude that popular participation is a necessary condition for the successful implementation of a basic needs strategy. If practised effectively, people's participation in development, especially at the local level, can contribute substantially to the satisfaction of basic needs through certain ways and means as identified and analysed above.

NOTES

1 The conclusion is most convincingly supported by the findings of a major 'dialogical' research undertaken among the vanguard group of a peasant movement in the state of Maharashtra, India – see G.V.S. de Silva, N. Mehta, Md. A. Rahman, and P. Wignaraja: 'Bhomi Sena: Struggle for people's power' *Development Dialogue*, 1979, vol. 2.
2 See ILO: *Meeting basic needs: Strategies for eradicating mass poverty and unemployment* (Geneva, 1977).
3 See ILO: *Poverty and landlessness in rural Asia* (Geneva, 1977) for clear empirical evidence in support of this conclusion; also Keith Griffin and Anisur Rahman Khan: 'Poverty in the Third World: Ugly facts and fancy models' *World Development*, vol. 6, no. 3, 1978, pp. 295–304.
4 This distinction is derived mainly from the relevant sections of the *Programme of Action* adopted at the ILO World Employment Conference (Geneva, 1976).
5 This is analogous to the Rawlsian principle of 'collective choice'; see J. Rawls: *A theory of justice* (Oxford, Oxford University Press, 1972).
6 For example see Gek-Boo Ng: *Mass participation and basic-needs satisfaction: The Chinese approach* (Geneva, ILO, 1979; mimeographed World Employment Programme research working paper; restricted).
7 See Franklyn Lisk: *Basic-needs activities and poverty alleviation in Kenya* (Geneva, ILO, 1978, mimeographed).
8 ILO: *The Kenyan rural access roads programme review meeting* (Geneva, Oct. 1977, mimeographed); see also J.J. Veen: *The rural access roads programme: Appropriate technology in Kenya* (Geneva, ILO, 1980).
9 Also, a particularly relevant empirical study in this context is Masao Kikucki, *et al.*, 'Economics of community works programs: A community irrigation project in the Philippines' *Economic Development and Cultural Change*, vol. 26, no. 2, Jan. 1978.
10 See V. Dujkanovic and E.P. Mach: *Alternative approaches to meeting basic health needs in developing countries* (Geneva, WHO/UNICEF, 1975); and UNICEF: *A strategy for basic services* (New York, 1976).

11 For example see Eddy Lee: 'Some normative aspects of a basic-needs strategy' in D.P. Ghai, A.R. Khan, E.L.H. Lee and T. Alfthan: *The basic-needs approach to development: Some issues regarding concepts and methodology* (Geneva, ILO, 1977).

2 Popular Participation in Decision Making with Reference to Development Planning: An Institutional Approach

Jean Majeres

In many developing countries the process of formal planning (for economic development and social progress) is centred around institutions that are characterised by the absence of or low levels of popular participation in decision making. Granted that the need for specialist technical inputs into the planning process justifies certain types of 'closed' institutions with restricted membership such as national or regional planning commissions and related advisory bodies, the broad political dimension of the process and its wider implications for the well-being of the population at large point to the necessity for popular influence on planning decisions through appropriate complementary institutional arrangements. This leads to the fundamental question of whether or not *formal* institutions within the administrative and political structures are appropriate and sufficient for ensuring popular participation in the decision-making process.

First, to the extent that formal institutions within the planning system tend to be concentrated at higher levels of administration and decision making they may not be amenable to mass participation which is essentially a local level or grass-roots phenomenon. Second, even when there is some decentralisation of decision-making powers and resources to lower level public institutions concerned with planning, the experience is often that such bodies seek or tend to alienate the broad mass of the local population from decision making through various means – e.g. bureaucratic obstacles or very narrow representation of diverse local interests on decision-making bodies. Third, there is also abundant evidence of such institutions being used by those in authority as means of furthering authoritarian or partisan forms of mass mobilisation with little or no impact on decision making with respect to planning. This has been found to exist even in political systems which favour participatory-oriented development and, accordingly, create formal institutions for involving the people in the making and implementation of decisions that affect their well-being. In fact, this sort of camouflage is often used by some 'reformist' regimes in the Third World to reinforce tendencies toward the concentration of political and economic power within a small but privileged group and to maintain control over the rest of the population.

Nevertheless, one should not conclude that popular participation in decision making cannot be effected through formal institutions within the planning system. There are at present some examples of institutions within the administrative structures that are instrumental in promoting popular participation in the development process. Analysis of the structure, methods of organisation and operation of such 'successful' institutions and their relationships with informal popular organisations will no doubt provide useful insights into the nature and requirements of an appropriate institutional framework for promoting popular participation in relation to the attainment of employment and basic needs objectives of development planning. At the same time, there is need for caution in generalising about the requirements of an institutional framework that is amenable to participatory-oriented development planning, given the differences in socio-political settings, types of programmes and activities, and so on, that provide illustrative examples for this study.

The analytical framework for this study, therefore, focuses on institutional development in the light of existing political and socio-economic factors that may both facilitate or frustrate the promotion of popular participation in the planning process. Within this framework, the aim is to identify salient features of participatory-type institutions concerned with development planning and to examine critically these in terms of their wider applicability to a variety of socio-economic systems and styles of development. The analytical framework also provides a basis for highlighting the more common weaknesses of institutional arrangements within the planning system which impinge on the effectiveness of popular participation in decision making. Finally, the analytical framework does not lend itself to a global evaluation of different types of institutions within the planning system in terms of suitability for meeting basic needs, nor is it the purpose of this study.

What follows has a more specific purpose: to investigate the usefulness of formal institutions in promoting popular participation in the planning process. As is now widely accepted in the literature, and increasingly among practitioners of development planning, popular participation in the development process can make a decisive contribution to the objectives of basic needs satisfaction and poverty alleviation. For this reason, the institutional framework required for promoting and sustaining genuine popular participation in decision making could be regarded as a major component of basic needs-oriented development planning. Yet, investigative and analytical studies on the institutional aspects of the basic needs approach, especially in relation to planning, are so far few and hard to come by in the 'basic needs' literature.[1] This study is therefore intended as a contribution towards filling this gap. It should, however, be regarded as a tentative inquiry with findings that are far from conclusive since, among its limitations, it is restricted mainly to *public institutions* that operate within the formal planning system. No doubt, more wide-ranging and sharper-focused analytical studies on the subject would be required for a fuller understanding of the issues and problems central to institutional development for basic needs-oriented planning. It is, therefore, hoped that this preliminary investigation could provide a direction for badly needed work in this area in the future.

INSTITUTIONAL DEVELOPMENT AND POPULAR PARTICIPATION

The Political Dimension

The active involvement of the broad mass of the population in decision making has been specifically identified as a major prerequisite for achieving the goals and objectives of basic needs-oriented development.[2] Yet in many contemporary developing countries popular participation in decision making is either non-existent or practised in forms and under conditions that significantly diminish its effectiveness. To improve on this state of affairs would involve organising the 'unorganised' and other disadvantaged socio-economic groups in order that their interests can be better articulated, represented and defended. Attempts at organisation by the poor and disadvantaged groups will, no doubt, have important political implications going beyond the recognition of fundamental human rights pertaining to freedom of expression and association and civil liberties. For example, legislation allowing freedom of association among rural workers may need to be complemented by such fundamental changes as the redistribution of political and economic powers in favour of poorer groups before a satisfactory level of participation in decision making can be achieved. There will also be a need for the development and strengthening of appropriate institutions through which rural workers can operate to influence decision making and to ensure fuller participation of their group or class in the development process.

From a political standpoint, the main obstacle to participation of poorer groups in decision making is generally related to the fact that this form of power sharing is likely to affect adversely the interests of privileged groups, and consequently alter the political power relationships in society. The need to overcome this obstacle reinforces the argument in favour of structural changes within the political system and in related administrative institutions with decision-making functions. To the extent that development (economic) planning is often undertaken within the administrative structure of government, a change in the distribution of political power, which consequently affects the nature of administrative decision making, will be crucial to popular participation in the development process. It is, therefore, desirable to take into account the political dimension of popular participation in developing an appropriate institutional framework for basic needs-oriented development planning.

Given the links between the distribution of political power among different socio-economic groups and popular participation in decision making through administrative institutions, a thorough understanding of the nature of existing obstacles to desirable political changes will be necessary in order to devise appropriate methods and policies for institution building. However, in a wider context, the political structure is not independent of the overall economic system and different forms of social organisation where development planning is concerned. Popular influence on the formulation of policies and strategies; the translation of policies and strategies into coherent action programmes; and the implementation of specific projects for poverty alleviation and meeting basic needs – i.e. the planning process – can be regarded equally as a function of prevailing economic and social conditions as of existing political power relationships in a given context.

A Conceptual Framework for Evaluating Public Institutions in the Planning System

Institution building will also require an appropriate conceptual framework for evaluating existing public institutions in the planning system in order to determine their suitability for promoting popular participation in decision making. In particular, the conceptual framework should be useful for analysing linkages and inter-relationships between different types and levels of institutions as well as for assessing the relevance of various policy alternatives in relation to the aim of developing and strengthening public institutions for fuller and more effective participation in decision making.

The main parameters requisite to the formulation of a conceptual framework for evaluating public institutions with reference to a basic needs-oriented planning system are the following:

1 *the prevailing economic system:* the means of production, the process of accumulation, the labour force, the economic relationships and interactions within the system;
2 *the existing class structure:* the different social classes or socio-economic groups and their state of well-being in terms of production and consumption of essential goods and services (standard of living, ownership of and access to productive assets, the distribution of income, access to private and public consumption goods); and
3 *the territorial division* (for example, region, province, district, town, village): the division of the entire population and the socio-economic characteristics of sub-divisions and their inter-relationships (the spatial distribution of physical and social infrastructural facilities, production and consumption, migration flows, flow of goods and services, and so on).

These three parameters are central to an evaluation of public institutions in terms of their actual and potential contribution to:

1 improvements in overall living standards and, in particular, the levels of consumption of goods and services 'basic' to the needs of the mass of the population;
2 reduction (in relative terms) of inequalities between different socio-economic groups; and
3 reduction of spatial or regional inequalities.

The application of the above conceptual framework to an evaluation of public institutions within the planning system will depend on the availability of data and information on economic, social, political and historical factors and their inter-relationships. In the context of many developing countries, this somehow implies a limitation on the use of the framework for analysis at the local level given the usual paucity of data and information at that level. In addition to the measurement of levels of participation in quantitative terms, the framework should also allow for the socio-economic analysis of different groups in order to capture the non-quantifiable factors that influence or determine levels of popular participation in the development process. This implies, for example, that a classification of agricultural holdings should not only be limited to differences by size, but also should reflect significant social and/or class differences between owners of different categories of holdings as well as their inter-relationships. Overall, an attempt to evaluate the suitability of public institutions would require an analysis of some very complex socio-economic phenomena such as: (a) the distributional aspect of one or more of the factors crucial to improvements in living and working conditions (for example, access to land, income, consumption and collective services) and (b) the specific socio-economic characteristics of different groups in the population and their inter-relationships (for example, landless labourers, peasants, share-croppers, landlords).

Finally, the framework should be useful for assessing the suitability of institutions with reference to popular influence on the planning and execution of concrete action programmes. In other words, when applied to public institutions, the framework should provide indications of why and the extent to which the masses are motivated to contribute to development efforts. In this regard, it has been suggested that the focus of institutional development should be on:

> that strata least prepared for abstract reasoning and most governed by immediate material needs. Their participation requires a symbolic frame of reference meaningful to them, certain concrete tasks through which they can relate themselves to wider processes, and a perception of convincing reasons why present efforts and sacrifices should lead to future gains.[3]

Accordingly, disadvantaged socio-economic groups and the poor in general can be critically examined with reference to the types of institutions and organisations relevant to their interests and to increasing their influence on public decision making.

The Development of Institutions as a Strategic Means for Increasing Popular Participation

The building up of institutions for promoting popular participation in decision making within the formal planning process is facilitated when based on existing forms of organisation of people into specific interest groups with aims and goals that are common to their memberships. In fact, there can be little doubt about the usefulness of popular organisations like trade unions, co-operatives, rural workers' and peasants' organisations, women's and youth organisations for promoting popular participation in public decision making. However, it should be stressed that the evolution of interest groups into effective organisations capable of influencing public decisions on matters of development planning could be a difficult and protracted process. This then might reduce the effectiveness of interest groups for institution building in many cases where there is an urgent need for popular influence on planning decisions. Therefore, attention should also be focused on the ways and means of immediately developing and strengthening the type of public institutions that are suitable for ensuring popular participation in decision making at all levels of formal planning and administration.

In this regard, however, there is the danger that public institutions can easily be manipulated by governments or power-holding groups to serve as a means of preventing, rather than encouraging, popular participation in decision making. For example, the dominating presence of government officials and bureaucrats in public institutions could undermine the capacity of such institutions to promote effective popular participation, as illustrated by the failure of the 'Basic Democracies' set up in Pakistan in 1962[4] and the weaknesses of the officially controlled 'Panchayats' and so-called 'Class and Professional Organisations' in Nepal.[5]

This is not to give the impression that public institutions cannot make a contribution to the promotion of popular participation in decision making directly and through their relationship with autonomous organisations or interest groups. In the latter context, there is evidence of the state institutions playing a catalytic role in the development and strengthening of popular organisations with potential to influence public decision making – as distinct from state-manipulated or controlled mass organ-isations – for example the case of the United Republic of Tanzania. Yet the role of the State and its institutions in promoting popular participation is a highly controversial issue and one on which it is difficult to generalise. On the relationship between the State and popular organisations, a study of popular participation in Latin America stressed the importance of an institutional arrangement that is characterised by 'a continual interplay of initiatives from above and below, along with an interplay of conflict and consensus at many levels of the social order, that would give full recognition to the human right of self-determination, and specify that opposition is a legitimate and essential component of authentic participation'.[6]

The existence of a political climate favourable to the evolution of popular organisation cannot be overlooked either. Where there is hostility or opposition to the idea of popular involvement or influence on decision making, one is unlikely to find a system of public institutions that will support the development of popular organisations. The fact of the matter is that popular organisations do not exist and operate in an entirely neutral political framework. For such organisations to work efficiently as a means of implementing development programmes it is essential for them to count on the support or at least on a favourable attitude of the State and its various institutions; a prerequisite for this situation to occur is, of course, that the priorities of the State (as a political entity) be in line, to the largest possible extent, with the objectives of these popular organisations, as harmonised and expressed in a coherent set of local priorities, at the various levels of decentralisation of the public institutions.

THE BASIC COMMUNITY AS THE FOUNDATION OF AN INSTITUTIONAL FRAMEWORK FOR PROMOTING POPULAR PARTICIPATION IN PUBLIC DECISION MAKING AT THE LOCAL LEVEL

On the basis of the experience of some developing countries, it has been observed that decentralisation of decision-making power and resources to local-level authorities is a viable means of promoting popular participation in the development process. With specific reference to the planning process, decentralisation could also lead to greater self-reliance at the local level. However, the potential of decentralised planning to contribute to popular participation and local self-reliance hinges crucially on the existence of appropriate participatory institutions at the national, regional and local levels (which together make up the *territorial/institutional* system).[7] More importantly, such institutions should be adequately representative in order to reflect fully the views of different interest groups in the community, especially those of minorities and particularly disadvantaged sections of society. Furthermore, if possible, broad-based representation should be recognised and guaranteed by law.

Available evidence from recent attempts to promote decentralised participatory development through the territorial/institutional approach suggests that efforts at institution building for development planning purposes are likely to be successful when these are initiated and based at the local level in the first instance, rather than at higher levels of decision making. Thus starting with local-level institutions as the foundation, higher-level institutions within the planning system could later be developed with the specific aim of providing a channel through which local-level institutions can transmit popular views to the centre. This would help to create the confidence of people at the local level (i.e. the basic community) in their own institutions as a means of participating in the decision-making process.

Contemporary examples of this type of institution-building are to some extent presented by the experiences of the *Ujamaa Villages* in the United Republic of Tanzania and of the *Fokonolona communities* in Madagascar, established respectively in 1966 and 1972. In pursuit of economic development and social progress, the governments of those two countries have attempted to implement national strategies that involved major restructuring of the decision-making process, with emphasis on the decentralisation of economic, social, adminsitrative and judicial functions and powers to local-level authorities and representative bodies.[8] Despite certain difficulties encountered, the experiences of both countries indicate that the decentralisation of administrative and planning functions is a major requirement for promoting broad-based participation in the development process at local level.

The experiences of countries which have achieved some success in promoting popular participation in decision making through adopting a global territorial/institutional approach to decentralisation of planning suggest that four important conditions should be fulfilled in order to establish and maintain an effective network of institutions at the level of the basic community. These are:

1 a representative local-level decision-making body;
2 an acceptable programme of local public works within the planning process;
3 the mobilisation of local financial resources; and
4 a system of external technical support.

The importance of the above conditions for institution building is obvious from the lessons of past failures and difficulties. For example, the Economic Commission for Latin America observed that traditional participatory organisations failed 'to gain a voice in the whole range of public sector activities that affect their lives or to grasp the inter-connections of these activities and possibilities for alternative allocations of public resources', because 'the planning bodies have not been able to envisage a realistic function for popular participation in their activities'.[9] A similar conclusion was reached with reference to Kenya, where a study of grass-roots 'Harambee' organisations identified 'inadequate integration of local and national planning and a lack of knowledge about how to merge the two' as a major obstacle to effective popular participation in local-level development projects.[10]

A Representative Local-Level Decision Making

Planning for the satisfaction of basic needs requires intimate knowledge of local conditions so as to identify correctly and assign priorities to fundamental needs of the community. This implies a thorough under-standing of the nature and causes of poverty, as well as the extent of basic needs shortfalls. The active participation of the local population in the making and implementation of decisions that are likely to affect both individual and collective well-being therefore becomes crucial in the planning process. Popular influence on public decision making could facilitate the implementation of local-level development projects through, for example, the resolution of local contradictions and conflicts; the taking of decisions consistent with local customs and traditions; and the adoption of working arrangements that do not conflict with other demands on local labour or interfere with existing social and cultural practices. A variety of local decision-making bodies may be established for the purpose of ensuring *adequate* local representation in public decision making.

The concept of a representative 'development council' at the local/community level is one which can be explored in this context. In order to ensure that the decisions taken by the council reflect diverse interests of the local population, representation might have to be based on legally fixed quotas for different socio-economic groups. In addition, each group should be responsible for electing (or selecting) its own members on the council. Through this form of representation, decision making is likely to be more consistent with the needs, priorities and development aspirations of the local community as a whole. In view of the variety of political and social systems that characterise Third World societies, the legal basis of representation on local-level decision-making bodies should be determined with reference to the existing pattern of government. For example, in African societies legitimate representation may be based on various combinations of formal democratic procedures and specific modes of traditional government. In fact, such an option may be necessary for integrating new institutions with existing social structures and customary law.[11]

Where the style of government is characterised by distinct hierarchical social/class structures, legitimate representation may be based on the need to ensure adequate participation of underprivileged groups in decision making – e.g. by allocating a number of seats on the council to disadvantaged minorities and the poorest social groups or classes. Although this might involve bypassing the formal democratic process of election, the guarantee of representation for the poorest groups in this manner should not be considered as undemocratic. On the contrary, the extension of decision-making power to those whose basic needs are least being satisfied does not in any way conflict with the primary purpose of democracy in relation to considerations of equity and social justice.

The diversity of modes of representation on a local development council can be illustrated by some concrete examples. In Viet Nam, an adequate representation of the poor and 'medium-poor' peasants in the decision-making bodies of production co-operatives is guaranteed by reserving two-thirds of the seats on the administrative committee and on the control commission for these low-income groups. Moreover, this means that effective control remains in the hands of the poorer peasants since the representation of intermediate, or 'better-off', peasants on these decision-making bodies cannot legally exceed one-third of the total number of seats. Furthermore, rich peasants are not represented on the decision-making bodies of co-operatives nor can landlords become members of co-operatives.[12] In the United Republic of Tanzania, a village council is elected annually by the village assembly and representation is based on formal democratic process (the only qualifications being that candidates must be members of the village and 18 years or older). In Madagascar, the *Fokonolona*, which is an assembly of all men and women over 18 years living in the Fokontany (the basic territorial community) elects a decision-making committee on the basis of formal democracy.[13]

The functions of the local development council or committee should be closely related to the organisation of various aspects of life and work in the local community. This would, in effect, give operational significance to the decentralisation of decision making from national or provincial level to local level. Furthermore, it is obvious that a local committee would be better placed to decide on and implement policies that pertain to local needs. Since certain major policy decisions will have to be made at higher levels of administration, the functions of local development council should extend to representation in provincial and national level authorities in order to ensure that local interests are taken into account at all levels of decision making. Such a provision would reduce the risk of conflicts between national and local policy decisions. However, the functions of local bodies should not be dominated by bureaucratic tasks that may impinge on their capability to plan and implement development projects at the local level.

In the United Republic of Tanzania, the functions of the *Ujamaa Village Council* cover the following areas: (a) finance and planning; (b) production and marketing; (c) education, culture and social welfare; (d) work and transport, and (e) security and defence. The Villages and Ujamaa Villages Act (1975) requires the Village Council to establish specific committees for at least these five areas of activities. However, since Ujamaa Villages, by law, own all capital goods such as heavy agricultural machinery, storage facilities, transport equipment, as well as control the use of land, the Village Council performs, in addition, important management and judicial functions.

As observed earlier, the relationship between the basic decision-making body and higher level decision-making institutions is of special importance, since effective decentralisation of decision-making powers and resources depends on a clear definition and division of responsibilities between different levels of administration. For example, the decision-making process may comprise, in addition to the local development council, a district development committee and a regional development committee at higher levels of administration, with each level having relatively autonomous powers. Yet, the composition of these higher-level bodies should reflect as much as possible the various socio-economic groups within their areas of coverage. In Madagascar a territorial/institutional decision-making structure was introduced in 1974; it is based on a four-tier territorial system (the *Fokontany*, the *Firaisampokontany*, the *Fivondronampokontany* and the *Faritany*) in addition to the Popular National Assembly at the top. Decision-making powers at each level emanate from the people; at the Fokontany level, representation is based on election within the community; and at the higher levels, Popular

Councils are constituted on the basis of representation from below in the form of presidents of lower-level executive boards, representatives of women and youth organisations and elected councillors. Decisions taken by the Popular Council are binding on the lower level institutions.

An Acceptable Programme of Local Public Works

The extent to which people are willing to contribute their time and labour or other resources to local development projects would, to a large extent, depend on their perceptions of benefits in relation to their inputs – i.e. barring situations wherein coercion and threats are used to obtain mass participation. This reasoning underlines the importance of involving representative local-level bodies in the planning and implementation of development programmes. Given the urgent need for integrated rural development in most Third World countries in order to reduce the urban–rural development gap, representative local-level bodies could play a key role in the execution of public works projects such as road construction, water supplies, irrigation schemes, health care and educational facilities. A major challenge to local-level planning authorities therefore is how to plan and implement local public works projects that would be catering for the needs of the broad mass of the population. To this end, local-level development councils would need to take into account popular views and preferences in the choice of development projects, as well as involve the local population in implementation and evaluation of such projects.

The legal or statutory basis of local-level development councils might impose certain limitations on their responsibilities and functions with respect to the implementation of public works projects. For example, local responsibility might not extend to certain key areas or sectors of economic activity, and the autonomous public spending power of local development councils may be limited by fixed financial ceilings. However, adequate decentralisation of decision-making powers and resources to representative local authorities should make it possible to attain a high level of popular participation in the planning and implementation of public works projects.

Local public works projects can also be effectively executed on a self-help basis, as is becoming increasingly common in several developing countries. Where there is a shortage of financial resources to satisfy basic needs of the population as a whole in essential services such as health, education and water supply, the mobilisation of often underutilised resources at the local level represents a viable approach to development at least cost. Linked to this is the use of labour-intensive methods to implement public works projects which can have both direct and indirect employment effects. But for such activities to be effectively and successfully implemented, it is necessary to organise them around local-level institutions that allow for broad-based participation in decision making as required for motivating people to greater efforts.[14]

In Pakistan, for example, the adoption of the 'Basic Democracies' strategy for local-level development included, as a major component, rural public works programmes. Starting with the experiment launched in the Commilla *Thana* in the former East Pakistan in the mid-sixties, public works projects were launched in several other areas of the country, and in some cases with impact on employment creation and overall rural development. Furthermore, the Third Five-Year Plan of Pakistan identified the 'Works Programme' as an important means for promoting popular participation in the development process. The implementation of Works Programmes led to the creation of co-operative and self-help type organisations at the village level, thereby extending the impact of the programme beyond what was originally envisaged.[15]

Specific organisational forms may be adopted for the implementation of local public works projects – for example, self-help or mutual aid teams, co-operatives, collective forms of production and ownership. The type of organisational structure adopted should be determined on the basis of a thorough assessment of local needs and priorities as well as the characteristics of the prevailing social system. Thus, it might be necessary in certain cases deliberately to bias ownership and control of resources and assets and decision-making power in favour of poorer groups in the community in order to obtain wide acceptability and support for local development efforts.

The implementation of local public works projects also provides an opportunity to develop and improve local planning, managerial and technical capability. The practical experience gained by local people from actively participating in the planning and implementation of public works projects could be extremely useful to the development of skills and positive attitudes towards regular work. In the long run this could lead to savings in financial resources spent on manpower training and development.

Finally, it is important that local public works programmes should be horizontally co-ordinated between various local communities within a district or region. The absence of a horizontal co-ordinating mechanism has often been a major reason for practical difficulties and failures, as became obvious from the later experience of the 'Basic Democracies' in Pakistan.[16] Also, the integration of village and district level programmes of public works into regional and national plans should be given particular attention in order to avoid conflicts. While the presence of members of local development committees in high-level decision-making authorities constitutes a way of ensuring representation of local interests in those bodies, it is necessary, in addition, to provide for regular consultations with the basic community on all major decisions pertaining to the livelihood of the local population. This also implies that officials of central government operating ministries based at the local level (for example, provincial and district) should consult with local authorities to ensure the harmonisation of decision making, particularly on matters over which local representative bodies do not have autonomous decision-making power.

Local Financial Resources

The implementation of local-level development projects would require, above all, financial resources to cover the costs of requisite inputs – even in the case of self-help projects where labour may be provided voluntarily. Local-level development authorities should therefore have access to requisite financial resources. In general, local-level development authorities obtain their funds from two main sources:

1 local taxation and levies; and
2 budgetary allocations and transfers from higher levels of government.

Local Taxation and Levies

The decentralisation of tax-raising power to local-level authorities is necessary for mobilising financial resources locally. Indirect taxation (for example, levies on production and on sale of goods and services) may be a feasible means of raising revenue locally, but this should be accompanied by appropriate pricing policies aimed at higher and more realistic producer prices for cash crops as well as improved internal terms of trade in favour of rural producers. Otherwise the imposition of taxation on rural producers could become an unbearable burden on a group that may already be disadvantaged vis-à-vis urban workers. There is also the risk that a high incidence of local tax on output could depress local production, if producers perceive that the net gain from higher levels of output (i.e. after tax) is not worth the extra effort and cost. Therefore, this form of resource mobilisation should be carefully worked out with reference to prevailing economic circumstances of the local community and the possible consequences on well-being and future growth. It should also be realised that the scope for local taxation in many developing countries might be limited by the existing low levels of income in rural areas and the narrowness of the tax base where the population is engaged mainly in subsistence production. A broader tax base might be obtained through the granting of tax-raising power to local authorities over large-scale commercial agricultural and mining activities in rural areas; however, the usual practice in most Third World countries is for the central government to retain control over direct taxation of such large-scale enterprises with a sizeable tax base. Whether or not the local communities where those

44

enterprises are based eventually benefit from tax revenues collected by the central government will depend on the criteria adopted for the transfer of financial resources to local authorities.

In more developed societies, local-level authorities might directly involve themselves in the operation of profitable commercial ventures that could yield revenue for development purposes. These, for example, could take the form of marketing contracts between local producers, preferably organised on a co-operative basis, and public and parastatal commercial enterprises for the supply of certain goods (for example, agricultural produce and raw materials). In this context the local development council could play a key role in organising the marketing of locally-produced goods. The involvement of the local development council in marketing activities could be beneficial to the community as a whole, not only from the standpoint of raising revenue for development purposes, but also in terms of protecting local producers against unfavourable commercial and trade practices and ensuring that legal minimum prices are paid to them. Such an arrangement should lead to the elimination of unscrupulous middlemen and the parallel take-over of their related distribution and retail functions (with respect to the supply of essential goods in the community) by the local development council or popular co-operatives.

Central Government Budgetary Transfers

Effective decentralisation of planning responsibilities must extend to the transfer of financial resources from central government to local-level authorities in order to give operational significance to the concept. The decentralisation of decision-making power to local-level authorities without at the same time providing them with the financial resources required to implement desirable development projects, could be a constraint on the effectiveness of such bodies to fulfil their statutory obligations to the local population. Ideally, the decentralisation of financial resources to local-level authorities should be based on the principle of 'self-determination' of essential needs. This means that local councils should be given authority over spending on development projects as determined by the actual needs and priorities of the local community. The provision of an annual development grant for financing specific development projects and the operation of essential services at the local level seems to be a most feasible arrangement in this regard. It may be necessary, in addition, to provide local councils with 'untied' funds on a regular basis to enable them to undertake activities for which the need might emerge only at short notice, in the course of the financial year after the budget has been finalised. However, it may be necessary for the central government to have some control over the spending of public funds by local authorities so as to avoid mismanagement of resources. But such control should not be exercised to the extent that it conflicts with the exercise of popular influence over the making and implementation of key decisions on matters of development at the local level.

A highly controversial issue in the financing of local-level development projects is that of revenue sharing or more precisely the formula for transferring resources from the centre to the local level. While broad principles relating to equity are often used as guidelines for working out an acceptable formula for revenue sharing, there is usually the problem of defining equity in practical terms. This problem cannot be resolved in a general way given the need to take into account specific economic and social conditions in each individual case.

Nevertheless, with reference to a basic needs approach to development, a suitable formula for revenue sharing among various regional and local authorities could be based on the following criteria: (a) the size of the local population; and (b) a coefficient for correcting existing inequalities, arising from past biases and distortions in development efforts between regions, districts and local communities – i.e. a sort of needs criteria. These two broad criteria are likely to lead to a more equitable distribution of public funds among the entire population of a country, as well as guarantee that, over time, poorer communities will progressively improve their situation vis-à-vis the rest of society.

Finally, the central government could guarantee bank loans or provide credits to local-level authorities for embarking on projects that have potential community-wide benefits. In the latter case, funds could be made available directly by the central government or through an appropriate institution, such as a development bank, to local development authorities and popular organisations like co-operatives and mutual aid societies. Since funds of this nature have to be repaid over a specified period, it may be necessary for these to be directed at economic ventures with tangible returns in addition to development potentials. For example, such credits could be used to support local economic activities relating to the production and supply of materials required for public works projects, the development of agro-based industries, the construction of low-cost housing units and so on. These are activities which also have potential income and employment benefits of relevance to the basic needs-oriented development strategy.

A System of External Technical Support

Often the implementation of local development projects is severely constrained by the lack of basic technology and requisite technical know-how. Similarly, the shortage of management skills at the local level has been identified as an obstacle to the efficient operation of local public services. The difficulties of overcoming these obstacles are further augmented by the fact that living and working conditions at the local level in most developing countries are generally not amenable to attracting skilled labour away from relatively more developed urban centres, where also wages and salaries tend to be higher. This situation underlines the need for a system of external technical support for local development efforts. This may be achieved by various means ranging from the redeployment of central staff to local-level authorities on a rotating basis to the establishment of government-funded multi-purpose development assistance teams and mobile workshops based at the district level from where they can serve different local communities.

However, it is important that the provision of external technical support should not act as a barrier to the development of local technical capacity and skills which are required for enhancing self-reliance at the local level. Therefore, the system of external technical support should be linked to the training of local-level officials as appropriate. For example, without incurring the expenses of formal training, local officials could acquire requisite practical skills by working alongside more experienced technicians and managers or other less formal on-the-job training programmes. This form of training could form an integral part of the overall system of 'learning' in local communities with the aim of making education more relevant to local needs and livelihood.

A properly trained polyvalent team of four or five officials, comprising, for example, a rural development planner, a quantity surveyor, an engineer and public health inspector or medical orderly, should be capable of providing the necessary technical support to a local development authority in the key areas of rural public works projects, agricultural development, primary health care, education, cottage industries and housing development. Similarly, mobile workshops based at the district level could meet the needs of local communities for heavy equipment and machinery in the undertaking of more complex technical operations and arduous tasks. By rotating equipment and skills between local communities it should be possible to make maximum use of available technical capacity which is an important consideration in a situation of capital scarcity.

Finally, it should be emphasised that the provision of technical support need not be based on highly qualified personnel and costly imported equipment. In this context, one may recall the well-known example of Chinese 'barefoot doctors' which, above all, demonstrates that in many areas of development the requisite training for improving on existing levels of efficiency can be undertaken at the local level at a minimum of cost. In the same vein, the need for equipment can be met from locally-based research and development efforts which rely on locally available materials and skills.

SUMMARY AND CONCLUSIONS

Evidence from many contemporary developing countries suggests that the promotion of popular participation in decision-making processes at all levels of government is far from easy and straightforward. To begin with, there can be conflicts between institutions and between the interests of various socio-economic groups. Such conflicts are, in fact, now widely regarded as unavoidable features of the development process itself. This makes the resolution of conflicts all the more important as a condition for fostering development. With reference to development planning, the resolution of conflicts could, perhaps, best be pursued through institutions and similar arrangements that allow for some degree of popular influence on the making and implementation of decisions pertaining to the allocation and use of developmental resources. Furthermore, if institutions within the planning system are to be useful as a means of promoting popular participation in the development process they should be accessible to the broad mass of the population at all levels of decision making. It may therefore be necessary to create new institutions at lower levels of administration and, accordingly, to decentralise decision-making powers and resources to those bodies.

The territorial/institutional approach to popular participation, which is the concern of this chapter, has been proposed as a way of resolving conflicts that may arise from the need to decentralise political and economic decision-making powers to local-level authorities. In terms of a strategy, this approach focuses mainly on institutional development as a means of achieving popular influence on public decision making. The role and functions of certain public institutions at the various territorial levels (local, district, regional, national) have been explored with reference to the planning process and the allocation of public resources. Within an institutional framework of the type presented, it is postulated that organisational efforts 'from below' and decentralisation of power and resources 'from above' could interact to produce a viable system for securing effective popular participation in public decision making.

The choice of the basic community as the main operational unit in the territorial/institutional system could be defended on a number of grounds. First, given the desire to extend the benefits of development to the mass of the population, it seems justifiable to direct attention at lower-level institutions that are reasonably accessible to the public at large, either directly, or through representation as well as at their relationships with higher-level institutions. With appropriate restructuring of both the basic and higher-level public institutions, popular participation could be enhanced through the opportunities provided for active involvement of local people in the making and implementation of decisions that affect their livelihood.

Second, the territiorial/institutional approach provides much scope for macro-planning at the centre, while at the same time allowing local-level authorities some degree of autonomy in decision making. Furthermore, it supports the evolution of the type of co-ordinating structure necessary for combining local priorities or basic needs with national priorities and options. The interaction between central and local-level institutions then becomes crucial for ensuring that there is consistency between nationally determined development goals and objectives and local needs and priorities.

Third, the territorial/institutional approach lends itself naturally to the decentralisation of decision-making power and resources since it advocates specific planning functions for clearly defined hierarchical levels of administrations, each being a relatively autonomous territorial unit or decision-making body. According to this approach, the de-centralisation of public decision making is directly linked to the decentralisation of financial resources and spending power, thereby giving operational significance to the concept of local-level planning. External technical support (from above) is recognised as a necessary input for local-level development, but at the same time the approach foresees the development of requisite skills internally through greater popular involvement in the development process.

Fourth, the approach allows for the creation of a structure that facilitates vertical (both downward and upward) and horizontal flow of information, which is an important prerequisite for effective popular participation in the development process. In particular, local-level institutions can be instrumental, through interaction with similar and higher-level bodies, in raising consciousness and increasing awareness among local people about economic and socio-political issues and alternatives. Thus, interest groups and organisations within the community, such as trade unions, rural workers' and peasants' organisations, co-operatives, women's and youth associations, consumers' associations, and so on, could make use of public institutions to articulate their needs more effectively and to defend their specific interests.

A further advantage of the territorial/institutional approach, from the standpoint of a basic needs-oriented strategy, is that it provides a viable mechanism within the planning process for (re)directing resources towards need-satisfying types of development activities and projects at the local level. Through popular influence on public decision making the pattern of resource allocation and utilisation could be re-oriented more towards the felt needs and aspirations of local communities. Linked to this, the approach is also amenable to the enhancement of local self-reliance which in turn can contribute to more efficient utilisation of both human and material resources at the local level, with considerable savings on scarce resources required for national development.

According to this presentation, it would seem that the usefulness of the territorial/institutional approach does not relate to *direct* employment and income benefits, since emphasis is placed mainly on its contribution to the provision of essential public services by local-level development authorities. Similarly, in terms of meeting basic needs, the approach may not have a *direct* link with the satisfaction of private consumption requirements at the household level. Nevertheless, the impact of popular influence on decision making in the planning process includes the potential to bring about desirable structural changes in the political, social and economic spheres. More significantly, these changes are known to have far reaching implications for employment creation through greater access to productive assets and socio-economic opportunities for hitherto disadvantaged groups, as well as for the attainment of a more equitable pattern of income distribution.

NOTES

1 This view is aptly supported by an examination of what is perhaps the most comprehensive bibliographical reference work on the subject to date: Jorge Garcia-Bonza: *Basic-needs analytical bibliography* (Paris, OECD Development Centre, 1980).

2 See ILO: *Employment, growth and basic needs: A one-world problem.* The international basic-needs strategy against chronic poverty and the decision of the 1976 World Employment Conference (Geneva, 1976), ILO: *Meeting basic needs: Strategies for eradicating mass poverty and unemployment* (Geneva, 1977).

3 Economic Commission for Latin America: 'Popular participation in development' *Community Development Journal*, vol. 8, no. 2, Apr. 1973, p.80 (this article is extracted from the United Nations publication, 'Social Change and Social Development Policy in Latin America').

4 See Nasir Islam: 'L'élaboration des politiques de développement et la participation sociale au Pakistan' *Revue Internationale des Sciences Administratives* (Bruxelles), no. 3, 1974, pp. 273–83.

5 See L.S. Baral: 'Class Organisations in Nepal: Social Control and Interest Articulation' *Asia Quarterly* (Brussels), no. 2, 1974, pp. 173–202.

6 Economic Commission for Latin America, op. cit., pp. 79–80.

7 This term is used to refer to the system of public institutions (with decision-making and administrative functions), composed of several hierarchical levels, each of which corresponds to a demarcated territorial area (e.g. country, region, district, village).

8 Some other developing countries have implemented institutional decentralisation on a sectoral basis, with the explicit aim of improving mass participation in specific sectors. An example is the educational reform in Peru, implemented in 1972 (Ley General de Educación, Decreto Ley No. 19326, Lima, Ministerio de Educación 1972). In this case, a fairly decentralised education structure based on a system of 'nucleos educativos communales', or NEC, which incorporates all educational services in the community, has evolved. This 'nuclear' system is defined as 'the basic community organisation for the co-ordination and management of the education services and other services used by education, within a specific geographical area, for the promotion of community life, thus confirming that

education should take place in and through the community, and that responsibility for its content, orientation, administration and direction should eventually be vested in the family and the community rather than be the exclusive preserve of education authorities. This, in turn, implies a steady movement towards decentralisation, towards a situation in which those most directly concerned will be able, as of right, to participate in policy-making, in the supervision and administration of the whole educational process', Judith Bizot: *Educational Reform in Peru* (Paris, UNESCO, 1975), p. 30.

9 Economic Commission for Latin America, op. cit., p. 90.

10 Mbithi and Rasmusson: *The structure of grass-roots harambee within the context of national planning* (Nairobi, University of Nairobi, 1974, mimeographed), p. 51.

11 As exemplified by the approach of the Fédération des groupements villageois de la Région de Bouaké in the Ivory Coast. See INADES (Institute Africain pour le Développement Ecònomique et Social): *Des paysans prennent en main leur développement* (Abidjan, INADES information, 1974), esp. p. 30 and ff.

12 See Vo-Nhan Tri: *Croissance économique de la République Démocratique du Viet Nam* (Hanoi, 1967), pp. 227–9.

13 The Government was aware that this mode of representation could result in relatively rich peasants, merchants, and leading citizens dominating decision-making bodies at local level, but it was assumed that such a situation would in fact lead to a greater mobilisation and organisational strength among the poorer sections of the rural population in order to defend their interests. This, however, was not necessary: with the exception of disputes over land, the poor did not find it necessary to organise themselves in order to promote their participation in decision making, since they so far have been able to secure adequate representation on decision-making committees.

14 See Costa, Guha, Hussain, Thuy and Fardet: *Guidelines for the organisation of special labour-intensive works programmes* (Geneva, ILO, 1977).

15 Nasir Islam, op. cit.

16 ibid.

3 Alternative Forms and Levels of Popular Participation: A General Survey*

Arnold Hughes

The Basic Needs Approach (BNA) to development – as endorsed by the ILO World Employment Conference (WEC), Geneva, June, 1976 – assigns an important role to popular participation in decision making in relation to the attainment of significant improvements in the living conditions of the broad mass of the population in developing countries.[1] With reference to the process of development as a whole, effective participation in the making and implementation of decisions crucial to human well-being implies popular influence in the formal choice of policy or action including the activities of those who have the responsibility for making such choices and for executing formal decisions and related development programmes.

According to the BNA, which advocates a re-orientation of development efforts towards the satisfaction of private and public consumption requirements for the entire population, popular participation is regarded as central to socio-economic development for four reasons.[2]

1 *By playing a part in the definition of basic needs.* This enables

*This chapter is a revised version of a longer study on the relationship between popular participation and basic needs satisfaction undertaken by an interdisciplinary group of researchers at the University of Birmingham, England, on behalf of the ILO – D. Curtis, K. Davey, A. Hughes and A. Shepherd, *Popular Participation in Decision-Making and the Basic Needs Approach to Development: Methods, Issues and Experience* (Geneva, ILO, 1979; mimeograph, World Employment Programme research working paper, restricted WEP 2-32/WP 12).

deprived socio-economic groups to make their needs felt to policy makers.

2 *By enhancing the generation of resources to meet basic needs.* Popular participation may increase the resources required for development by harnessing and channelling local knowledge, skills, labour, and even land and capital to needs-satisfying programmes and projects.

3 *By improving the distribution of goods and services.* Access to public decision making is regarded as a means of ensuring a more equitable distribution of the benefits of economic growth and development.

4 *By fulfilling a psychological need for participation.* Popular participation is both a means and an end in itself in the sense that people desire and get innate satisfaction from active involvement in the making and implementation of decisions which contribute to the satisfaction of their basic needs.

This chapter presents a general survey of alternative forms of participatory practices and institutions. Central government institutions and national political organisations are specifically excluded from the survey, since the focus is mainly on participation as practised at the local level through popular organisations and related institutions that are to a large extent controlled by the people themselves. Nevertheless, the fact that state institutions within the administrative structure and the political system often interact with and, thereby, may influence local-level popular organisations should be recognised. Therefore, in evaluating the effectiveness for meeting basic needs of the various forms of popular participation covered by this survey, the role of the state has to be taken into account.

The attitude of governments towards popular participation is crucial to its success. Governments may favour increased opportunities for mass participation for ideological reasons or because it generates public support and enthusiasm among the majority of the population. In this context, the ruling political parties and related institutions assume numerous detailed participatory and developmental functions in addition to exercising overall guidance of other agents of participation. On the other hand, it must be recognised that where governments are authoritarian-personalist, oligarchic, or radical-collectivist, there is a tendency for the authorities to prevent, limit or manipulate popular involvement in decision making. Too much participation may be viewed as politically threatening or economically damaging so that *de-participation*[3], a conscious attempt to reduce participation, comes to be favoured.

Usually, official attitudes towards popular participation are ambivalent. While political institutions, ideological declarations and policy statements may proclaim the value of popular participation, the practice may be less consistent with such proclamations. Hence, one finds examples wherein participatory processes are periodically undermined by the withholding of information, resources or real freedom of action, or attempts by governments to use popular participation as a means of co-opting popular effort and support for centralised decisions, rather than for delegating real power over decision making and resources to local-level bodies concerned with development.

At the same time, it should be noted that not all political cultures or individuals rank participation highly among their social needs. Social deference, alternative means of redress for grievances, lack of skills to play a proper part in participatory institutions, fear of assuming public responsibilities, and so on, may result, at least temporarily, in a low demand for public access to decision making. Also, not all development initiatives are equally suitable for popular participation. Large-scale and technically complex schemes may require a high degree of centralised control and expert knowledge, whereas local and fairly basic improvement projects may be left entirely in the hands of participants. There may be occasions when the four directions through which popular participation can contribute to basic needs satisfaction as mentioned above clash: the generation of capital for national development may require restraining the redistribution of goods and services, or the definition of needs at the local level may interfere with attempts to determine needs nationally.

Where participation does occur, it may take very different forms, ranging between the genuinely effective or merely symbolic type. Participation may be direct or through the mediation of others; it may be obtained through formal institutions or through informal processes of action and discussion. It can be unfettered or regulated, but political and administrative constraints vary over time. Which combination of these forms will be more amenable to basic needs-oriented development strategies depends upon the prevailing economic, social and political structures and the resultant distribution of power and resources within the society in a given context.

With reference to the different types of participatory institutions included in this general survey, it should be realised that it may be extremely difficult to make a comparison from the standpoint of effectiveness for meeting basic needs. That is therefore not the purpose of this exercise which covers a wide spectrum of organisations and institutional arrangements all of which are regarded as participatory by their protagonists. Thus, accepting that participation is subject to numerous definitions and quite differently interpreted and practised[4] – i.e. ranging from token investment of people at one extreme to autonomous decision making at the other – the methodology adopted is that of identifying different types of participatory institutions and then critically assessing each type separately in terms of its impact on basic needs-oriented development objectives. The survey also makes reference to country examples of popular participation – through a number of institutional arrangements – to illustrate salient features of the concept as may be relevant to the evaluation.

EVALUATION OF PARTICIPATORY INSTITUTIONS

The following types of participatory institutions are identified for evaluation from the standpoint of effectiveness for contributing to fulfilment of basic needs-oriented development objectives and goals:

1 Representative local government and other forms of local administration;
2 Self-help associations;
3 Agrarian associations;
4 Women's organisations;
5 Youth organisations;
6 Trade unions;
7 Industrial democracy;
8 Craft guilds and small business unions;
9 Employers' organisations and professional associations.

Typological classification inevitably involves problems of demarcation. Overlap and arbitrary distinctions are unavoidable, as, for example, it has been found convenient to discuss rural co-operatives under 'Agrarian associations', but industrial co-operatives as a form of 'Industrial democracy'. The amount of attention devoted to individual institutions varies considerably. This reflects differences in the significance of these institutions to the BNA and as well as in the amount of information readily available. In a general survey of this nature and given the limitation of a chapter-length contribution, the coverage of undoubtedly complex processes and agencies has had to be brief. Thus the findings reported do not constitute a definitive evaluation of informal and non-governmental participatory organisations, and any judgements concerning the impact of participation upon the fulfilment of basic needs should be considered as tentative.

Representative Local Government and Other Forms of Participation in Local Administration

Local government – in the sense of authorities with a predominantly representative constitution and a comprehensive concern for the affairs of specific geographical areas – is an important institution for promoting popular participation. Such authorities may be found at various levels of government and administration within a country (e.g. from the village to district, province, region) and their powers vary accordingly.[5]

Characteristics of Local Authorities

The representative character of local authorities, which makes them more participative than other branches of government, is derived from the elective nature of most of their membership, the small geographical scale of their operations, and the relatively restricted nature (in terms of volume and complexity) of their functions. Even so, significant variations do exist among such bodies which have a considerable bearing on their suitability for effecting a basic needs-oriented development strategy.

Status. Local authorities may have complete autonomy within a circumscribed area of activity or be mere extensions of a national bureaucracy. All authorities are subject to some kind of external control, regulation or restriction, for example in the definition of their powers, in their access to resources, or in the supervision of their duties.

Membership. Typically, this is elected but this may be directly or indirectly chosen, may be nominated by government or the ruling party, or may have ex-officio or special interest representation added to it. The powers of members may vary as well from overall policy making to executive management.

Functions. These include the provision of services (social, environmental, utilities, protection); representation (of local opinion within such bodies or to higher public authorities); regulation (making and/or enforcing legislation and arbitration); development (directing economic enterprises, extension services, provision of infrastructure, communal mobilisation); raising revenue (rates, fees, and other forms of local taxation); and planning and co-ordination (land use, social and infrastructural investment planning, input/output production planning).

Resources. Financial resources include grants or other central government budgetary allocations; centrally and locally derived taxes; fees, loans from the public and private sectors; profits on commercial enterprises; and dividends on investments. The degree of fiscal autonomy and forms of revenue source vary radically between local authorities. Human resources include elective and nominated or ex-officio members together with paid employees. Staff may also be deputed from national civil or unified local government services. Occasionally traditional office-holders are co-opted, and obligatory or voluntary efforts from the public may be made use of in the implementation of local development projects.

56

Local Authorities and Basic Needs Fulfilment

Several factors determine the contribution which local authorities, as a type of participatory institution, can make to the successful implementation of basic needs-oriented development strategies. These can be presented in terms of the following questions:

Are local authorities representative of those most deficient in basic needs satisfaction? Local authorities represent the general public rather than the needy in particular and even their ability to represent the former will be affected by such factors as the extent to which members are popularly elected, as opposed to being nominated by government (Malaysia) or on an ex-officio basis (as in the Sudan); the size and composition of the electorate and the criteria for voting; choice of candidates (political or financial/educational constraints); the degree to which non-elected members are representative of the mass of the population (e.g. traditional rulers in various independent African states); the general political climate which permits or restricts free expression of popular feelings at all levels; the socio-economic environment and the bias within, in favour of elite interest groups[6] (which may act out of self-interest or be regarded as more capable spokesmen for local communities); and the extent to which local representatives make decisions relating to the planning and implementation of development programmes and projects in their areas. The nature and complexity of these factors and the realisation that representing the views of the public at large is not necessarily the same as furthering the interests of those most deprived of their basic needs, leave some doubt about the ability of local government to minister to the needs of disadvantaged groups, apart from publicly provided facilities which are shared with other groups. In many cases it is unlikely that local authorities would initiate and promote the kind of positive intervention necessary to provide households and individuals with a satisfactory consumption level of basic needs and livelihood. For these reasons, spontaneous or officially-sponsored bodies have been created to provide a focus of local development co-operation with comprehensive improvement schemes (as in Jakarta and Lusaka). Institutions which support and encourage the participation of the whole community in the decision-making process (town meeting, village assembly, parish council) tend to be severely restricted in scope and powers and may fail to attract widespread public support.

Do local authorities control the allocation of critical resources? Two sets of issues arise in assessing the control or influence of local authorities over the allocation of resources necessary to the fulfilment of basic needs – functional responsibilities and resources. Functional responsibilities such as those which have been itemised above are much more restricted in practice with respect to local authorities in the Third World. A number of basic needs services – for example education and health – are as likely to be vested in central government agencies as in local authorities. While the latter may sometimes undertake limited development functions (for example agricultural extension or industrial promotion) they rarely have much influence over wider market, fiscal and price mechanisms. With regard to resources the critical issue is whether local authorities have sufficient means to support the implementation of basic needs-oriented policies. What assistance can be expected from central government? How effective are they in raising local revenues? Deprived areas are short of human as well as financial resources. They often fail to attract or retain competent staff as required to provide basic services. The ability to mobilise communal labour depends on several factors – a tradition of collective efforts; skill levels among the local populace; availability of surplus labour; administrative capacity.

How much discretion do local authorities really enjoy? External controls may be helpful if they oblige local authorities to provide basic services and enforce standards of efficiency and probity. They can be harmful if they impose unrealistic standards. They can be helpful if they direct resources towards deprived groups but harmful if they favour entrenched local elites. They can encourage greater participation within local authorities or discourage it through bureaucratic delays and interference.

Do representative local authorities have the information and understanding to perform their role? Are local authorities aware of the extent of deprivation in their midst? Can they identify, measure and rank the priorities in terms of need? This awareness rests on the abilities and integrity of the members and staff of local authorities. All too frequently abysmal standards of morality, responsibility and competence prevail and several local authorities have at various times been suspended on the ground of mal-administration (including Banjul, Freetown, Calcutta and Delhi).

To summarise, local representative institutions are well placed to articulate local perceptions and priorities but in practice lack of information, sectional self-interest, lack of resources or restricted powers may prevent them from fully appreciating the needs of deprived groups or acting to remedy them. Local authorities may generate additional resources in several ways – of these, 'self-help' projects offer the best prospects of success though difficulties exist in raising sufficient revenue to maintain these and other services. Also local taxation is often unpopular, difficult to collect, and subject to abuse.[7] While successful municipal enterprises do exist, many are inefficiently run or misused. Lack of financial resources may also hamper the provision of general services. Politically competitive local government can be effective in extracting resources from central government and in redistributing them at the local level, but too frequently the local beneficiaries are not the poor, so much as elite groups and political factions controlling the local authorities.[8] Evidence exists to show that not only are deprived groups overlooked but local authority powers are used to extract rather than redistribute resources among political opponents of those in office.

The ability of local authorities to generate popular satisfaction will depend on how far they are seen to, and can articulate and gratify public wants. The danger exists that, if local authorities prove incapable of meeting popular needs (some of which may be unrealistic), or are subject to improper pressures, the general public will become alienated, if not hostile towards them.

Some Other Forms of Participation in Local Administration

In addition to predominantly representative multi-purpose local authorities other forms of participatory arrangements may exist at the locality level. However, their scope is more narrowly defined and the element of local control is restricted. Three general types can be identified:

Agencies which Permit only Limited Popular Participation. These include development committees or teams set up to co-ordinate the activities of several government agencies; boards established to administer particular services or utilities; and special authorities which manage the comprehensive development of a specific area. In practice these are predominantly bureaucratic or centrally directed bodies, with only a limited element of popular representation. Given their composition, power and responsibilities, they are not likely to offer much scope for public involvement in decision making.

Single Purpose Representative Bodies. These are agencies which are predominantly managed by local representatives but have only specified responsibilities, for example Local Education Committee, Housing Management Association. They are localised in scope but deal with issues of great popular concern and for this reason interest and participation tend to be high. They can be most effective in harnessing local energies and extracting resources from higher levels of authority. Their drawbacks to a basic need strategy is their reliance on government resources and on the support of local dignitaries or elites who may distort the allocation of services in favour of their own socio-economic group. They are mainly concerned with the provision of specific services and, as such, can offer considerable satisfaction to those who participate in their decision-making process.

Process of Consultation or Information. Public referenda, public enquiries or other forms of consultative mechanisms afford the masses the opportunity of informing those in power of their feelings. In the case of referenda, care must be taken in phrasing issues not to exclude options or to be too open-ended. There is also the danger that over-vocal activist groups, whose interests may not be identical or similar with those of the deprived, are better placed to influence decisions in their favour. A conscious effort is required to ensure that the voices of less well-endowed groups are heard. A variety of additional means of informing government of popular needs exist in the Third World ranging from the 'wall-posters' of China to the 'executive visits' of the late Liberian head-of-state to the countryside to hear public complaints and receive requests for aid.

'Self-Help' Associations

Increasingly 'self-help' projects are recognised as an important element in the development programmes of Third World governments and inter-national aid agencies and, as a strategy, the practice appears to have much to contribute to the satisfaction of basic needs. The current revival of interest in 'self-help' as a development strategy may be attributable to the attention which economists and others are now paying to China's development pattern which strongly emphasises local self-reliance and mass mobilisation and provides an alternative to existing models of development. A key feature of this development appears to be a 'do-it-yourself' approach to optimising locally available productive resources – human and material – and enhancing local capacity for welfare oriented activities.

Characteristics of 'Self-Help' Schemes

'Self-help' associations are voluntary groups of citizens engaged in the planning and implementation of community improvement projects. Where the government lacks resources for local development a strategy through which people are mobilised to do things for themselves has obvious attractions. The activities engaged in by self-help groups are mainly concentrated upon the provision of common services such as schools, water supply, clinics, and in most cases they concern the construction rather than the running of such facilities. 'Self-help' groups may be little more than adjuncts of local national government or party-directed schemes or may be completely autonomous of the state, relying instead on entirely local inputs or direct assistance from international aid agencies. Where the participation of the central government is involved, official assistance is usually provided on a 'matching fund' basis, in direct proportion to local contribution (usually voluntary labour). By such means it is possible for poor countries to compensate for a lack of public financial resources by the use of usually abundant supplies of under-utilised labour and the benefit of local knowledge and material resources. Indeed, the potential of self-help in development lies in its ability to create capital out of otherwise underemployed labour; this being one of the few resources which many developing countries have in plentiful supply.

'Self-Help' Development Strategy and the Basic Needs Approach

This is analysed with reference to the four areas already identified:

The Definition of Needs. In as much as 'self-help' schemes originate within local communities they provide a forum for expressing local needs and priorities. 'Self-help' associations thus have a potential to promote popular participation in the identification of local needs as well as in the making and implementation of decisions requisite to the satisfaction of those needs. In this way 'self-help' activities at the local level as a development strategy can be said to be consonant with the BNA. In practice though, several factors may operate to prevent the satisfaction of basic needs through self-help development efforts. Radical cadres, local notables or influential interest groups may seek to determine needs on behalf of the community, and the views of political out-groups or deprived elements can thus go unheeded. The skills, confidence and influence needed to advance a case may be most lacking in lower-income or low status groups. Community Development officials may unduly influence the choice of projects or encourage unrealistic schemes, given the availability of local financial and material resources. The mere avail-ability of 'matching funds' may lead to demands and support for ill-thought out projects, and local pride can lead to the adoption of prestigious new ventures in preference to more need-satisfying development projects. On the other hand, local self-help groups may only go for the kind of schemes that the government is known to favour and be willing to support, even if they do not reflect the felt needs of the community. Finally, governments may impose allegedly voluntary tasks on local communities even when the benefits to local people are far from clear or ignore local opinions once a scheme has been completed.

Generation of Resources. 'Self-help' associations undoubtedly can and do contribute to economic development through the generation and mobilisation of local resources for productive ventures and community services. The potential of self-help associations to raise capital for local-level development – beyond what the government can afford – is considerable as can be deduced from the experience of Kenya (*Harambee*) or the Gambia (*Tesito*) where they are allotted an important role in rural development programmes. Voluntary effort has also made a positive contribution to urban improvement schemes in some developing countries.

At the same time 'self-help' associations may become a drain upon central government resources. The 'demonstration effect' of successful projects, the promptings of enthusiastic Community Development officials, or the knowledge that 'matching funds' are available, may lead to governments being inundated with demands for assistance, with the possible danger of over-concentration of facilities.[9] Over-concentration of projects may lead to increased spending of scarce financial resources, given that often local communities are not able to maintain a facility or hire the staff to operate it, and as such the government has to meet recurrent costs. Local priorities may clash with national ones and, because of the political pressure of the 'self-help' movement, resources may have to be diverted to it which would otherwise have been employed more productively. Ill-conceived or badly implemented self-help projects may waste resources or even damage the environment, leading both the government and the public to lose faith in the self-help principle.[10] Schemes that had public support may fail to retain popular enthusiasm as costs in time or money are seen to outweigh the original benefits.

Distribution of Resources. Conflicting views are held about the distributive effect of 'self-help' schemes. In principle, the fact that 'self-help' generates resources for public consumption which otherwise would have remained untapped (or retained for personal consumption by the rich) suggests some benefit to the community at large. The concentration of 'self-help' projects at the local level in a number of Third World countries, particularly in the less-developed areas, lends weight to this belief. However, the actual distribution of goods and services depends in part on the efficiency of voluntary 'self-help' schemes but more importantly on the power structure within the community. Without a radical shift in the distribution of power between social classes it is unlikely that the 'self-help' movement can achieve a great deal of re-distribution of resources, even though modest shifts or the generation of relatively little new wealth can be of some significance to those most in need. It has been observed in East Africa[11] that the main beneficiaries of community development schemes have been relatively privileged social groups – those with the initial resources, skills or influence to help ensure that 'self-help' schemes reflect their particular needs. Particularly deprived socio-economic groups and individuals may end up putting more effort into such schemes, relative to what they eventually obtain from them. For example, women can end up contributing most of the labour input to a 'self-help' project while their menfolk enjoy the benefits. Where the benefit desired is not confined to a target group identified on the basis of need, it is inevitable that other socio-economic groups will gain from it as well. Government preference for higher productivity may lead it to favour 'self-help' schemes which benefit the more productive large-scale farmers rather than smallholder peasant producers. Political influence may also adversely affect the distribution of benefits within a community.

Satisfaction. Very high levels of perceived satisfaction may be obtained by individuals and social groups from 'self-help' projects but the sense of well-being and efficacy will depend on how far such ventures satisfy the basic needs of the participants. Too much government interference or too little state support; poorly conceived or executed schemes; squabbles over individual contributions to or benefits from a project; lack of technical resources to maintain a scheme: all these can materially affect the sense of satisfaction to be obtained from being involved in a 'self-help' activity.

The implementation of 'self-help' projects can contribute to the promotion of genuine and effective popular participation as required by the BNA but only if a number of conditions are met. A number of these have been reviewed above: 'self-help' projects must reflect real need, particularly the needs of the most deprived; and government must exercise both firmness and discretion to ensure that schemes are technically feasible and potentially beneficial, that they can be reconciled with over-all national priorities and resources, and that they do not unduly favour elite groups in local communities. Yet these may not be easy to accomplish even given widespread public support or a high level of motivation. Government involvement may be resented or can cause delay in implementing a project with consequent fall-off in local interest and enthusiasm; a desirable stress on economic growth may lead local decision-making bodies to favour more obviously productive schemes or the more 'efficient' groups in a locality; or the 'self-help' movement may be used to reward local political allies and to defuse potential unrest.[12] In such cases it is unlikely that the aims of the 'self-help' movement will be achieved and dissatisfaction with central government and local authorities will increase while apathy or internecine conflict will be intensified at the local level.

Agrarian Associations

A variety of participatory organisations can be found in the rural sector although their value to a basic needs-oriented development strategy differs widely. All are subject to restrictions and opportunities presented by the diversity of political, economic and social relations occurring among agrarian communities in the Third World. Factors such as the location of political power in society, the attitude of authority towards rural associatons which seek to alter the status quo, the modes of agricultural production, the existence of a tradition of collective action on the part of cultivators, or relations between rural and urban groups are known to have an important bearing on the expression and fulfilment of rural needs and demands. A review of the more common forms of agrarian-based associations[13] provides a useful insight into the inter-actions of these factors and the impact on rural levels of living.

Peasant Organisations

These can be and have been important (and sometimes unique) vehicles for promoting participation of the rural poor. Their importance can hardly be over-emphasised in the context of a great part of the Third World, where there exists a close relationship between deprivation and rural existence. A considerable number of obstacles lie in the path of a successful peasant organisation, some of which are relevant to other forms of participatory organisations, but others rather specific to rural livelihood.

First, quasi-feudal and clientelist social and economic relations prevail in many parts of the Third World. Small farmers may be tied to large landowners by legal, economic and social bonds and the latter may be strongly opposed to many of the reforms favoured by peasant organis-ations, for example, land redistribution or rent reduction. Where rural landowning elites are nationally powerful, opportunities for non-violent reform may be rather limited. Also the social characteristics of rural society may inhibit collective action in other ways as, for example, the highly individualistic character of peasants, suspicion of outsiders who might attempt to organise them,[14] rival forms of group identity based on religion, caste or language, and parochialism deriving from geographical remoteness.

As a deprived stratum of society peasants frequently lack political education or skills relevant to comprehending their predicament and resolving it through collective action. In consequence, peasant move-ments may fall under the control of demagogic or unscrupulous leadership. While strong leaders are sometimes called for, the danger exists of leaders either abandoning their followers or turning their organisations into docile bodies in return for political office or economic rewards. Often peasant organisations lack formal constitutions or proper rules of conduct which enables leaders to run them as personal fiefs. Better-off farmers may play a disproportionate role in the activities of peasant unions, often to the detriment of poorer farmers.[15] Urban groups may have ambivalent attitudes towards farmers; they may seek their co-operation but also despise them for not eagerly implementing their policies or may even abandon them if alternative resources (for example, mineral wealth) become available.[16] In collectivist/authoritarian political systems, state-sponsored peasant or farmers' organisations may be granted monopoly status, and ideological, factional or personal factors may lead officials and their local allies to misuse their positions.[17] Central governments and over-large post-colonial bureaucracies often rely on the taxation of peasant production to sustain them. Peasants may be exhorted to increase output but see little of the profits of such increased production.

An effective participatory role for peasant organisations will rest upon several factors. The role of the state is important, in so far as the government must provide the legal basis for unions to exist and operate effectively, as well as the machinery for preventing abuses and exploitation by false leaders or opposition from entrenched interests. Educational facilities must be provided to enable farmers to comprehend the purposes of their organisations and master their procedures. The success registered in Japan, and now being emulated in Malaysia and the Philippines,[18] shows what can be obtained through partnership between government and farmers. A tradition of successful collective action is of great help[19] but success will depend on continuing achievements as well as past victories. Overall, it is important that the interests of all peasants are represented in free and independent agrarian-based organisations, otherwise discontent may lead to fission or withdrawal.

Traditional Communal Organisations

Given the primacy of local and communal ties in rural society any alternative to peasant organisations are likely to be communal in nature. These – based on such affinities as village, district, ethnic sub-group, caste, religion or language – may prove more attractive and effective than novel entities such as peasant organisations. In their favour are their local origins and the existence of enshrined patterns of behaviour to minimise abuse of leadership. They may be elitist or democratic in structure and local or national in organisation. In India[20] caste associations (*Sabhas* and *Sanghams*) have mobilised on a national scale the dispersed votes of the lowliest, and won major concessions. In Africa, 'tribal improvement unions' have similarly linked remote rural areas with national policies through the leadership of educated 'sons abroad' in the major cities.[21] Religious movements such as the Muslim Brotherhoods (*tariqas*) of Senegal, led by saintly families, have also provided leadership against government exaction for peasant communities.[22] Communal associations, depending on their individual composition, have been effective in voicing grievances, obtaining redress and generating new resources through collective labour. The sense of satisfaction thus generated can be very high, notably among threatened groups or those bound by religious ties.

Against these achievements some drawbacks must be recorded. Many communal associations are elitist in leadership (with sometimes excessive deference paid them) and participation may be restricted. Elitist leaders may use their positions for the good of the community but they may also be selfish or anti-modernistic. Extreme partisanship or obscurantism on the part of communal associations may lead to intense conflict and violence with the state or among rival groups as happened in India, Nigeria and Malaysia. Governments anxious to establish their national and secular credentials may find it inexpedient or impossible to work with communal associations and the latter may withdraw into sullen isolation. Communal organisations with trans-national allegiances (for example world religious bodies) may arouse the suspicions of the government because of their divided allegiances.[23] Given the 'total' concerns of communal associations, individual government departments may find it difficult to deal with them. Finally, communal associations may not be able to contain tensions arising from economic and social modernisation; religious bonds may decline and individualism may weaken common ties.

Agricultural Workers' Organisations

To the extent they seek to articulate the needs of the rural landless (perhaps the most deprived socio-economic group covered in this survey) agricultural workers' unions may be considered a suitable vehicle for promoting mass participation, and a number of observations can be made regarding their suitability to a basic needs-oriented development strategy.

Farm workers were among the last to be organised economically in developed countries because of their physical dispersion, low pay, poor education and close ties to their employers. The same is true of the Third World today, with the additional problem of migrant labour. To begin with, migrant labour is extremely difficult to organise because of its geographical mobility, uncertain legal status and ambivalent economic identity. At certain stages in his annual work cycle, the migrant may be a labourer, a trader, a farmer or a rentier, but as a labourer he may operate as a share-cropper hoping to obtain permanent rights to land. The latter hope may result in organisational quiescence. Even in cases where farm labour is of local origin, landowners may turn to 'imported' labour with a view to under-cut local workers and reduce their capacity to organise in defence of their interests. Competition between alien and local workers can effectively destroy the basis for any economic solidarity among agricultural labourers. To these problems must be added the attitudes of certain governments that create obstacles, legal or otherwise, to the organisation of rural farm workers and the uncertain qualities of union leadership at the grass-roots level.

While the needs of the rural landless are very real, providing them with institutional support is difficult. Plantation workers, with their physical concentration and stable work environment, have proved less difficult to organise but other landless elements may slip through any organisational net because of their collective disadvantage. Though caste and other communal associations may offer some redress, and political action in concert with other elements in society may lead to major land reform programmes,[24] the well-being of the landless labourer is still threatened by powerful landowning elites opposed to such radical changes. In other situations there may not be enough land to redistribute. The experience of societies undergoing earlier modernisation shows that in a number of cases the rural landless were obliged to emigrate or seek work in the rapidly expanding cities of the urban sector. A similar fate seems to have overtaken the rural poor of the Third World today. Ameliorative policies must, therefore, not be confined exclusively to the countryside; yesterday's rural landless are today's urban squatters. Hence, urban 'self-help' and informal sector job-creation schemes seem to be a necessary adjunct to the organisation of the rural poor in their places of origin.

Co-operative Enterprises

Together with 'Community Development', co-operation has come to be regarded as something of a universal panacea for the problems of rural development in the Third World. Its achievements, despite inescapable difficulties, recommend it as a means of implementing a basic needs-oriented development strategy. Since the co-operative movement as a type of participatory institution encompasses a wide variety of forms and levels, what follows has to be selective.

Co-operative enterprises in the rural sector may take the form of:

1 *Producer co-operatives* involving the joint farming of land and sharing of its produce or income from it (for example, kibbutzin, communes);
2 *Marketing co-operatives* through which farmers collect, store, and sell their crops direct to wholesale buying outlets;
3 *Supply co-operatives* in which farmers join to acquire bulk supplies of inputs or to share ownership and use of water sources, equipment and other productive assets;
4 *Processing co-operatives* whose members jointly own ginneries, refineries, mills, canneries, and so on, required to process produce;
5 *Credit and savings co-operatives* through which farmers obtain seasonal or longer-term loans, normally for farming investment; and

6 *Consumer co-operatives* for bulk purchases and retail distribution of consumer goods.

This classification, which refers largely to agricultural production, also applies to other sectors of rural production, for example cottage industries. Considerable variations may exist in the size and level of operation as well, for example primary societies, secondary bulking and processing societies, and apex institutions whose functions may be extremely diverse. Not included are traditional forms of co-operation involving pooling labour and credit or sharing communal natural resources.

Co-operative Enterprises and the Basic-Needs Approach.[25] Co-operatives can make an important contribution to basic needs satisfaction through their potential for promoting and ensuring popular participation in the development process in the following ways:

1 *Defining needs:* A successful co-operative movement can effectively influence national planning decisions while within each co-operative enterprise members can help determine local decisions;
2 *Mobilisation of resources:* Productivity and output can be enhanced by improving inputs and outlets crucial to rural production (water, seeds, fertilisers, marketing, preservation of produce, processing, and so on). Economies of scale may also be obtained through common ownership and maintenance of equipment, and so on;
3 *Distribution of benefits:* Co-operators and their families can obtain a share of profits previously taken by middlemen; and
4 *Satisfaction:* Effective participation and economic success can generate high levels of satisfaction and self-confidence.

To obtain these objectives several conditions need to be met: two inter-linked factors seem to be of crucial importance – *the degree of loyalty and solidarity among members* and *the effectiveness of co-operative management.* Tentative analysis of various national experiences suggests a number of conducive factors:

● local initiative and enthusiasm in setting up co-operatives;
● a strong sense of affinity undivided by class or communalism;
● effective leadership responsive to members' needs;
● sufficient autonomy to enable members to obtain meaningful participation in planning and management; and
● the availability of sufficient state support – extension services, credit facilities, audit and scrutiny by outside experts.

Conversely, the effectiveness of co-operatives as a vehicle for promoting popular participation is likely to be significantly reduced in

68

instances where the idea and organisational form is imposed on a community for ideological or administrative reasons; the membership is racked by class or communal antagonisms; the leadership lacks competence or integrity; state support or supervision is lacking or operates to frustrate the goals and aspirations of the majority of the membership.

Capable and respected leadership protects co-operatives from outside interference or internal malpractices. However, in several instances, speculation by office-holders, petty tyranny and sheer incompetence on the part of officials are a major source of popular complaint and loss of enthusiasm. There are even cases where the practice of 'co-operation' has become synonymous with embezzlement and self-enrichment of the leadership as concluded in various reports by commissions of inquiry investigating mismanagement and related abuses of co-operatives.

Political interference in the activities of co-operatives can be damaging particularly when responsible positions are given to clients of political leaders. A failure or unwillingness to scrutinise their actions enables them to misuse co-operative funds and resources. In other instances loans advanced to co-operators with the necessary political connections may be put to improper use and not repaid. Lack of membership solidarity has been endemic in Asia and Africa, partly as a result of political interference but also because of sharp cleavages within the local societies to which the co-operators belonged.

While high levels of solidarity protect co-operatives from external pressures, in several Latin American cases this solidarity has worked to the disadvantage of other social groups.[26] Economically successful co-operators may be backed by the state in their disputes with less successful and impoverished elements. Co-operatives have, in some instances, spawned privileged and selfish communities. In Peru, co-operators who had gained from earlier land reform programmes, sought to prevent others from obtaining land or exploited the labour of landless peasants.[27] In Africa, a relatively privileged co-operative element has been observed and income inequalities in rural society have been known to increase as a result of the operation and activities of co-operative enterprises.[28] Governments sometimes take an indulgent attitude because the co-operators are 'progressive' farmers whose activities contribute to efficient, purely growth-oriented development strategies. Such instances illustrate the potential conflict between the objectives of economic growth and egalitarian distribution. Where capitalist-type farming is well advanced, co-operatives may be little better than 'nurseries' for rural capitalism or be relegated to the position of a poor relation.

State (in addition to political) interference can also be a source of dissatisfaction. Central government, with its large bureaucratic base, may be interested in co-operatives in order more effectively to extract resources from the rural sector. Not all such resources are invested in productive ventures and social services that benefit rural inhabitants. Attempts by farmers to resist may lead to coercive measures being taken against them. In China,[29] some balance between a monopolistic political centre and local autonomy within the communes seems to have been arrived at: the state determines overall economic priorities and production quotas but local communes are granted considerable autonomy in fulfilling targets and disposing of profits.

As noted elsewhere in this survey, relations with central government or ruling party are a crucial and sensitive issue. Some decentralisation seems necessary but the state must, at the same time, provide essential support. The right balance must be determined empirically. Allowing co-operators to use local languages would also seem desirable. Educating and training co-operators in the mysteries of procedure is also vital to success – an informed membership is less likely to be fooled or brow-beaten by despotic or dishonest leaders. Finally, increased autonomy may be strengthened by promoting integrated co-operative activities as, for example, the linking of the provision of credit with the bulk purchases of agricultural inputs and the marketing of farm produce.[30]

Women's Organisations[31]

While it is not easy to generalise about the circumstances of women globally, the ILO[32] recognises that the plight of women in the Third World demands redress both within the household and the community at large. Political emancipation has often favoured men more than women (as indicated by the preponderance of men in political office at all levels). Modernisation of agriculture in many instances has increased the burden of women and undermined a precarious economic independence[33] for, in addition to domestic and food-crop production, women may be called upon to labour on cash crops and to replace their menfolk who have moved to the towns or mines to find work. Their traditional handicrafts may be overtaken by mechanisation, and male domination of rural development agencies may restrict women's chances to obtain credits for self-employment. Denial of education and job skills, competition from men, and male prejudice towards non-household employment among women restrict opportunities for advancement so that hawking, petty trading or even prostitution may be the only openings available to them. Frequently, in town and countryside alike, participatory institutions are dominated by men, and women are held back by institutional and cultural barriers.

Women and the Basic Needs Approach

Increasing female participation in decision making through women's organisations alone is unlikely to prove very successful, though these have a part to play. In rural areas there is some scope for re-directing traditional associations among women, towards wider participatory goals. In the Ivory Coast,[34] the Government is seeking to utilise such bodies in agriculture and there are possibilities for their use in such activities as disseminating information on child welfare or family planning. The capacity of traditional women's organisations to undertake modern participatory functions will be determined by their original purpose, their adaptability to change and the attitudes of men as much as women to their new roles.

In urban areas organisations of professional women are restricted by the paucity of educated women, but they can act as pressure groups to advance female causes or supervise remedial programmes of action.[35] Yet the lack of formal education should not, and in practice does not, constitute a barrier to organisations by women in defence of their interests. For example, non-professional women, organised in market or craft associations, may exercise some influence on wider events as well as on their members' living conditions through their control of retail trade.[36] This has existed historically in many parts of West Africa and, more recently, during the colonial and post-independence era, 'market women' have been able to take successful direct action on a number of issues.

Participation of Women in the Decision-Making Process

Auxiliary wings of ruling parties can be found which provide women with a national and local organisation to represent the interests of their sex, for example in Guinea where women play an important and influential role in the Party and the State through such representation.[37] Women may also be given nominated seats in political assemblies or on important policy bodies to ensure a measure of female representation. Such opportunities can increase the part played by women in the making and implementation of key decisions that have a bearing on their well-being and their position in society. Yet such opportunities may be constrained; in Mali, the National Union of Malian Women has had its activities suspended by a suspicious government. Politically-orientated women's movements may be an additional means of regulating society as well as a source of genuine participation. Where the regime enjoys the support of women, and this is necessary for its political survival, important legal and practical concessions may be granted in return. Radical regimes stress the full emancipation of women as an essential element of their ideologies and major gains have been won in countries such as China and Cuba. Elsewhere, a male-dominated social system may set limits to female emancipation.

Regardless of political ideology the extension of full participatory rights to women will depend on breaking down male prejudices and privileges and the creation of adequate educational, training and other facilities (creches, canteens, family planning clinics) for women. Such comprehensive changes can only be brought about by positive governmental action. Once women are given the basic skills, time and opportunities they will be able to participate both through their own associations and, more importantly, through all other institutions at present dominated by men.

Youth Organisations

Young people constitute an increasing proportion of the unemployed in both developed and developing countries and, therefore, any attempt to implement a basic needs strategy within the context of national development must take account of the needs of youth and provide specific policies aimed at increasing opportunities for their involvement in the development process. Their large numbers and concentration in urban areas, often with high aspirations and limited opportunities, suggest an urgent need to institutionalise channels for a more effective and constructive participation in decisions which affect their future; otherwise, the combination of idealism and self-interest on the part of youth together with the breakdown of traditional family life might result in extremist alternatives to meet their demands. Yet many governments seem to waver between identifying actual needs and aspirations of youth on the one hand and attempting to manipulate and control young people on the other. The main types of youth organisations are outlined below.

Government/Ruling Party Sponsored Youth Organisations

Many ruling groups in the Third World actively recruited young people when they formed opposition movements to colonial rule and now claim to represent youth in their ideologies and policies. Youth wings attached to the ruling party are a familiar phenomenon as are state-sponsored national students' unions, 'young pioneers' associations, or national service corps. At one level such bodies provide young people with corporate recognition within the political system and the opportunity to engage in constructive national mobilisation. Youth groups may be given control over development projects or police and internal security roles (as in Mali or Guinea under Sekou Touré),[38] as well as consultative status. At the same time governments seek to manipulate and regulate youth through officially-sponsored organisations, and indoctrination and surveillance are as important functions as participation and representation. It is not unusual for the leadership of youth groups to be purged periodically to ensure loyalty to the state.[39] Within such constraints state-controlled youth organisations may be given a say in decision making; have an opportunity to contribute to development policies through work programmes and ideological campaigns; benefit from heavy investment in

72

education and sport even when full employment is not possible; and obtain a sense of satisfaction from such purposeful association with national objectives.

Autunomous Modern-Sector Youth Organisations

This category covers a range of activities – youth wings of rival parties; independent students' unions and school pupils' unions; church or other religious youth groups; social and sporting clubs; associations of unemployed youth, etc. Some may be elitist or confrontationist, as is often the case with students' unions, while others may be purely recreational in purpose. Several of them may have a national or even international representation; others may be parochial in location and concern. Sometimes, as in the Gambia, they may be grouped into a national youths' council which discusses with or confronts the government; in other instances they may be too divided and fragmented to comprise a unified and effective interest group in society. Their participatory capabilities, as such, much depend on the attitude of the regime and their internal characteristics.

Traditional Age-Grade Associations

These are common in parts of the Third World, notably parts of Africa, and represent a means of instilling into the young the values of society and providing them with purposeful functions within the community. Sex-based, age-grade associations usually have, or had, ritual, leisure, defence and police, and heavy work roles in society. Modernisation and the growth of central government power have destroyed or undermined some of these functions, but 'self-help' projects, as in East Africa, have made use of inputs from such organisations. Up-dated versions of such traditional groupings, as in the form of improvement unions and so on, may enable them to continue to play a constructive part in community development at the local level – heeded by society in return for their contribution to the needs of the community.[40]

No participatory or development strategy can ignore the young; they are both beneficiaries of and contributors to such policy. As already noted, the energies and idealism of youth are vital resources for a basic needs strategy but insensitive reactions on the part of governments or the older generation can easily alienate the young and push them into an oppositional role damaging to all concerned.

Trade Unions

The historical experiences and achievements of trade unions in advanced industrial societies indicate a significant participatory role for them in the newly industrialising states of the Third World, where a range of problems affecting wage-earners and the working class in general are evident. Yet, although trade unions across the world have a number of common features, wider political and social factors may result in different roles and capacities.

Characteristics of Trade Unions in the Third World[41]

Third World trade unions share with those in developed industrial countries the functions of representing and promoting the interests of wage and salary earners through industrial combination. To that extent their constitutions and modes of action are often similar, for example:

- trade unions are found in the public and private sectors though general and company unions are more widespread than craft or industry based organisations;
- power notionally resides in an (annual) congress which debates policy, approves resolutions and elects an executive council;
- there is the customary hierarchy of representation from plant/workshop through district/regional committees and meetings to national organisations which may be affiliated to the major international trade union federations – ICFTU, WFTU, WCL and regional groups within the Third World;
- trade unions may advance their members' interests within the place of employment, through independent political action, or by means of affiliation to political organisations and parties;
- and trade unions may enjoy the customary legal rights to negotiate with employers and to withhold labour when in dispute.

Yet these outward similarities to labour organisations in advanced industrial states can be misleading. In practice things tend to be very different. This can be accounted for by the peculiar societal constraints under which trade unions operate in the Third World and also by the internal shortcomings of the unions.

Societal Constraints. In many Third World countries the proportion of the working population engaged in wage or salaried employment is still significantly low – averaging 15–20 per cent – though with considerable variation depending on the level of modernisation or industrialisation. Thus in such countries as Argentina or Egypt, wage employment is high, whereas in many African countries with low levels of industrialisation it is minuscule. Industrialisation is also unevenly spread within individual countries and modern sector employment is principally in commercial and public sectors rather than manufacturing. The fact that trade union activities in developing countries have been confined mainly to modern sector employment effectively limits the participatory capacity of this

74

type of organisation. Another societal constraint to organising workers in the Third World is that the urban labour force still retains strong physical and cultural ties with rural society and as a consequence lacks strong class consciousness which, in developed countries, contributes immensely to workers' solidarity and unionisation. In the so-called informal sector many employees may be relatives of employers or tied to them by cultural and social bonds and therefore difficult to unionise as well. The threat of unemployment may lead wage-earners to seek to improve their living conditions by less controversial means than union membership, for example working longer hours, taking on several jobs, attaching themselves to economic patrons.

Internal Weaknesses of Trade Unions. For a variety of reasons workers may prefer to join other forms of voluntary associations, such as communal ones, rather than trade unions. Union strength is further weakened by excessive numbers of small trade unions and frequent rivalries between competing central federations based on personal and ideological differences on the part of leadership. The fact that many unions were set up through outside support (ICFTU, WFTU and WCL), government intervention (as with colonial administrations) or employers' initiative, also serves to undermine independence and weaken membership solidarity through common struggle. In general, many Third World trade unions find it difficult to raise funds internally because of low wage levels and inability of members to pay regular dues. This encourages reliances on foreign patrons, governments and employers to provide financial support or 'check-off' facilities. As far as leadership is concerned, standards tend to be low due to lack of training, education and experience. In addition, experience and bargaining techniques acquired during the colonial era may no longer be appropriate or advantageous.

Relationship with Government and Employers. Government is often the major employer of labour and may set limits to free collective bargaining, restrict strike action, and impose pay 'ceilings'. Unions as such may have to operate within rules and regulations that leave them with little room for manoeuvre. Unions may be viewed by government as a rival source of political power and as centres of radical subversion. Emphasis on rapid economic growth often leads governments to adopt a 'productionist' attitude towards unions.[42] The latter are expected to discipline the labour force in the interests of the nation; to increase production, restrict wage demands and avoid disruption rather than to press demands of their members. This constant search for political security and economic growth leads governments of all political persuasions to adopt authoritarian or paternalistic attitudes towards trade unions. Many trade unions are compulsorily affiliated to a government-sponsored central organisation, and union leadership may be selected by the ruling party or a military junta rather than by the members themselves. In return for certain privileges ('check-off' system, offices, funds, etc.) and, perhaps, a restricted participatory role in decision making, unions are expected to support government policies. Despite the legal recognition of trade unions, industrial action may be proscribed and union leaders imprisoned. Urban wage-earners may be viewed as a privileged section of society by governments anxious to shift priorities to rural development. Governments may even side with expatriot employers against workers in order to maintain foreign investment; many large expatriot employers, while often providing better working conditions than local entrepreneurs, may decide to withdraw if labour increases wage demands.

Despite legislation supporting and guaranteeing the existence of trade unions and their rights to bargain, employers may refuse to recognise trade unions, employ too few people to be affected by prevailing labour legislation, or set up exclusive or rival company or house unions to head off worker militancy. Further, employers enjoy a considerable advantage in negotiating with trade unions – much greater financial resources, information, skilled staff, and so on.

In the main, labour organisations in the Third World are numerically weak, inadequately organised, poor and sometimes badly served by their leaders; furthermore, their constitutional rights are frequently cast aside by unsympathetic governments.

Trade Unions and the Basic Needs Approach

Articulating Needs. Do unions in the Third World *effectively* voice the needs of the working people? In the main, the answer to this question is no, because only a small minority of working people belong to trade unions, though, given the necessary ideological and organisational attributes, trade unions may promote the interests of the 'working class' in general, as well as those of their own members. Yet in many Third World countries it is doubtful if this takes place given the difficulty of maintaining democratic practices within unions and of operating independent of outside influence. Politically controlled, autocratic or corrupt leadership frequently prevents the rank-and-file from playing a proper role in union activities. Government action in many cases further restricts trade unions from adequately voicing the needs of their members, and deprives wage-earners of a forum for articulating their needs and taking action in support of their demands. It is difficult to reconcile a regimented 'productionist' attitude on the part of governments with the participatory requirement of the basic needs approach to development. Partial or token participation is more likely to be granted though some qualified gains may be obtained by such means.

Generation of Resources. Trade unions have much to contribute in this respect, as the frequent 'productionist' exhortations of governments suggest. Economic development lays great stress on new skills and attitudes on the part of the work force and unions can play a part in socialising new entrants into the labour force in industrial routines and skills. Knowledge of work processes may enable trade unions to contribute to greater efficiency and productivity though experience elsewhere shows that trade unions may resist technological and work changes as well.

Distribution of Goods and Services. Where free collective bargaining is permitted, trade unions have proved very successful in improving the living conditions of their members and, in alliance with radical forces in society, have helped to bring about a more equitable distribution of essential goods and services. The ability of unions to improve their members' living standards or those of society rests in part on whether trade unionists and wage-earners form a 'labour aristocracy' or serve as points of redistribution to needy social groups. The evidence remains somewhat ambiguous.[43] More importantly, the position taken by governments will determine the role of unions in this capacity.

Satisfaction. As with other institutions surveyed in this chapter, the ability of trade unions to provide 'psychic' satisfaction to their members depends on how representative and successful unions are. Leadership shortcomings and government interference have caused considerable dissatisfaction in many instances (for example, Ghana, the United Republic of Tanzania)[44] and led to rank-and-file rebellion against leaders and government policies.

It is unlikely that full participation in decision making will be granted to trade unions in most Third World countries for some time. Union weaknesses and authoritarian governments indicate a subordinate and carefully regulated role for trade unions. However, opportunities do exist for unions to take limited action in defence of the interests of workers (strikes, go-slows, passive resistance) and to throw in their support behind factions sympathetic to labour where political leadership is divided.

Industrial Democracy

The term 'industrial democracy' has been used to cover several types of participatory arrangements in industrial enterprises. These include collective bargaining; various forms of employee participation at different levels of the enterprise and in different areas of managerial responsibility; worker 'self-management' collectivities; workers' control; industrial co-operatives and common ownership enterprises.

Levels of Participation

Three main levels of decision making and participation by workers in industry can be identified.[45]

1 *The Job:* Workers may be granted discretion regarding job activity, subject to the overall constraints of the work process (that is production system and technology). Skilled workers are more likely to be given such discretion than the unskilled.

2 *The Work Group:* Participation is again normally confined to aspects of the production system, discretion of management in arranging work procedures to meet pre-determined production quotas.

3 *The Plant or Enterprise:* Much interest is now shown in worker participation in higher levels (management) of decision making. Representation may be by direct election or through trade union or shop steward representatives.

In addition to the above, trade unions and labour-based political parties may represent worker opinion on national/regional planning authorities.

The highest level of worker participation is found in countries with the greatest public ownership or active state intervention in privately-owned industry. However, general economic and political constraints on complete autonomy in decision making occur everywhere.

Scope of Participation

There are two aspects of importance in this regard. The first concerns the range of issues in which employees participate. Worker participation may focus on personal, social or economic (including technical and business issues) decisions. The areas of decision making in which worker participation is limited may have greatest immediate relevance to workers, and therefore their outcome may be determined at higher levels or by extraneous factors. The second is the degree of influence exercised by workers. This encompasses co-operation (rights of information, protest, suggestion, consultation); co-determination (rights of temporary or permanent veto, co-decision, arbitration); and self-management (autonomy in decision making).

Co-operation implies restricted employee participation with ultimate decision making in hands of management. Co-determination implies shared decision making within defined limits. Self-management implies that workers make autonomous decisions.

The Context of Industrial Democracy

This has an important bearing on the scope and effectiveness of workers' participation. The important distinction here is between industrial democracy, resulting from the active struggle of employees for a greater say in decision making, and that stemming from management or government initiative. This distinction may affect worker commitment and attitudes, and, hence, the effectiveness of this type of participation for satisfying basic needs.

Objectives of Industrial Democracy[46]

Four schools of thought on industrial democracy have been identified:

1 *The 'management' school* advocates participation of low intensity and narrow scope as conducive to greater productivity and harmony.
2 *The 'humanistic psychology' school* advocates participation of high intensity and narrow scope (i.e. considerable autonomy at job/workgroup levels). Expected benefits are the same as for (1) above with the additional improvement in the mental health of the workers. Also like (1) above this is concerned with improving industrial relations within the existing system of power.
3 *The 'democratic theory' approach* advocates high intensity and wide scope for participation as a training in participatory democracy as well as in industrial power-sharing.
4 *The 'participatory left'* in Europe advocates high intensity and wide scope as well, both for improved industrial efficiency and for cultivating a revolutionary consciousness requisite to a worker take-over.

Experiences of Industrial Democracy

In this section, within the limits of space, we go on to consider how participation in industrial democracy has been introduced in various parts of the world and the degrees of success and failure of these varying experiences. However, it should be noted that despite widespread agreement on the utility of industrial democracy much resistance has been met in trying to implement its more radical aspects.

European Experiences. Industrial participation seems to have gone furthest in countries which have suffered economic devastation from war or undergone radical changes in the ownership of the means of production.

Industrial co-operatives are a common feature of the socialist economies of Eastern Europe. These co-operatives are usually organised according to the main industrial groups or sectors and combined in a national central union which is responsible for economic planning and the provision of managerial, development and research services to members. In addition to production of consumer goods, they are also particularly active in the provision of services such as housing, credit and savings. Initial financing is usually by the State but the co-operatives are expected eventually to generate their own investment funds. Profits from their production and marketing activities are split between members' accounts and reserves for reinvestment. In Poland, for example, where perhaps the most participatory arrangements in the Eastern European countries were introduced in the post-war reconstruction period, industrial co-operatives accounted for 7.6 per cent of the GNP in 1976 with a total membership of 867 000 in over 1500 enterprises within 15 main industrial groups. In 1975 they produced 11 per cent of the country's consumer goods and 59 per cent of its services.[47] In theory, industrial co-operatives and their central unions are democratically controlled through a hierarchy of elected committee members, which allows for indirect participation of the membership in decision making and management. In practice, however, overall powers and activities are subject to rigid state control.

Yugoslavia is, perhaps, the most outstanding experiment in industrial democracy, with elected workers' councils responsible for appointing the Directors and management boards of all industrial enterprises.[48] In practice though, worker autonomy is constrained by the reliance on the market mechanism for resource allocation in the Yugoslavian economy. This gives the banks, which provide over half the investment funds, and top management, a predominant influence in investment planning and technical decisions. Evidence suggests some scepticism on the part of workers over the extent of their influence on these critical decisions and a growing dependence upon trade unions and secondary employment to safeguard their interests. Nevertheless, workers' opinions (though less so those of women and less-educated workers perhaps) have undoubtedly been important in determining wages and working conditions and in reducing wage disparities. Participation also appears to ameliorate much of the alienation normally associated with repetitive factory tasks.

Ironically, it was in 'fascist' Spain under General Franco that one of the most successful workers' co-operatives, the Mondragon enterprises, developed.[49] By 1975 there were 58 related enterprises with some 13 000 members. Apart from manufacturing, the co-operative movement has a bank, insurance society, and even educational and research institutions. Funds are obtained from high membership fees, the bank's resources and company profits. The elected boards of management allow considerable latitude to hired managers and these, together with the expertise and financial support of the bank, ensure a profitable record. In other European States and North America there is considerable resistance to industrial democracy. The practice of 'worker directors', which originated in the Federal Republic of Germany,[50] has now been extended to several neighbouring States but workers' co-operatives are rare and have a mixed record.[51] Worker attitude is not entirely favourable to the extension of industrial participation; many employees prefer to leave high level decisions to professional management or else regard such innovations as 'worker directors' as a means of curbing labour militancy and dividing the workforce.

Third World Experiences. Several Third World countries have experimented with worker participation in decision making and management within the industrial sector.

In *Peru*[52] the radical military regime introduced 'Industrial Communities' (ICs) in most manufacturing enterprises in 1970, whereby all employees belong to 'ICs' and a fixed portion of company profits/stock is handed over to them. 'IC' representation on boards of management is proportional to the amount of company stock they own. There is evidence that these innovations did lead to greater reinvestment of company profits as well as increased earnings for employees. Yet against these gains must be noted the claims that the industrial, as opposed to agricultural, workers were already a relatively privileged section of society; that reinvested profits lead to unemployment because of capital-intensive emphasis; and that foreign investors were scared away by the precipitate action of the government in imposing 'ICs' upon employers.

In *Chile*[53] workers' control was also introduced under the Allende regime (1970–73) but it is not clear what remains of it today. Workers' councils were introduced at shop-floor (Production Committees), intermediary (Co-Ordinating Committees), and management (Administrative Councils) levels by state fiat and independent action by employees. Democratic control was further strengthened by the creation of parallel assemblies which elected and invigilated the worker representatives. Trade unions maintained a separate existence. Among the gains claimed for the system were reduced absenteeism, theft and disruption; improved product quality; and the stimulation of worker creativity through having to cope with the effects of the American trade embargo. It has been further claimed that reinvestment was greatest in those enterprises where participation was highest. Participation was highest in enterprises where conflict with management existed; where employees had assumed control; where lower levels of management were sympathetic; and when participants had affiliations with like-thinking political groups.

India,[54] despite its democratic political record, has not taken to industrial participation in a big way. There was some cautious establishment of joint industrial councils before the Emergency in 1975–76 and an apparent intensification of these during that period. Employers strongly resisted such innovations; managers in the state sector found problems in introducing them; and trade unions clashed over who should represent the work force. Indications are that the councils tend to limit their activities to wage bargaining.

In *Egypt*[55] worker participation was introduced in the 1950s when half the seats on boards of management were given to workers' representatives. With a strong trade union tradition, board meetings have often been stormy. Workers also possess block representation in parliament.

In *Algeria*[56] the rapid departure of the French in 1962 forced workers to take over the running of abandoned estates and factories, and self-management ('auto-gestion') became part of the national ideology. The consolidation and extension of state power has led to encroachments on self-managed enterprises with complaints of bureaucratic interference and political patronage. Opposition from a new class of technocrats and state managers and a weak working class identity has led to a loss of momentum in the self-management sector.

In *The United Republic of Tanzania*[57] Workers' Councils were introduced by government in 1970 for all enterprises employing more than ten persons. With a relatively weak trade union organisation this innovation has been regarded more as an attempt to regulate the workforce and increase production than a statement of ideological solidarity with wage earners. Workers' Councils form an additional layer of bureaucracy within the work-place and they have been criticised for being tools of government and management. Management dominates the Councils, particularly in investment and planning areas. Evidence exists though of worker participation having some influence on planning decisions but too frequently the Councils are distanced from the work force to ensure direct participation in decision making.

Industrial Democracy and the Basic Needs Approach

This albeit brief and incomplete survey shows that a number of participatory arrangements exist within the industrial sector to provide workers with varying degrees of opportunities to attain the objectives of a basic needs-oriented development strategy. The evidence shows that successful participation in decision making can occur, leading to the generation of economic resources, the redistribution of profits in favour of wage earners (if not society as a whole) and the creation of 'psychic' satisfaction from such involvement. Complete autonomy is seldom achieved, principally because of wider economic forces which restrict options; political considerations which determine ultimate criteria; lack of managerial expertise and specialised skills or deference to management cadres among workers. Opposition from employers has also prevented the wider adoption of industrial democracy. If workers' representatives are to play a fuller and more informed part in industrial decision making, governments and management must resist the urge to manipulate or intimidate workers' councils as well as provide assistance with training schemes. Workers must ensure a place for women and less-skilled employees in participatory arrangements and ensure that gains achieved in higher productivity through participation do not go entirely to the work force but are fed back into society as well. Otherwise the danger exists of industrial democracy benefiting only the relatively favoured few.

Craft Guild and Small Business Unions

The role of these organisations in generating growth and providing employment is now widely recognised by the governments of developing countries and such international agencies as the ILO. Despite differences in origin and organisation, these two kinds of petty entrepreneurship have much in common. They seek to regulate entry into the so-called 'informal business sector' and to control prices and output as much as the quality of goods and services. They may be regarded as contributing to a basic needs strategy principally through their ability to provide goods and services of a kind and at a price that are relevant to the satisfaction of the basic needs of the masses and, to a lesser extent, through their job-creating potential. They also contribute to a wider distribution of such goods and services. Their particular skills and knowledge may be of use to government in drawing up and implementing local development programmes either through formal consultative mechanisms or informal contacts. Conversely, such organisations may thrust their views on government through various forms of direct or indirect action. In as much as they defend and promote their members' interests such bodies are significant to the promotion of popular participation in decision making.

Against these positive attributes must be noted the generally limited skills and knowledge of these organisations and their highly localised distribution. The particularistic interests of their members can lead to attempts to regulate prices of goods and services to their advantage or to efforts to keep down the wages of their employees who are normally not unionised.

Employers' Organisations and Professional Associations

Employers' organisations and professional associations are pre-eminently a feature of advanced western economies where they are often credited with considerable political influence and economic power. More recently they are to be found in the Third World as a consequence of economic and social change and industrial development.

Characteristics of Employers' Organisations/Professional Associations

The complexity and specialisation of modern economic activity, increasing competition, and the growth in state and trade union power, have all contributed to the emergence of defensive organisations among employers and professions. They may serve one industry/profession or act as umbrella organisations for a number of related activities. They usually have local and national representation and some may be particularly political, others vocational, and yet others social in orientation. They may be oligarchic or democratic in structure. Their influence on decision making varies with the government in power and the characteristics of each organisation. Three principal functions can be identified:

1 *Representational.* To determine a common policy among members and to advance it. Wage negotiation with trade unions may also be undertaken.
2 *Promotional and common services activities.* To provide members with specialised facilities – research, information, statistics, product/service promotion.
3 *Commercial and professional regulation.* To control competition, prices and fees, and entry to membership; to maintain standards and professional conduct.

Relevance to the Basic Needs Approach

In the Third World the late development of industry and its uneven distribution has an important bearing on the emergence of employers' organisations. Historically, commerce and the professions were the first to develop; hence, Chambers of Commerce often had corporate representation in colonial legislatures, and legal and medical associations, together with journalists, have a long record of seeking to articulate general interests as well as those of their professions. In many Third World countries (with certain important exceptions in Asia and Latin America) manufacturing industry is still limited; further, much of it is in state or foreign hands. In many authoritarian countries governments may seek to curb the liberal professions and regulate the affairs of commerce and industry. Even where the political climate is permissive these organisations may be too small, fragmented and inexperienced to play any role approximating those of their counterparts in Europe, North America or the Far East. State attempts to create an indigenous business class, as in Nigeria, may eventually lead to powerful employers' organisations.

While recognising that these are elitist or class based bodies, created primarily to further their members' interests, they may contribute to the successful implementation of a basic needs-oriented development strategy in some of the ways suggested below:

1 By providing representative and specialist opinion or knowledge, as, for example, in national parliaments through nominated/corporate membership (the Gambia, Egypt); on national economic planning councils or other official permanent or *ad hoc* bodies;[58]
2 By acting as 'leaders of national opinion' on more general issues – either in response to government or in oppposing it (for example Ghana 1978);[59]
3 In generating economic resources through the provision of specialist services to members and the support of policies aimed at increased productivity and output, although members' needs may differ from those of the community;
4 By contributing to redistribution objectives through their support for 'indigenisation' policies aimed at reducing alien control of the domestic economy, but this could lead to a costly protectionism with high priced and inferior goods and services. They may sponsor various forms of charitable activities with partial redistributory effects (for example disaster appeals, voluntary projects).

To the extent that sectional interests coincide with popular needs these organisations may contribute to basic needs satisfaction, but they are essentially too elitist and class based bodies to be genuinely broad based. Thus, there are limits to their ability and willingness to engage in wider participatory roles. The roles they do adopt will ultimately depend on the governments in power: right-leaning regimes may rely heavily on them but left/populist administrations may proscribe them or otherwise regulate their activities.

SUMMARY AND CONCLUSIONS

It is easy to become sceptical and pessimistic about the workings of any human institution and the foregoing discussion may have succumbed too frequently to this temptation. As this survey has tried to argue, it seems necessary to examine a variety of participatory organisations, with different forms and at varying levels, in order to:

1 determine the efficacy of each type for implementing basic needs-oriented development strategies (particularly in relation to the four objectives identified at the beginning of this chapter); and
2 identify obstacles to participation, with a view to indicating how they can be overcome.

Clearly, participation allows opportunity for the people involved to define their basic needs as they perceive them and to express demands or priorities requisite to the satisfaction of those needs within a specified time dimension. Thus, workers may demand improvements in earnings and working conditions, local communities may claim roads or more frequent bus services, or self-help groups may contrive clinics or schools. The success of such demands will depend on the extent to which interest groups control or influence decision making within representative bodies and other participatory organisations. In other words, the capacity of participatory organisations successfully to take action to meet their demands is directly related to the opportunity and power to influence the making and implementation of key decisions at all levels. In terms of affecting decisions at higher levels of government or commercial machinery, participation may be effective in agitation for broad goals such as 'more education', or 'higher crop prices', and consultative mechanisms may contribute information which influences planners' choices. Attempts, however, at 'planning from below' – i.e. involving the people in more precise operational choices by governments of investment priorities, resource allocations, regional locations, and so on – have only rarely proved effective. Such involvements are too sporadic and tend to be distorted by differential access to information and the ears of planners.

Two dangers are clear from this survey as far as *definition of needs* is concerned. First, the demands expressed may represent the preferences of activists with the information and ability to make a case and be heard, rather than of those who might be regarded objectively as being most deprived of their basic needs. Second, as discussed in reference to self-help groups, the levels and types of needs which participants may express could be those they realistically expect to be met, rather than those things which they want more but entertain no hope of getting.

The survey offers many examples of participation aiding *growth in resources* required to meet basic needs. There are clear cases of farmers' co-operatives providing vital marketing and processing outlets; of workers' participation increasing productivity and stimulating reinvestment of profits; of slum dwellers voluntarily clearing sites for services and contributing labour for housing and environmental improvement. These cases are usually marked by attractive opportunities which the participants wish to exploit, and a perception that co-operation will remove constraints.

The effectiveness of participatory institutions in promoting equitable growth is often limited by lack of control over critical resources. Self-management enterprises may be dependent upon banks or multi-national companies for investment capital; local authorities may have to beg for capital loans from central government; and self-help groups may lack technical expertise. Most significantly, such institutions tend to lack control or influence over many of the macroeconomic decisions pertaining to prices, import controls, investment priorities, and so on which lie with government or the wider market forces but have a profound effect upon the provision of a basic livelihood.

Participation can generate growth; it can also inhibit or misdirect it. Elected leaders who are corrupt or inept can squander scarce local financial resources or manpower on prestigious office blocks or lavish entertainment; once prosperous enterprises taken over by co-operatives may experience decline in efficiency and product, broken down machinery, rising overdrafts. Growth may be achieved which benefits participants unevenly or disadvantages wider sections of society vis-à-vis a privileged socio-economic group.

Many participatory institutions are basically concerned with *distribution* – with improving wages at the expense of shareholders; farm gate prices at the expense of middlemen; or services for the many through taxing a few. Again there are examples of success such as workers' participation restraining disparities in remuneration or improving working conditions; of rural organisations facilitating land reform; of self-help groups stimulating a wider spread of services in rural areas. A number of factors however vitiate the effectiveness of participation in improving distribution. Co-operative mismanagement may so reduce production that there is less income to distribute. Participation may only benefit the relatively privileged who can best exploit the opportunity it affords. They may even do so at the net expense of the most needy. Trade unions, representing a relatively advantaged urban work force, may force up wages and thereby the cost of mass consumption goods or services, or persuade governments to control urban food prices, again at the expense of small rural producers. The evidence repeatedly reveals cases where the most needy have been excluded from the benefits of development or further impoverished as a result of ill-conceived and restricted forms of participation – land reform benefiting 'progressive' peasants but not the poor and landless labourers, wage increases that raise income levels of middle-level unionised wage employees while bypassing the majority of low-income workers and reducing job opportunities for the unemployed.

The enhancement of *psychic satisfaction* is the most difficult to assess of the four means through which popular participation can contribute to basic needs satisfaction. This has been subject to minimal research outside Western industry. An obvious difficulty is that of measuring results. Crude observation suggests that people often derive some innate satisfaction from participation in the making of decisions that affect their livelihoods – e.g. identification with 'their' co-operative factory or local authority, whether it brings them any material benefit or not. This can even extend to some of the more symbolic forms of participation encouraged by governments, such as plebiscites or demonstrations, which have little to do with genuine decision making. But where there is an increasing gap between expectations and reality, where people are being too clearly manipulated to serve the interests of the leadership, satisfaction can give way to apathy, cynicism, obstruction and hostility.

The biggest question surrounds the whole assumption on which this objective is based – that people do want to participate in decision making. The concept stems in part from egalitarian political theory and partly from the human relations school of management theorists nursed in the individualistic culture and private enterprise economy of the United States. Does it apply equally in societies where decision making is traditionally the preserve of a spiritual elect, of a dynastic leadership, or gerontocracy, or of males? Does it apply with the same force in societies with greater traditions of deference and a greater sense of collective identity? Some cultural milieux may encourage an appetite for a say in decisions (though even in these there is a tendency to leave issues to the 'experts'); others may induce people to fear and evade personal responsibility or to seek satisfaction from informal influence, through a patron for instance, or to achieve their ends by such means as bribery or crime. Even within participatory political cultures the incidence of participation varies significantly as does the kind of people who seek to participate. For example, in developed countries local government elections are notorious for low participation and educated middle class people are far more likely to participate than the uneducated poor.

There is evidence that participation is more effective where it is spontaneous – where it has been demanded and achieved by the participants, perhaps with a struggle or as a result of a tradition of collective action rather than where it is conferred from above. This suggests that people participate more actively, vigilantly and perhaps with greater sacrifice if they have come together out of a sense of opportunity or necessity with no feasible or preferable alternative to co-operation. Institutions imposed for ideological reasons or administrative convenience are less likely to arouse the same sense of involvement and will require strong and sustained external support and bring about very obvious improvements in conditions of life to achieve comparable loyalty on the part of their members.

It is inevitable that the conclusions of so brief a study of so wide a field should be short on guidelines and long on caveats. What is clear is that there is no simple equation between participation and the fulfilment of basic needs. Efficacy in terms of basic needs objectives is dependent upon a complex range of factors such as – how far institutions represent those with the most urgent needs; the extent of their control over critical resources; the degree of real discretion in exercising their role and freedom from manipulation from privileged groups and those in authority; or their command of relevant information and skills.

Above all, participation is critically dependent upon the attitudes of government – dependent for legal sanction and enforcement, for political tolerance or encouragement, for access to resources of land, capital, information and skill. Whilst national government is outside the purview of this study, it has to be recognised that the political and cultural environment of many countries in the Third World is not very conducive to effective mass participation at most levels. Indeed, there is a trend away from unrestricted large-scale mass involvement towards 'de-politicisation' and 'de-participation' on the part of many Third World regimes. Personalist rulers, military juntas and radical 'guided democracies' alike seek to set limits to the amount of popular involvement in decision making. They may also wish to determine what kind of participation can be practised. Concern for maximising economic production and savings through centralised planning and investment may also encourage governments to seek obedience and sacrifice; participation may be seen as distorting priorities and inflating consumption through spiralling demands. 'Bureaucratic' development may be preferred, particularly in former colonies where a strong bureaucratic element exists together with a tradition of state-managed development. Investment choices critical to basic needs satisfaction may be heavily dependent upon the preferences of external donors and multinational enterprises, rather than local institutions, which may conflict with the self-reliant aspirations of some states. Low levels of education and technical skills, combined with traditions of subservience to authority may compound the indifference of rulers to power-sharing. Such concerns and practices may produce symbolic or low levels of participation designed to legitimate a regime and maintain national stability rather than improve the conditions of the masses.

Against the background of various country experiences, it is difficult to determine conclusively what conditions – i.e. socio-economic factors, political systems and particular moments in the development process –are favourable to popular participation for meeting basic needs. Even the least sympathetic regimes may tolerate or even encourage some form of participation for reasons not related to basic needs satisfaction of the masses, such as to undermine a political opposition or to provide a safety valve for political ambitions at local levels. Other governments may have a deeper and more lasting interest in participation, stemming from ideology or from what they see to be the imperatives of economic and social development. Yet popular participation in decision making may conflict with the goals of economic and social development when these are sought exclusively or mainly through growth of large, formal sector operations such as mineral exploitation or plantation agriculture.

However, there are indications that where governments are disappointed with the result of centralised planning and large-scale, capital-intensive investment, and where they are pessimistic about access to resources in an age of world recession, interest in participation may be less ephemeral and opportunist, and more courageously experimental. Some Third World countries seem to have reached precisely this position.

The experience of participatory institutions surveyed here strongly suggests that the introduction of genuine forms of mass participation requires some form of continuing government commitment to the concept as well as to the objectives of the basic needs approach to development. Government can play an important supporting role, for example, in the vetting of self-help schemes for feasibility, the provision of supplementary resources and technical and managerial expertise or even institutions that promote participation, the supervision of the actions of local bodies and leaders to ensure probity and full access for non-elites and less articulate groups. Similarly, and perhaps most important, government can play a leading role in the provision both of increased levels of general education (literacy and numeracy) and training in the aims, procedures and operations of participatory institutions with the aim to increase popular access to information and knowledge which is so crucial to the promotion and sustaining of mass participation.

Finally, does the evidence suggest any role for external agencies, such as the ILO, in stimulating broad-based participation? There are a number of possibilities. External agencies can continue to exhort governments; this is not particularly productive but would-be participants can occasionally exploit pious conference resolutions to which their governments have formally subscribed. International agencies can seek to incorporate elements of participation in the running of projects which they finance. They can also reinforce participatory institutions with resources where they exhibit promising signs of life. Finally, they can continue the process of education by disseminating experience of participation through training programmes, research activities, seminars, conferences, and so on. Caution must be sounded however. External support for participatory institutions can be dangerous if it arouses government suspicion. There is a tendency too for donors to espouse promising institutions too liberally; the effect is to expand the scope of their activities rapidly, outpacing the growth of their capacity for effective self-management.

This brief survey has looked at institutions separately and globally, without going further to consider their interaction – for example, to assess the effect of institutions such as co-operatives and rural local government, or trade unions, employers' associations and workers' participation upon each other or their collective impact upon the provision of basic needs. Likewise, the inter-relationship of various ways through which popular participation can contribute to basic needs satisfaction has not been explored in detail. The conflict between defining and satisfying needs in situations of general shortage has been noted; so has the clash between generating and distributing resources. To comprehend these interactions fully would require deeper studies, ideally of a number of selected countries. This would also improve understanding of the effect of historical contexts upon these institutions, a factor whose importance emerges clearly from the current study.

Caution must indeed be the keynote of this conclusion – caution over the validity of judgements reached after a short survey; over the promotion

90

of common approaches in widely varying social and economic environments; and, finally, over the extent of present understanding of why the same institutions can work so well in one case and so badly in another.

NOTES

1 For details see ILO, *Employment, growth and basic needs: A one-world problem.* The international basic-needs strategy against chronic poverty and the decision of the 1976 World Employment Conference (Geneva, 1976).
2 As implied by the WEC *Programme of Action* (ILO, Geneva, 1976).
3 For a discussion of this concept and its application to Africa, see N. Kasfir: *The shrinking political arena* (London, 1976).
4 See, for example, C. Pateman: *Participation and democratic theory* (Oxford, 1974); M. Poole: *Workers' participation in industry* (London, Routledge and Kegan Paul, 1975); Economic Commission for Latin America: 'Popular participation in development' *Community Development Journal*, vol. 8, no. 2, 1973; and S. Rokkan: *Approaches to the study of political participation* (Bergen, 1962).
5 A useful review of the variety of local government systems may be found in S. Humes and E. Martin: *The structure of local government* (London, Oxford University Press, 1969).
6 See G. Hunter: *Modernising peasant societies* (London, Oxford University Press, 1969).
7 See K. Davey: *Taxing a peasant society* (London, Charles Knight, 1974).
8 There is substantial literature on factional manipulation of local politics. African examples are provided in C. Leys: *Politicians and Policies* (Kampala, 1967); J.P. Mackintosh: *Nigerian Government and Politics* (London, 1966); and D.C. O'Brien: *Saints and Politicians* (Cambridge, 1975).
9 An example from Lesotho is described in R Feecham, *et al: Water, health and development* (London, 1978). This problem of 'system over-load' is now a familiar one in the literature on self-help development.
10 See R. Chambers: *Managing rural development* (Uppsala, Scandinavian Institute of African Studies, 1976) for East African examples.
11 ibid.
12 As illustrated in Feecham, op. cit.; R.B. Charlick: 'Participatory development and modernisation in Hausa Niger' *African Review*, vol. 2, no. 4, 1972; and D. Collier: *Squatters v. Oligarchs* (Baltimore, Johns Hopkins University Press, 1976).
13 For a more exhaustive survey see ILO: *Agricultural organisations and economic and social development in rural areas*, Studies and Reports, New Series, No. 77 (Geneva, 1971).
14 See R. Redfield: *The little community/peasant society and culture* (Chicago, 1960); H. Landsberger (ed.): *Latin American peasant movements* (Ithaca, Cornell University Press, 1969).
15 See, for example, C. Beer: *The politics of peasant groups in Western Nigeria* (Ibadan, Ibadan University Press, 1976).
16 For Venezuela, see D. Warriner: *Land reform in principle and practice* (Oxford, Clarendon Press, 1969).
17 For Ghana under Nkrumah see B. Beckman: *Organising the farmers: Cocoa politics and social change in Ghana* (Uppsala, Scandinavian Institute of African Studies, 1976).
18 See B. Galjart: 'Peasant co-operation, consciousness and solidarity' *Development and Change*, vol. 6, no. 4, 1975.

19 See ILO: *Agricultural organisations and economic and social development in rural areas* op. cit.
20 See L.I. Rudolph and S.H. Rudolph: *The modernity of tradition* (Chicago, University of Chicago Press, 1967).
21 For Nigerian examples see A.C. Smock: *Ibo politics: The role of ethnic unions in eastern Nigeria* (Cambridge, Mass., 1971).
22 D.C. O'Brien: 'A versatile charisma: The Mouride Brotherhood 1967–75' in *Archives Européennes de Sociologie*, vol. XVIII, no.1, 1977.
23 The Catholic Church in Latin America and fundamentalist Muslim sects (e.g. the Muslim Brotherhood in the Sudan) have encountered serious difficulties of this kind.
24 For example, as in China, Viet Nam, Mexico and Peru.
25 Much of the material in this section is to be found in three publications by the United Nations Research Institute for Social Development: O. Fels Borda: *Co-operatives in Latin America* (Geneva, 1970); R. Apthorpe: *Co-operatives in Africa* (Geneva, 1972); Inayatulla: *Co-operatives in Asia* (Geneva, 1972); and R. Hewlett and J. Markie: 'Co-operative farming as an instrument of rural development, China, Viet Nam, Tanzania and India' *Land Reform, Land Settlement and Co-operatives*, no. 2, 1976.
26 See, for example, J. Strasma: 'Agragrian reform' in D. Chaplin (ed.): *Peruvian nationalism: A corporatist revolution* (New Jersey, 1976).
27 Strasma, op. cit.; D. Cuche: 'Pouvoir et participation dans les cooperatives agraires de production au Perou: Le cas des cooperatives cotonnières de la côte sud' *Communauté*, no. 40, 1976.
28 Apthorpe, op. cit.
29 Hewlett and Markie, op. cit.
30 For a successful Indian example see Hewlett and Markie, op. cit.
31 Two useful general bibliographies are M. Buvinic: *Women and world development: An annotated bibliography* (Washington, DC, 1976); and S. Smith Saulniers and C.A. Rakowski: *Women in the development process* (Austin, Texas, 1979).
32 ILO: *Employment, growth and basic needs* op. cit.; ILO: *Women in rural development: Critical issues* (Geneva, 1980).
33 See, I. Palmer: 'Rural women and the basic-needs approach to development' *International Labour Review* (ILR), vol. 115, no. 1, 1977; Martha F. Loutfi: *Rural women: Unequal partners in development* (Geneva, ILO, 1980); Z. Ahmad: 'The plight of rural women: alternatives for action' ILR, vol. 119, no. 4, 1980.
34 Cote d'Ivoire; Services Communautaires: *Animation feminine rurale au pays Dida* (Abidjan, mimeographed, 1973).
35 For example, see S.A.A. Chip: *The role of women elites in a modernising society: The All Pakistan Women's Association* (Paper presented to the 9th Congress of Anthropological and Ethnological Sciences, Chicago, 1971).
36 D. Remy: *Social networks and patron-client relations: Ibadan market women* (Washington, DC, mimeographed, 1974).
37 C. Riviere: *Guinea: The making of a people* (Stanford, 1976).
38 Riviere, op. cit.; for Mali under civilian rule see F. Snyder: *One-party government in Mali* (Newhaven, 1965), also various references in *West Africa* (London, 1966–68).
39 See, for example, N. Chazan: 'The manipulation of youth politics in Ghana and the Ivory Coast' *Genève-Afrique* (Geneva, ACTA Africana), vol. 15, no. 2, 1976.
40 See, for example, C. Meillassoux: *Urbanisation of an African community: Voluntary associations in Bamako* (Seattle, University of Washington Press, 1968).
41 Much of this section derives from the following sources: B.H. Millen: *The political role of labour in developing countries* (Washington, Brookings Institute, 1964); W. Falenson: *Labour in developing countries* (Berkeley, 1963); W.H. Friedland:

Unions and industrial relations in under-developed countries (Ithaca, Cornell University Press, 1963); V. Alba: *Politics and the labour movement in Latin America* (Stanford, Stanford University Press, 1968); R. Sandbrook and R. Cohen (eds): *The development of an African working class: Studies in class formation* (London, Longman, 1975); B.C. Roberts and L.G. de Bellecombe: *Collective bargaining in African countries* (London, 1962).

42 See Sandbrook and Cohen, op. cit. This general propostion is illustrated with a number of African examples.

43 There is considerable controversy surrounding this subject. See the chapters by Pearce, Jeffries and Saul in Sandbrook and Cohen, op. cit.

44 For Ghana see R. Jeffries: *Class, power and ideology in Ghana: The Railwaymen of Sekondi* (Cambridge, Cambridge University Press, 1978); for the United Republic of Tanzania see H. Mapolu: 'The organisation and participation of workers in Tanzania' *African Review*, vol. 2, no. 3, 1972; and Bienefeld's essay in Sandbrook and Cohen, op. cit. Relations between trade unions and government in Africa are surveyed annually in C. Legum (ed.): *African contemporary record* (New York/London, Africana Publishing Company, 1968/69).

45 Poole, op. cit.

46 E.S. Greenberg: 'The consequences of workers participation: A clarification of the theoretical literature' *Social Science Quarterly*, vol. 56, no. 2, 1975.

47 T. Janczyk: *The co-operative movement in Poland: Selected problems* (Warsaw, Naczelna Rada Soldzielcza, 1977).

48 E. Kolaja: *Workers' councils: The Yugoslav experience* (London, Tavistock Publications, 1965); J. Obradovic: 'Workers' participation: Who participates?' *Journal of Industrial Relations*, vol. 14, no. 1, 1975; see also N. Pasic, S. Grozdanic and M. Radevic: *Workers management in Yugoslavia: Recent developments and trends* (Geneva, ILO, 1982).

49 A. Campbell, *et al.*: *Worker-owners: The Mondragon achievement* (Anglo-German Foundation for the Study of Industrial Society, 1977).

50 A. Szakartz: 'Workers' participation in management: The German experience' *Industrial Relations* (Sydney), vol. 16, no. 1, Mar. 1974; F. Furstenberg: 'Workers' participation in management in the Federal Republic of Germany' *International Institute of Labour Studies Bulletin*, June, 1969.

51 For the United Kingdom see Pateman, op. cit., and L.J. Tivey: *The politics of the firm* (London, 1978).

52 W.F. Whyte and G. Alberti: 'The industrial community in Peru' *Annals of the American Academy of Political and Social Sciences*, vol. 431, 1977.

53 A. Zimbalist and J. Petras: 'Workers' control in Chile' (Institute for Workers' Control, Pamphlet No. 47); A. Zimbalist: 'Workers participation in the management of socialist industry: An empirical study of the Chilean experience under Allende' (unpublished Ph.D. thesis, Harvard University, 1974).

54 S. Kannapan and V.N. Krishnan: 'Participative management in India: Utopia or share?' *Annals of the American Academy of Political and Social Sciences*, vol. 431, 1977.

55 Information supplied by Mohamed Badran (Institute of local government studies, University of Birmingham, United Kingdom).

56 I. Clegg: *Workers' self-management in Algeria* (London, Penguin, 1974); L. Dominelli: 'Autogestion in Boufarik' *Sociologia Ruralis* (Assen, the Netherlands) vol. 14, no. 4, 1974; H. Ait Amara: 'Enquête sur la participation dans l'autogestion agricole algérienne' *Communauté*, vol. 29, 1971.

57 Mapolu, op. cit., and Bienefeld in Sandbrook and Cohen, op. cit.

58 On the importance of employers' associations in national economic planning see *International Labour Review*, vol. 93, no. 4 (France); vol. 94, no. 6 (Japan); and vol. 95, no. 6 (Latin America).
59 See various references in *West Africa* (London), 1977–78, on the activities of professional organisations under military rule.

PART II

PARTICIPATORY DEVELOPMENT: NATIONAL EXPERIENCES

4 Mass Participation, Development and Basic Needs Satisfaction: The Chinese Approach

Gek-boo Ng

This case study of China's experience in using mass participation to promote economic and social development among its entire population has two purposes. The first is to show that in general, mass participation could be an important instrument for achieving the objective of basic needs satisfaction in an originally poor and underdeveloped country like China. Here, our basic premise is that mass participation, no matter how it is defined, would only be useful to the satisfaction of basic needs if it makes a direct or indirect contribution to either one or some combinations of the following broad goals: (a) sufficient mobilisation and use of local resources (both human and material); (b) improvement in allocative efficiency; (c) increased access to productive assets and employment opportunities; and (d) reduction in income inequalities.[1] The second objective is to illustrate how the Chinese Government actually makes use of mass participation to achieve basic needs and other related socio-economic objectives of development. Significantly, it will be shown that in order to realise the full potential of popular participation as an effective means of fulfilling basic needs satisfaction, the practice must be complemented by the provision of an appropriate institutional/administrative structure as well as a political system and a socio-economic framework that allow for the active involvement of the people in the decision-making process at all levels.

The People's Republic of China has been selected as a case study for two main reasons. First, the level and state of socio-economic (under) development prevailing in China immediately after the revolution in 1949 was not much different from those which characterise many developing countries today. Upon taking over the reins of government, the Communist Party was confronted with the serious development problems of high unemployment, stagnant production, low factor productivity, high rates of illiteracy and infant mortality, widespread poverty and regional inequalities. Second, mass participation has been an integral part of the Chinese approach to development since the revolution. It is known to have played a vital role in the progress achieved in the areas of social reforms, indigenous capital formation and industrialisation, rural development, technological development and overall economic development. With specific reference to the development process itself, mass participation is also recognised by the Communist Party both as a means for combating bureaucratic obstacles and raising administrative efficiency and as a way of guaranteeing the right of the people to involve themselves fully in all aspects of decision making. The fact that China shared, and still shares, a number of common features with many contemporary developing countries (most important of all the rural base of the majority of the population and the dominance of agriculture among productive activities) suggests that the Chinese experience of broad-based participation in the development process could be of some relevance to Third World countries today.

The scope of this case study, however, is limited. Although overall emphasis is on the role of mass participation in promoting socio-economic development and meeting basic needs satisfaction, the analysis refers particularly to rural China where the majority of the country's population live and work. Furthermore, the discussion does not include, in any detail, the ideological dimensions of participation in a socialist framework, nor does it go into the question of whether participation is seen as an end in itself in the specific context of China. The objective is to present and examine a range of evidence from the Chinese experience to support the main thesis that genuine and effective mass participation in development can contribute immensely to the satisfaction of basic needs for the population as a whole. To this end, the chapter elaborates on the key factors behind the success of the Chinese 'model' of participatory development, and also draws attention to certain pitfalls or obstacles of which one should be aware.

THE ROLE OF MASS PARTICIPATION IN BASIC NEEDS SATISFACTION: SOME EVIDENCE ON THE CHINESE CASE

A simple way of verifying the importance of mass participation for satisfying basic needs country-wide is to investigate the extent to which the masses at all levels are actively and meaningfully involved in the processes of social reforms and economic development, and to show how mass involvement in these processes have in turn contributed to the satisfaction of the basic needs among the population as a whole. Four areas, namely, social reforms, policy implementation, development of domestic technological capacity and the provision of health services, are selected for this investigation.

Social Reforms: Agrarian Changes and Agricultural Collectivisation

A well-known Indian economist observed that social transformation has contributed much to the rapid scientific and industrial progress attained in Western countries, Japan, and the Soviet Union.[2] Indeed, it would be hard to disagree with the view of Professor Mahalanobis concerning the importance of effective social reforms, in support of technological progress and rural development, as a necessary condition for achieving economic development and social progress in many developing countries today. For our purpose, however, the crucial issue concerns the role of mass participation in promoting social changes required for implementing a basic needs-oriented development strategy.

The use of mass mobilisation to promote and support agrarian reform was a key policy measure adopted by the Communist Party of China (CPC) in the 1940s in the 'liberated' areas.[3] But the confiscation of land belonging to landlords and rich peasants, as a policy measure, was not implemented on a nation-wide scale until 1950 when the 'Law of Land Reform' was officially proclaimed.[4] The impact of land reform on the satisfaction of basic needs in the rural areas can be judged to be quite significant from two standpoints. First, the achievement of the objective of 'land to the tillers' released land for the landless and poor peasants who were previously underemployed or unemployed, due either to landlessness or to the uneconomic size of their holdings. The consequent increase in labour inputs provided much of the impetus for growth of output and overall agricultural development. Second, as the highly unequal pattern of land ownership was eliminated, the pattern of income distribution in rural China improved substantially, that is in favour of lower-income groups. The complete implementation of the land reform programme by 1953 indeed had a positive impact on the production process. In particular, it led to the creation of incentives and, hence, increased productivity among the majority of the rural population since their 'production enthusiasm' was no longer discouraged by the high rents imposed by landlords and rich peasants. Together, the expansion in agricultural output and the improvement in income distribution combined to bring about dramatic increases in the real incomes of the rural masses. Furthermore, the consequent increase in the purchasing power of the rural masses, with respect to the consumption of manufactured goods, resulted in higher effective demand for industrial output, thereby providing additional wage employment opportunities in the urban areas as well.[5]

The most salient feature of the land reform programme in China in the early 1950s, however, was not its success in achieving the goal of 'land to the tillers'. What perhaps distinguishes the Chinese experience from those of many other countries which have adopted similar programmes of agrarian reform is the top priority that was given to the active involvement of the masses in the whole process – from planning right through to implementation. As early as the mid-1940s a fundamental principle of the CPC with regard to the movement to reduce land rents was that the eventual outcome should be 'the result of mass struggle, (and) not a favour bestowed by the Government'.[6] This principle was adhered to by the CPC in its implementation of the land reform programme in the early 1950s, as was explained later by Mao in his 'Reading Notes on the Soviet Text':

> On page 339 it says that the land taken from the rich peasants and given to the poor and middle peasants was land the Government had expropriated and then parcelled out. This looks at the matter as a grant by royal favour, forgetting that class struggles and mass mobilisations had been set in motion, a right deviationist point of view. Our approach was to rely on the poor peasants, to unite with the majority of middle peasants (lower middle peasants) and seize the land from the landlord class. While the party did play a leading role, it was against doing everything itself and thus substituting for the masses.[7]

The underlying reason for Mao's emphasis on the role of mass participation in land reform was not difficult to understand, as he further observed that:

> In some countries of Eastern Europe the co-operatives were not organised very energetically, and even today they remain uncompleted. The main reason is not that they lacked tractors (they had many more than we, comparatively speaking), but that their land reform was a top-down royal favour. Land was expropriated by quota (in some countries no expropriation was carried out on farms under 100 hectares); the work of expropriation was carried out by executive order. We did quite the reverse. We put a mass line into effect, roused the poor and lower-middle peasants to launch class struggle and seize all the land of the landlord class and distribute the surplus land of rich peasants, apportioning land on a per-capita basis. (This was a tremendous revolution in the rural areas.)[8]

Clearly, in Mao's view, any land reform movement without active mass participation could lead to the slow progress in collectivisation and mechanisation in the long run as in the case of Eastern Europe, and, even worse, to the regaining of political power by landlords and rich peasants

100

almost immediately. Mass mobilisation, as such, was considered by the CPC to be an essential requirement for the successful implementation of the agrarian reform programme.[9]

Mass participation, however, is unlikely to be sustained unless the achievements of land reform can be maintained and consolidated over a period of time. This is by no means an easy task when the masses are initially very poor in terms of their access to farm implements and capital. As a matter of fact, indebtedness, due to poverty, illness or natural adversities, did give rise to considerable transactions in land ownership and to polarisation in income distribution immediately after the completion of the land reform programme in China. Mainly as a result of poor farming conditions agricultural productivity failed to rise on a steady basis and at a sufficiently high enough rate to justify the output from the manufacturing sector of farm and sideline products.

To overcome this initial obstacle to the implementation of the land reform programme, the CPC eventually decided to launch a complementary programme for organising individual peasant households into mutual-aid teams, which in turn were to be amalgamated into agricultural producers' co-operatives and which finally were to be grouped into people's communes. Mass participation played a very important role in facilitating this process of collectivisation. First of all, mass participation and popular support for the collectivisation programme, as reflected by the initial enthusiasm of peasant producers to operate on a co-operative basis, made it possible for the process of agricultural collectivisation to progress well ahead of schedule. In mid-1955 the CPC had estimated that by 1958 only about half of the rural households would be participating in the so-called semi-socialist agricultural producers' co-operatives (APCs),[10] and, as such, the process should not be expected to attain complete national coverage until about 1960.[11] But mainly as a result of active mass participation in the process of collectivisation, it was reported that 96.3 per cent of all peasant households had in fact joined agricultural producers' co-operatives by the end of 1956. More significant is the breakdown of this total – 87.8 per cent of rural households had progressed to membership of advanced agricultural producers' co-operatives, leaving only 8.5 per cent in the elementary APC category.[12] This is quite a remarkable achievement when compared with the situation the previous year (1955) when only 14.2 per cent of rural households belonged to the elementary type of producers' co-operatives.[13] By the end of 1958 the process of collectivisation was virtually completed with 99.1 per cent of rural households already organised in 26 578 people's communes.[14]

The rapid pace of collectivisation was far in excess of what had been expected by the CPC leadership, including Mao himself, when the policy of 'agricultural co-operativisation' was adopted in 1955. The participation of the masses, with their 'enthusiasm towards collectivism' and their creativity, was widely regarded as the key factor responsible for the rapid progress in the evolution of agrarian institutions. Indeed, as a result of active mass involvement in deciding upon such matters as modification of co-operative management methods, including job assessment of individual members and the distribution of collective income, it was possible to correct managerial and organisational mistakes more quickly and overcome essentially local problems related to the planning and implementation of communal production activities. Yet one should not lose sight of the fact that the incentives for peasant households to join voluntarily and participate in the newly established co-operatives were mainly related to the belief that concrete benefits in the form of increased output and income would accrue from collectivisation. There was indeed visible evidence of these from existing co-operatives for those peasants who were still hesitant to see.

The active participation of the masses in the process of collectivisation had much relevance for the successful implementation of a basic needs-oriented development strategy. First, as the collective system was established on the basis of mass participation starting at the grass-root level, it was amenable to the type of administrative structure required for institution building in the context of local level development planning. Appropriate participatory institutions at the local level have served to ensure that the interests of the masses are adequately reflected in decision making as well as to act as a safeguard against possible usurpation of people's rights. Second, mass participation, as used to facilitate the evolution of Chinese agrarian institutions, provided the basis for realising a more egalitarian pattern of income distribution in the rural areas as well as for sustaining this trend on a longer-term basis. The progressive reduction of intracollective income inequality during the process of collectivisation, in particular, is consistent with the basic needs-oriented goal of raising the levels of household income among the poor to enable them to satisfy their essential private consumption requirements. In the case of China, this is synonymous with the introduction of basic foodgrain ration policy among member households in the people's communes which was aimed at ensuring that even the poorest households were provided with their basic needs.[15]

But the overall significance of the Chinese pattern of agrarian reform for a basic needs strategy lies in the fact that the change in production relationships (including the pattern of ownership of the means of production) also became a major incentive for the masses to participate and contribute substantially to development efforts. It has been observed that in situations where the mass of the population is oppressed and exploited by a privileged minority, effective broad-based participation is usually difficult to achieve. On the one hand, the poor are less likely to be interested in participation within the *existing* institutional framework that is regarded by them as biased and unjust, nor will the ruling class willingly agree to the structural changes that would promote the participation of the masses in the decision-making process. In China, effective and meaningful mass participation in the development process was not achieved until the system of ownership was changed to provide the poor with access to productive assets. Apart from the land reform programme itself, the abolition of the entitlement of landowners to rental income in the advanced producers' co-operatives was a key underlying reason for higher rates of labour force participation in collective farms.[16] Increased productivity and total output, due to greater participation and commitment by the labour force, can be regarded as relevant for meeting basic needs especially when these are accompanied by improvement in the pattern of income distribution.

Policy Implementation

As already mentioned, the CPC, upon taking over the government, was confronted with a number of critical socio-economic problems which apparently could not be solved in the short run. On the one hand, factory productivity was extremely low and the existing economic infrastructure was grossly inadequate to support any significant expansion of agricultural production. To improve factory productivity and economic infrastructure would require considerable financial resources much in excess of what the new regime could mobilise at the time. On the other hand, there were serious problems relating to foodgrain marketing. At a time when it was vital to control inflation urgently, there was widespread speculation and black marketing in agricultural products, especially foodgrain, which gave rise to additional difficulties for the new regime in its efforts to adopt appropriate policies for absorbing unemployed and underemployed labour into productive activities. In addition, these difficulties were compounded by the rapid growth of population which itself was the result of improvement in living conditions among the poor following the end of the civil war. Clearly, problems of such complexity and magnitude had to be resolved fairly quickly if the CPC was to win the support of the masses and consolidate its power base. The ability of the new regime to tackle these problems effectively was therefore the major challenge facing the CPC during the period of transition when the objective was to change the production system from semi-feudal and semi-colonial to socialist.

Essentially, the main task was to formulate and implement a development strategy that would break through the existing vicious circle of poverty, stagnating growth and capital scarcity. Apart from launching various complementary programmes of social reforms, the CPC's package of development policies included specific measures for relieving unemployment. Thus in the 1960s, the CPC introduced family planning as a means of controlling the flow of new entrants into the labour force in the long run, and, as a short-term measure, urban youths were sent to work in agriculture in the rural areas. The introduction of an agricultural procurement scheme for controlling foodgrain marketing was also designed to encourage the mobilisation of the rural population in support of human capital formation. Thus, the participation of the masses was again used by the authorities as an important catalyst in the implementation of various policy measures. As will be illustrated below by selected examples, mass participation was indeed crucial in removing certain socio-economic and institutional constraints to the development objectives of the new regime.

First, in common with other socialist countries during the period of transition, the new regime's biggest problem in the early 1950s concerned supply management of foodgrain. Given the low level of agricultural productivity in contrast to the big increase in demand for food as a result of urban industrial development and improvement in income distribution, this problem was particularly acute during the period of transition when both commerce and agriculture were still privately owned. The existence of black marketing in foodgrain made it extremely difficult for the Government, with little financial resources of its own, to compete with the private enterprises in the open market, especially whilst at the same time seeking to reduce income inequality and to control inflation. The Government eventually took the bold decision to control foodgrain markets by introducing 'The Scheme of Planned Purchase and Planned Supply of Foodgrain' in 1953.[17] But even legislative measures plus price incentives were found to be inadequate for getting the peasants to sell their surplus foodgrain to the official buying agents. This was due partly to the co-existence of parallel private commercial activities which effectively sabotaged official efforts, and partly to the expectation of peasants for higher prices as well as their desire to keep surplus foodgrain for themselves in case of shortfalls in household requirements. In the event, the Government launched a massive political campaign to gain support for its foodgrain policy. A key feature of this campaign was the direct appeal to the loyalty and patriotism of the masses to throw their weight behind a policy that was aimed at improving the conditions of the poor and reducing social inequalities. The fight against speculation and black marketing was thus carried out with a political movement for educating and mobilising the masses. It is now widely accepted that price distortions and other anomalies in the marketing of foodgrain in China during the transitional period and even later could not have been tackled with any degree of success by the Government without the continued involvement of the masses in the implementation of requisite policy measures.[18]

Second, the new regime was confronted with the problem of finding jobs for some four million urban unemployed, nine million former employees of the administrative and military services of the old regime and the tens of millions of jobless and underemployed rural peasants.[19] Given the magnitude of the employment problem as indicated above and the precarious financial state of the new regime, the only practical solution available to the Government was to mobilise and channel the surplus labour to agricultural production in rural areas. Mass participation was again used to effect such a large scale mobilisation of labour even before the establishment of the commune system in 1958, by which time the unemployment problem was largely solved.

Labour accumulation, defined as the use of surplus labour for farm infrastructural works (i.e. soil improvement, land levelling, deep ploughing, irrigation, terracing and development of waste land, and so on), has been a salient feature of rural development in China. It was estimated that around a hundred million people participated annually in farm infrastructural works projects during the slack seasons for the period 1971–75.[20] Assuming that the average total population during this period was about 800 million, of which 75 per cent was in the rural areas, and that the rate of participation was 46.65 per cent, the proportion of the total rural labour force engaged in infrastructural works projects would have been in the region of 40 per cent.[21] Preliminary data for the last few years suggest that the degree of mass participation in infrastructural works projects has in fact been increasing.

From the standpoint of a basic needs-oriented development strategy, the significance of mobilising the rural masses to participate in farm infrastructural works projects deserves special mention. From the outset, labour accumulation through mass participation was not seen by the authorities simply as a means of promoting employment, but also as an important way of solving critical problems of agricultural development. The problem of lack of development capital, or low level of domestic capital formation, for instance, was largely overcome by the mobilisation and financing of required labour inputs by the rural collectives themselves.[22] As a result of accelerated capital formation through labour accumulation in rural China over the last few decades, the ability of the collective economy to withstand natural disasters has been significantly augmented. Floods and droughts, which occurred periodically and brought about famines and flights of refugees in pre-liberation China, have now been brought under control.[23] Furthermore, as food and agricultural production became less vulnerable to the vagaries of the weather, the accumulation of agricultural surplus also became more of a certainty with favourable income and consumption implications for the mass of the population and consequent growth of the national product. Mass participation in the implementation of infrastructural projects in China contributed significantly to the promotion of self-reliant attitudes in tackling development problems at the local level. This is a factor which assumes much importance in the context of present day capital-scarce developing countries.

Third, mass participation has also been instrumental in the implement-ation of family planning programmes in China.[24] The introduction of family planning was originally greeted with much scepticism, if not

105

opposition, for a variety of reasons. To overcome possible obstacles to the implementation of the programme, the Government carried out mass campaigns at all levels of the administration to publicise and explain the importance and advantages of family planning. These mass campaigns were found to be very useful as they stimulated and encouraged frank discussions, often in the form of local study groups, which clarified issues and thereby helped to convince the sceptics about the value of the programme. It would seem that China has achieved remarkable success in implementing its family planning programme, as can be deduced from the decline in the population growth rate per annum from an average of 2.7 per cent in the early 1950s to an estimate of around 1.4 per cent in 1978.[25] In some of the more successful counties, like Jutong in Jiangsu Province, the population growth rate in 1976 was estimated at only 0.325 per cent per annum. In this case, success was officially attributed to the fact that the county set up a special team consisting of 40 000 members for directing the mass campaigns in support of family planning.[26] The rapid decline in birth rates in China is particularly important for the satisfaction of basic needs among the rural masses from two standpoints. First, it helps to ensure that increase in output is not simply eaten up by population growth, thereby making possible accumulation of surplus; and, second, it allows for female labour to be more effectively mobilised to participate in collective farming which in turn contributes to increased output.[27]

Domestic Technological Capacity

The vital role of science and technology in the process of economic development is now widely recognised. In the WEC 'Declaration' and 'Programme of Action', the need to develop and adopt appropriate and optimal technologies in developing countries is especially stressed as an essential component of a basic needs strategy aimed at increasing employment and eliminating poverty.[28] An adequate domestic technological capacity is a fundamental prerequisite for developing and adapting technologies that are appropriate to a country's specific development needs. Without such a capacity there is the real danger of choosing the wrong types of technology with reference to local conditions and situations, often with adverse consequences for overall development. In China, as will be illustrated below, mass participation has played an important role in the development of indigenous technological capacity.

In the field of industry, workers are generally encouraged to participate in the development of new techniques on the basis of their own practical experience. Mass mobilisation is also used to undertake specific tasks which require localised experience and know-how, thereby contributing to the development of domestic technological capacity. Thus, when it became necessary to overhaul and remodel the 100-year-old poorly

106

designed boilers of the Shanghai public utility system, the task was approached by mobilising some 200 000 local artisans who were able to complete the job within the relatively short period of 80 days. Exhibitions focusing on new and advanced industrial techniques are held on a regular basis throughout the country as a means of securing mass interest in technological development and, thereby, encouraging innovation among workers in neighbourhood factories. In addition, ordinary workers are exposed to lectures and demonstrations by qualified technicians, engineers and university researchers as a way of keeping them in touch with the latest techniques as may be relevant to their vocation or trade. The overall effect of this interaction between experts and the masses is reflected in significantly higher rates of productivity in industry, often at little or no cost to the enterprises concerned. Mass participation, in short, provides the motivation and ingenuity required for the development and introduction of productivity-raising techniques in Chinese industry.

In agriculture, the Chinese model of participatory development pays particular attention to domestic technological formation through the setting up of a nationwide scientific experimentation network at the county, commune, production brigade and production team levels. Most communes and brigades today possess their own experimental plots and stations. It was reported in 1977 that the total arable land allocated to experimentation and seed development under this programme was some three million hectares and the number of people involved exceeded fourteen million.[29] As a result of mass participation in agricultural experimentation, a number of important scientific and technological 'break-throughs' in Chinese agriculture have their origin in the peasantry. For example, advanced techniques such as the development of a variety of short-stalk rice seedlings and simple but practical farm equipment were actually developed by the peasants themselves in Jiang Province.

The significance of mass participation in the development of domestic technological capacity in China is perhaps most obvious in terms of its contribution to a highly efficient network of extension services for the diffusion of information and knowledge. This has served to ensure that appropriate scientific and technological innovations benefit as wide a coverage of the rural population as possible. One such case concerns the widespread adoption of new varieties of Chinese-developed hybridised paddy rice – an achievement which would not have been possible but for the efficient network of agricultural extension services. In all, over two million hectares of farmland were covered by the introduction of the new varieties between 1973 and 1977, resulting in an increase in output estimated at two million tons over this period. By 1979, mainly as a result of the activities of the extension services the new varieties were introduced to another 6.5 million hectares of farmland. Most of the credit for the progress in agricultural science and technology and for the progressive attitude of collectivised peasant producers to innovation in Chinese agriculture is now generally attributed to the fact that the masses themselves have been involved in experimentation and extension services at all levels.[30]

The Provision of Medical and Health Services in Rural Areas

The importance of adequate medical care and health care in the development process hardly needs elaboration. For example, lack of medical care or poor health services can lead directly to low levels of productivity through ill health; high rates of infant mortality as a result of inadequate medical facilities can lead to high birth rates as low-income peasant families seek to guarantee an optimal household size. There are also indirect consequences of inadequate health care facilities for a basic needs-oriented development strategy. If access to satisfactory medical and health care facilities is not easy and readily affordable for the poor, they might have to sacrifice consumption of other basic needs in order to obtain available medical services whatever the cost when confronted with a situation of extreme desperation. As a consequence, they will experience a further drop in living standards and greater immiseration.

Thus, from the viewpoint of basic needs satisfaction, the provision and delivery of medical and health services must fulfil two conditions. First, available services must be reasonably adequate and efficient in the sense that general treatment for common illnesses can be provided locally and when needed. Next, such services must be accessible to the masses in terms of the cost of treatment.

The Chinese success in the provision of health care for the rural masses is now widely recognised.[31] It is also commonly accepted that one of the major factors behind the Chinese success in providing the rural population with adequate medical and health services is mass participation and mobilisation, as is explained below.

In the early 1950s, the most urgent task confronting the new regime in the field of health concerned the need to eliminate smallpox, plague, cholera and venereal diseases, and to reduce the incidence of other infectious diseases and local and occupational health hazards. The eventual success of the authorities in coping with such a wide range of health problems could be traced, to a large extent, to the mass health campaigns that were launched periodically to promote environmental sanitation, for example, keeping out the four pests, namely, rats, mosquitoes, bedbugs and flies, and personal hygiene. In addition to educating the masses about the necessity of adopting sanitary habits, the various health campaigns also promoted physical exercise as a source of good health.

The mass campaign to control schistosomiasis provides a good example of the use made of mass participation to meet the health needs of the population in China. Schistosomiasis was the most notorious parasitic disease in central and south China in the immediate post-liberation period. At one time the disease affected some 10.5 million rural inhabitants. To combat and control the spread of the disease the authorities launched a series of mass campaigns in the mid-1950s aimed at eliminating the carrier of the disease – in this case, the snail – from habitable areas. Essentially, local population groups in affected areas were mobilised to collect and destroy snails, to implement soil and water sanitation projects and to administer therapy to infected humans and draught animals. In all, some two million people were reported to have been engaged in snail control and related sanitation projects during 1959–60.[32] Thus, through effective mobilisation of the masses it has been possible to encourage the people themselves to take action to solve their own pressing health problems.

Mass participation has also contributed much to solving the once serious problem of shortage of medical personnel, medicines and basic health facilities. Given the relatively poor state of health and medical facilities in China in the 1950s and the scarcity of resources to provide immediately the necessary services, the urgent task of meeting the health needs of several hundred million peasants would have proceeded at a very slow pace even with the best of intentions and commitments. The approach adopted instead was to mobilise the masses at all levels for the purpose of creating an effective network of health care facilities consisting of hospitals at the county level, clinics in the communes, health stations in the production brigades, and health aide services in the production teams. The problem of personnel to man these various institutions was effectively tackled by the training and use of 'barefoot doctors'.[33] As far as the provision of medicines is concerned, this was taken care of by the establishment of the co-operative medical service, at the commune level, which purchased essential drugs in bulk with money from a special fund contributed to by commune members; each member contributes a small sum annually to the co-operative medical fund and in return receives reasonable medical care for a small nominal charge. The people were encouraged and advised by the barefoot doctors to collect locally available medicinal herbs for the collective use of the co-operative medical service, thus reducing considerably the operating cost of the service.

The active participation of the masses in planning and operating their own medical and health care facilities has contributed to an adequate spatial distribution of such facilities throughout China today, with guaranteed access for all those needing medical treatment. Together with improved conditions of public health, the provision of adequate health facilities locally has contributed to higher productivity and output in industry and agriculture through reduced rates of absenteeism in work places.[34]

POLITICAL COMMITMENT AND INSTITUTIONAL REQUIREMENTS FOR EFFECTIVE MASS PARTICIPATION IN DEVELOPMENT: SOME ELABORATIONS ON THE CHINESE CASE

In the international development strategy for the second United Nations development decade, the importance of securing the active support and participation of the masses in the development planning process was strongly emphasised.[35] Yet, at the end of the decade, it can hardly be said that the overall performance of developing countries in promoting effective mass participation in their development process has been satisfactory. Although one of the main reasons for such a state of affairs is often identified as the lack of political will at the highest level, it is not true in all cases that governments are either disinterested or indifferent to the option of using mass participation as a means of achieving their development objectives. An equally important reason for the poor performance of developing countries in this regard seems to lie in complex political and social requirements for initiating meaningful mass participation as an integral part of the development process itself. In other words, effective mass participation may still not be achieved even when there is the political will and commitment on the part of the leadership. In this section, we will make use of the Chinese experience to demonstrate that success in promoting meaningful mass participation in development depends critically on the existence of an appropriate institutional framework – i.e. one which is conducive to, among other things, the decentralisation of decision-making powers, popular influence over the allocation of key resources and the distribution of benefits, and the actual involvement of the people themselves in the planning and implementation of local-level development projects.

Decentralisation and Institutional Arrangements

Decentralisation of decision-making powers is generally regarded as a major prerequisite for fulfilling the objective of popular participation in the development process. Given the differences that may exist between regions within a country, in terms of socio-economic and cultural characteristics, it becomes extremely difficult to plan and direct a variety of local development programmes from the centre, particularly where some of these might relate to essentially local problems. Hence, a centrally designed policy package is unlikely to be strictly relevant to specific local problems, and, even where this may be so, it is less likely to be implemented efficiently without the active involvement of the local people or their representatives. This implies that power and authority should be decentralised to local decision-making bodies. It is important for such bodies to have a say in what is going on in their localities, since decisions taken at the local level are generally more likely to be in accordance with local interests and priorities and, hence, more readily acceptable. This in turn makes it much easier to obtain broad-based support for development efforts at the local level.

There are two fundamental issues pertaining to the scope and possibilities for decentralising decision-making powers from higher to lower levels of administration. The first concerns the capability of the local administration to tackle effectively its own local development problems, given the usual scarcity of requisite skills and financial resources at the local level. In part, this can be overcome by the decentralisation of resources (including as well the authority to collect and spend money locally on development projects) to train and recruit the necessary skilled labour that is not available locally. The second is that, even when decentralisation of decision-making powers is accompanied by the transfer of resources required to implement local decisions, the process could still fail to serve as a means for effectively involving the masses in the development process if the right type of institutional arrangements for promoting popular participation is absent or ineffective.

The CPC's decision to decentralise its administrative machinery was not adopted and put into practice until the authorities had acquired sufficient lessons and experience from nearly a decade of post-liberation socio-economic development planning. This was explained by Mao in his 'On the Ten Major Relationships' – the most important work of Mao on economic management during the 1950s:

> The relationship between the central and the local authorities constitutes another contradiction. To resolve this contradiction, our attention should now be focused on how to enlarge the powers of the local authorities to some extent, give them greater independence and let them do more, all on the premise that the unified leadership of the central authorities is to be strengthened. This will be advantageous to our task of building a powerful socialist country. Our territory is so vast, our population is so large and the conditions are so complex that it is far better to have the initiative come from both the central and the local authorities than from one source alone. In short, if we are to promote socialist construction, we must bring the initiative of the local authorities into play. If we are to strengthen the central authorities, we must attend to the interests of the localities. . . We should encourage the style of work in which the local authorities are consulted on the matters to be taken up. It is the practice of the Central Committee of the Party to consult the local authorities; it never hastily issues orders without prior consultation. . . But, provided that the policies of the central authorities are not violated, the local authorities may work out rules, regulations and measures in the light of their specific conditions

and the needs of their work. . . The central authorities should take care to give scope to the initiative of the provinces and municipalities and the latter in their turn should do the same for the prefectures, counties, districts and townships; in neither case should the lower levels be put in a straightjacket. The provinces and municipalities, prefectures, counties, districts and townships should all enjoy their own proper independence and rights and should fight for them. To fight for such rights in the interest of the whole nation and not of the locality cannot be called localism or an undue assertion of independence.[36]

Broadly speaking, decentralised planning in China is characterised by two important features. The first is its flexibility: planned targets for each administrative level are fixed with a certain degree of flexibility and in so doing the concept of decentralisation of decision making to local authorities is given practical significance in the sense that such authorities have some scope for making adjustments to policies and targets on the basis of local conditions and initiatives. This flexibility applies to both factory units and people's communes.

With respect to agricultural planning, the central plan itself usually covers a wide range of rural socio-economic activities and sets forth targets for the various rural collectives.[37] However, the collectives are not expected to, and do not in most cases, exhaust all of their resources in order to fulfil the targets set by the state plan. In fact, a certain proportion of cultivable land outside the target acreage indicated in the plan remains at the disposal of the collectives for their own use. Land still left idle may be available for cultivation and the target acreage can also be expanded through intercropping or raising the cropping index.[38] Moreover, rural collectives at all levels still enjoy a certain degree of autonomy under the ownership system. As provided in the state plan, and depending on local conditions, each collective can formulate its own annual and long-term production plans, decide on the method of distributing collective income, and allocate manpower and collective surplus. The rationale for allowing a certain degree of flexibility in production planning at the micro-level is not hard to find: it provides a safeguard against the defects of centralised planning by allowing for adjustments and modifications due to peculiar local conditions and circumstances as well as permitting the application of local initiatives to unforeseen local problems.

The second characteristic of the Chinese pattern of decentralised planning relates to its process. In general the preparation and finalisation of a five-year development plan or an annual plan has to go through several levels of administration. First, the State Planning Commission, the central government economic planning machinery, completes a draft plan at the national level, which is next referred to the provincial administration, then on to the administrations at the prefecture and county levels respectively. It is the county administration that allocates planned targets to its own communes, who then finally distribute and allocate these targets among their own production brigades and teams at the lowest level of administration. But there is also consultation between the higher and lower-level authorities at each stage of the process of plan preparation and finalisation, thereby providing an opportunity to reach a consensus on key decisions including the allocation of targets. Thus, the entire process involves both 'top–bottom' and 'bottom–top' consultations. In this way, the suggestions and criticisms of the actual production units are brought to the attention of the administrations at various levels, and appropriate modifications and revisions are made, before the plan is finalised and adopted for implementation.

The Chinese system of economic planning is of much relevance to a basic needs strategy, particularly with reference to the role of mass participation in the making and implementation of decisions. To begin with, the system strongly emphasises the decentralisation of decision-making powers and resources as a way of actively involving the masses in the development process. A good practical example of this feature of Chinese planning is provided by the implementation of the highly decentralised programme to provide industrial support to agriculture. Under the general guidelines for providing industrial support to agriculture, the state administrations at provincial, prefectural and county levels are empowered to formulate their own plans of action. This decentralisation provides flexibility for production planning in the manufacturing sector, so that in each locality industrial output can be modified to meet the urgent needs of the agricultural sector. Furthermore, decentralisation reduces bureaucratic obstacles and, in this regard, helps to ensure that local resources are mobilised and allocated quickly and more effectively towards solving the immediate problems of agricultural production and rural development.[39]

The Chinese experience, however, also shows that the commitment of the central authority to mass participation, through decentralisation, is not on its own sufficient for achieving basic needs satisfaction. Proper institutional arrangements have to be established for promoting mass participation. The masses have first to be organised on the basis of an appropriate institutional framework before they can be mobilised to participate and make a contribution to economic development.[40] In China the urban masses are organised through neighbourhood or street committees, and in the rural areas they are organised through the people's communes. The significance of an appropriate institutional structure for supporting and promoting effective mass participation can be best illustrated by the operation of the commune system.

The commune system has a three-tier structure, consisting of the people's commune itself, being the lowest unit of the state administration; the production brigade, which is the lowest unit of the CPC political machinery; and the production team which corresponds to the 'basic accounting unit' in the sense of an autonomous economic management body at the grass-roots level. On average, there are about 25 households in a production team. Given the relatively low level of agricultural mechanisation in rural China, the production team is a small enough unit to monitor the work performance of each individual member and to determine rewards to members based on their productivity. Accordingly, individual participation in collective productive activities in the rural areas is supported by a built-in mechanism of economic incentive. Furthermore, team members can also be engaged for work on the relatively large-scale economic undertakings (i.e. infrastructural works, industrial enterprises, and so on) under the ownership of the production brigade or commune, with remunerations based on an agreed payment system or method of sharing benefits. As a result of these practical arrangements, the efforts of individuals are considered by the workers themselves as closely linked to the promotion of collective as well as individual welfare. Motivation, derived from both expected economic and political gains, is thus a major factor behind the successful operation of development-oriented participatory institutions in China.

Local Leadership and Administrative Capability

The political will of *national* leadership and appropriate institutional arrangements are necessary but not sufficient conditions for achieving the effective participation of the masses in the development process at the local level. First, it is not unusual, particularly within a decentralised system of planning, for local leaders to act contrary to the wishes and intentions of national authorities with regard to implementation of local development programmes. Thus, it may be possible for national commitment to popular participation to be ignored or translated into action in a highly authoritarian or paternalistic manner at the local level. But on the other hand, as already argued, decentralisation of decision-making powers could itself be a positive factor in promoting mass participation, particularly where local authorities are inspired by the political will and commitment from above. In fact, local-level decision-making bodies are usually in a better position than national authorities to promote broad-based local participation by virtue of their 'closeness' to the people concerned. Ideally, given the necessary commitment to mass participation at the national level, local leadership of the right type can play a key role in giving proper and adequate expression to basic needs-oriented development planning through organising the people for productive activities on the basis of local interests, needs and aspirations. In China, local contingents of committed cadres and administrators have been instrumental in organising the masses in agriculture and industry for effective participation in the development process at all levels. This is particularly important if one takes into account the fact that meaningful

114

mass participation is not often spontaneous; it usually requires the organisational ability or even the initiative and inspiration of capable and committed leadership. Thus, it can be argued that political commitment to popular participation at the national level without the support of competent and honest local leaders could end up simply as an empty verbiage.

The issue of leadership in the context of promoting mass participation gives rise to a number of important questions which need to be answered. For example, what is the actual role of local leaders or cadres in initiating meaningful mass participation? What are the best criteria for selecting local leaders or cadres? What types of training should be given to local leaders and cadres to improve their organisational and administrative capability? In which ways can the alienation of the local leaders and cadres from the masses be avoided with reference to the making and implementation of local decisions?

In China, local cadres played a prominent role in promoting and sustaining mass participation for implementing the agrarian reform programme. Not only was their role confined to raising the consciousness of the peasantry about their new rights to land, but they were also indispensable in organising the hitherto landless and land-poor peasants into agricultural co-operatives and collectives as a way of consolidating their agrarian gains. In the early years of the movement to collectivise peasant production, the elementary agricultural producers' co-operatives survived initial difficulties and problems mainly as a result of the administrative skills and hard work of the local cadres. This was most obvious from the role played by local cadres in organising and uniting the masses to resist frequent attacks from former landlords and rich peasants.[41] Guidance and advice were also provided by local cadres to co-operatives and collectives on the introduction of new techniques to farming, the organisation of production and the marketing of output under the new socialist system.

Good leadership is regarded as essential for promoting mass participation in the development process at the grass-root level for two obvious reasons. First, in view of their direct interaction with the local population, local administrators and cadres are better informed about the range and variety of local problems which can impinge on development efforts and, hence, they are better suited than 'outsiders' to provide appropriate solutions to local problems. In this regard, they can contribute immensely to the successful implementation of local development programmes and projects. Second, again in view of their familiarity with the local scene and conditions, local cadres tend to be more sensitive to the socio-economic, cultural and traditional complexities of a particular rural society, and as a result adopt policies and methods which take full account of the socio-economic framework within which they are intended to operate. An outsider, on the contrary, might easily overlook or not be aware of apparently minor but important local details which can have grave consequences for local-level development.

The quality of local leadership is largely determined by the criteria applied for selecting or electing local leaders. In contrast to the practice in many developing countries today wherein local administrators are recruited from outside the local community with much emphasis placed on some level of formal educational achievement,[42] the CPC has always given preference to the use of endogenous cadres who have the advantage of being members of the local community, often from among the masses, and as such are extremely familiar and knowledgeable about local affairs. These people are then given the necessary training and political education which equip them for their leadership role. Following reforms and the spread of the educational system, the new generation of cadres are now also recruited from outside the masses. These are often young people who have undergone formal schooling including courses on socialist theory and practice of economic management and production techniques. In addition, they receive ideological instructions which are regarded as essential for their integration into the masses after graduation.

Clearly, if the local cadres themselves become an elite class, their effectiveness in promoting mass participation will be severely reduced. Thus, once cadres are trained and recruited, measures have to be taken to prevent them from alienating themselves from the masses. The policy of the CPC to have local cadres integrated with the masses is implemented through the activities of the 'May 7 Cadre Schools' and the application of the principles of democratic management in both factories and agricultural communes.

The 'May 7 Cadre Schools' were set up as a result of a directive issued by Mao himself on 7 May 1966. The 'directive' emphasised the need for cadres in all types of state institutions to be integrated with the masses through their direct participation in various forms of manual work.[43] Hence, special 'Schools' were set up throughout the countryside 'to train a corps of cadres, armed with Marxism–Leninism–Mao Tse-tung Thought, who are willing to work at any level, whether as leaders or led, who have close ties with the masses and who serve the people wholeheartedly.'[44] The participants are drawn from among administrators at all levels of the state machinery, including the People's Liberation Army and officials from the State Council. During the training period the participants have to study political theory as well as engage in collective farming activities together with the masses. Although their salaries as state administrators and officials remain unchanged, the participants are expected to live and to work with the peasants of nearby villages during the course of their training. The rationale of this is that state officials – who as a result of educational reforms are progressively being recruited from outside the masses – should be close to the masses in order to understand better the socio-economic problems of development at the grass-root level. This, in

116

fact, has been an effective means by which the CPC is able to combat bureaucratism and to prevent the emergence of a new elite class from within the ranks of state administrators.

The CPC has also adopted other measures for orientating the training of cadres towards the idea of effective mass participation in the economic management of production units. Concrete measures, in the form of specific regulations and rules governing the activities of cadres, have been institutionalised as important features of the operation of production units at all levels. In addition, the masses themselves are made aware of the code of conduct laid down for cadres, thus providing a safeguard against possible abuses of power in a situation where, as a result of administrative decentralisation, individual factories and communes enjoy a relatively high degree of autonomy in management functions. These measures plus the institutionalisation of the principles of democratic management in effect are designed to foster the integration of the administrative and technical cadres and the broad mass of the population. Again, the aim is to prevent elitism and improve managerial efficiency, as clearly laid down by the 'Ankang Charter' issued by the CPC in 1960.[45]

In particular, the 'Ankang Charter' stressed the need to launch mass movements for technical innovations, characterised by administrative and technical cadres engaging in direct productive work alongside workers with the latter participating in factory management. By doing so co-operation among workers, management and technicians is enhanced. In a way the overall objective could also be seen as a means of improving industrial relations in support of higher productivity and economic growth.

In the rural areas, similar measures have also been introduced by the CPC for promoting the integration of cadres with the masses. As mentioned already, cadres at various levels of collective production are expected to participate in manual work. In the early 1960s the minimum number of working days per annum devoted to manual work on collective farms was fixed at 60 and 120 respectively for cadres at the commune and brigade levels. These requirements were extended to 100 and 200 respectively in the 1970s. The minimum number of working days per annum for cadres at the production team level is now fixed at 300. The participation of cadres in manual work on collective farms at the county, commune and brigade levels is now recognised as one of the criteria for achieving the status of a 'Tachai-type county'.[46]

There are also strict regulations governing the remuneration of local cadres who work on collective farms. Under the work-point system all work done by cadres should be assessed on the same basis as work performed by other members of the production unit. Cadres at the team level, in particular, receive basic incomes similar to those of 'ordinary' members of the unit, with a small addition in the form of special 'work-point allowance' by way of compensation for their extra administrative duties. Such allowances for cadres at the team level, however, are limited to a maximum of one per cent of the total number of work-points of their associated production teams. In addition, no cadre at the production brigade and team levels is permitted to receive work-point allowance in excess of the equivalent of 120 working days. Moreover, all compensatory allowances allocated to cadres must first of all be assessed by the assembly of members' representatives and be approved finally by the county administration.[47]

The application of the principle of democratic financial management to production at the level of the people's communes has also contributed to the fulfilment of mass participation in rural development planning. According to this principle, management is made accountable to the masses and as such the bookkeeper of the commune is obliged to present the collective accounts periodically to the people at public meetings for their examination and scrutiny. At these meetings ordinary members have the right to ask for explanations of all items of expenditure, and to suggest modifications for adoption. At the end of each year the general assembly of all members also decides on the methods of allocating foodgrain and collective surpluses to various needs, duly taking into account the tripartite interest of the State, the collective and the individual. The key feature of this arrangement is that the mass of the population is given the opportunity to discuss and decide on how and on what collective revenue should be invested in within the local community.[48]

Measures for Sustaining Mass Participation

Once the framework for promoting mass participation has been established, a more important, and perhaps difficult, task seems to be the creation of the right types of conditions for sustaining mass participation over time. The important question then is how to maintain or even build on the initial momentum which might have been derived from the desire to satisfy a specific need, once this has been fulfilled and new demands and higher aspirations take its place. The problem becomes even more difficult when the authorities, as is usually the case, are confronted with popular demands that are more difficult to satisfy.

Experience has shown that a critical factor for sustaining mass participation concerns the extent to which the masses (who have participated individually and collectively in development efforts) perceive rewards and benefits received in relation to their inputs. Essentially, this consideration focuses on the related issues of incentive and motivation which are now widely recognised as important conditions for mobilising the masses for effective participation in the development process.

The situation in contemporary rural China provides a useful illustration of how the authorities have made use of incentives to motivate the masses and sustain their interest in participatory development. First, over time,

118

the effective rate of agricultural tax has been progressively reduced concomitantly with expansion in output as a way of providing material incentive to producers. For the same reason tax exemptions have been granted for the cultivation of waste land and for the development of communal enterprises. There are also price incentives offered to producer collectives in the form of higher producer prices for marketable surpluses, including a premium price with respect to the voluntary sales of surplus products, and the deliberate intervention by the government to stabilise and even reduce the prices of manufactured goods as a means of improving the internal income terms of trade of agriculture. Further incentives aimed at stimulating rural production and raising income levels include the provision by government of grants and low-interest loans to communes for the development of infrastructure and the widespread adoption of mechanical aids in agriculture. In particular, state subsidies are given to worthwhile rural industrial enterprises for technical innovation and development related to agricultural production.[49] Finally, by way of incentive, individuals are encouraged to pursue certain economic activities in their free time as a way of augmenting household incomes and supply of consumption goods as well as of raising the aggregate output of the collective economy.[50]

There can be no denying that these various incentive schemes have been instrumental in sustaining mass participation and interest in collective production in rural China. The fact that they have contributed significantly to improvements in the material well-being of the rural masses underlies their importance as sources of motivation for continued interest by the people in the collective system of farming that today distinctly characterises rural development in China. The operation of the system of incentives itself is based on reward according to efforts: the masses themselves have become aware, on the basis of past experience, that the more they participate and the harder they work the more benefits they will in turn receive in terms of household consumer goods and collective services.

With regard to the latter category of benefits, the role of the state has been particularly crucial for sustaining mass participation. This can best be illustrated by the policies aimed at improving health and medical services in rural areas. The mass movements for improving health facilities would undoubtedly have faded away had they not been backed by several positive measures appropriately taken by the State. For example, out of the realisation that the health facilities introduced in the rural areas could become inoperational due to lack of equipment, steps were taken to increase the supply of necessary equipment (for example X-ray machines, microscopes, surgical kits, operation tables, shadowless lamps, high-pressure sterilisers) and pharmaceutical products in the manufacturing sector, apparently at the production expense of other less essential goods. State intervention also resulted in the reduction of the prices of medicines in the 1970s on average to about one-fifth of early 1950s prices. In addition, urban medical colleges and hospitals have been supporting the running of rural health services through the provision of free vaccination and immunisation, the training facilities for rural-based barefoot doctors, and the sending of qualified medical and health personnel to the rural areas. It is estimated that more than 100 000 urban medical and health personnel were voluntarily transferred to rural areas during 1965–75. During the same period, mobile medical teams, equivalent to about 800 000 person-trips, were regularly sent from urban hospitals to the rural areas for the purpose of treating the seriously ill, training barefoot doctors and helping to establish commune clinics and hospitals.[51] The support provided by the State in the area of rural health services has thus contributed immensely to increasing the confidence of the rural masses in the participatory institutions established to minister to their health needs.

The need to sustain mass participation as a useful means of promoting people-centred development does not imply the unnecessary prolongation of any mass movement or campaign merely for the sake of keeping the masses on their toes, otherwise the result could be counter-productive. What is required, from the viewpoint of sustaining meaningful mass participation, is to create sufficient levels of consciousness among the masses so that they can discern and analyse the nature of their problems and, accordingly, take action to improve their situation. In this they may require outside assistance in the form of education, information dissemination and technical support; but, importantly, such assistance should not take the form of, or be regarded as, a substitute for local initiatives. Outside assistance should serve as a catalyst for raising the level of local consciousness and for supplementing local development efforts where there is clearly a need for this, and any assistance so provided must allow for the active participation of the people themselves. Indeed, this has been the cardinal principle underlying the Chinese model of participatory development and, perhaps, the most important single factor that has contributed to the sustaining of mass interest and commitment to this pattern of development over the past three decades.

SUMMARY AND CONCLUSIONS

The preceding examination of the Chinese experience of using mass participation to promote economic and social development leads to several important conclusions and provides some useful lessons for other contemporary Third World countries. Above all, it provides concrete evidence to support the hypothesis that popular participation can be an important means of achieving basic needs-oriented development objectives and goals, provided that it is pursued within social, economic and political structures that are amenable to the genuine involvement of the mass of the population in the making and implementation of key decisions at all levels. More specifically, the Chinese experience shows that popular influence over the allocation and use of productive resources, in conjunction with the necessary structural changes, could in fact lead to reduction in income inequalities and improved access for the majority to essential public services and facilities through more efficient supply management.

One important point that emerges from the above examination of the Chinese system is the obvious need to establish an appropriate institutional framework for promoting and sustaining popular participation as a major force in the development process. This is related to the key prerequisites of a decentralised process of decision making, an effective organisational structure at the local level and a flexible planning system. The Chinese experience has shown that decentralisation of administration cannot serve the interests of the people without competent and dedicated local leadership which can adequately and truly represent diverse local interests and aspirations. Hence, it is necessary to introduce safeguards to ensure that the wishes of the masses are reflected in programmes and projects being implemented in the name of local development. In China, these safeguards take the form of rules and procedures pertaining to the conduct of local cadres and are institutionalised within the framework of the production system at all levels. Accordingly, the risk of abuses is significantly minimised, if not eliminated altogether. The institutions and institutional arrangements that characterise the Chinese system, though socialist in orientation, have to a large extent been developed or adapted with due regard to the existing socio-cultural values and traditional practices and modes of life; reforms, changes and adaptations have been implemented primarily for the purpose of correcting social injustices and overcoming obstacles to development and progress. This is most obvious in the field of medical and health care where the efforts to satisfy basic health needs are pursued through a combination of modern and traditional forms of treatment. Even in the area of technology, adequate attention is given to local know-how and traditional skills as the basis of innovation. Such a self-reliant style of development, as already argued, holds much potential for saving on scarce development capital and resources – a major obstacle to development in many Third World countries today.

The foregoing is not to give the impression that Chinese development since the liberation in 1949 has not been without its problems and shortcomings – an aspect which has not been highlighted or discussed in detail in this chapter. For example, there are the social costs of mass mobilisation, within a socialist framework, which manifested themselves in overall decline in living standards amidst the difficulties of the early transition period. There have also been excesses and abuses on the part of over-zealous ideologists during certain mass campaigns, the most notorious example being the array of abuses committed during the Cultural Revolution.

Similarly, economic performance has on some occasions drastically fallen short of expectations for reasons connected with maladministration by cadres.[52] Even today shortages in housing and certain essential commodities, and inadequate transport facilities, especially in large cities, attest to the shortcomings of a system that is still undergoing evolution.

Despite these weaknesses, past and present, the development path of China since the liberation has, on the whole, been interesting and certainly one that is characterised by massive strides towards economic development and social progress. One reason why the system has been able to progress towards its stated goals and objectives, in spite of obstacles and setbacks from time to time, could well be the continued existence of conditions and institutions that are amenable to the genuine and effective participation of the masses in the development process at all levels. The survival of these conditions and institutions over time can in turn be attributed to the predominance of the principle of mass participation in Chinese socialism, as is indicated by its entrenchment in the highest organ of the state, the Constitution of the PRC:

> The State adheres to the principle of socialist democracy and ensures to the people the right to participate in the management of state affairs and of all economic and cultural undertakings, and the right to supervise the organisation of State and its personnel.[53]

Finally, what is the relevance of the Chinese approach and experience of mass participation for Third World countries? Given the differences in socio-economic and political systems between China and other developing countries it may be misleading to suggest that the experience of China can be replicated *in toto* in those countries. At the other extreme, it would equally be misleading to argue that because of differences in political and economic systems, level of development and size, the Chinese experience is of no relevance outside her borders. What this study has shown is that, irrespective of the system concerned, there are certain conditions which can be regarded as indispensable to the promotion and sustaining of genuine popular participation in the development process. Based on the premise that such participation itself serves to facilitate the process of development, the study has identified and analysed the most important of these conditions in an operational context. The results of this study, in effect, represent useful guidelines for adopting and promoting participatory styles of development, with allowance for appropriate modifications and adjustments according to prevailing socio-economic and political structures in each individual case. Thus, in conclusion, the study can be said to be of much relevance to any developing country that may wish to use popular participation as a means of promoting socio-economic

122

development, as advocated by the basic needs approach to development.

NOTES

1 These goals are not necessarily mutually exclusive. Both the increase in resource supply and the improvement in allocative efficiency through mass participation would lead to expansion in the production of goods and services required to satisfy basic needs, possibly with no change in the pattern of income distribution in the short run. However, it is strongly argued that structural changes and increased access to productive assets could cause a redistribution of income in favour of the poor and low-income groups within the economy over time. At the same time, policy measures could be deliberately introduced to facilitate income redistribution. A crucial assumption then is that improvement in the pattern of income distribution is a major prerequisite for satisfying basic needs on a sustainable basis, even if the Government succeeds in maximising local resource supply and allocative efficiency.

2 P.C. Mohalanobis: 'The Asian drama: An Indian view' *Economic and Political Weekly,* Special Number, July 1969, pp. 119–32.

3 The term 'liberation' refers to the 1949 victory of the Communist Party of China (CPC).

4 *People's Daily Editorial,* 30 July 1950.

5 Taking northeastern China as an example, the effective demand for cotton cloth in 1947, the year of liberation and land reform, was 800 000 bolts. This amount increased to 1 200 000 in 1948, 3 200 000 in 1949, and 9 million in 1950–*People's Daily Editorial* op.cit.

6 Mao Tse-tung: *Selected works of Mao Tse-tung* (Peking, Foreign Language Press), vol. 4, 1965, p. 72.

7 Mao Tse-tung: *A critique of Soviet economies* (New York, Monthly Review Press, 1977), pp. 44–5.

8 ibid., p.93.

9 Mao Tse-tung: *On the question of agricultural co-operation* (Peking, Foreign Language Press, 1955), pp. 26–7.

10 For definition and operational details of APCs, see *Model regulations for an APC* (Peking, Foreign Language Press, 1976).

11 Mao Tse-tung (1955), op. cit.

12 *Ten great years: Statistics of the economic and cultural achievements of the People's Republic of China,* introduction by Feng-hwa Mah, Occasional Paper no. 5, Programme in East Asian Studies, Statistical Bureau, Western Washington State College, Bellingham, 1974, p. 29.

13 ibid.

14 H. Soo: *The socialist road of China's agriculture* (Peking, People's Publishing House, 1976), p. 102.

15 G.B. Ng: 'Inequalities and the commune system in rural China' (Geneva, ILO, 1976; mimeographed World Employment Programme Research Working Paper), pp. 32–3.

16 H. Soo, op. cit., p. 92. In Shansi province, for example, the abolition of rental income in 1956 was accompanied by an increase in the rate of attendance of around 10 per cent for male labour force and 30–40 per cent for female labour force. Accordingly, additional labour inputs were available for developing farm infrastructural works, including the expansion of nearly 300 000 hectares of irrigated areas in that year.

17 See *People's Daily Editorial,* issues of 23 Nov. 1953, 30 Nov. 1953 and 1 Mar. 1954.
18 This is argued in G.B. Ng: 'Incentive policy in Chinese collective agriculture' *Food policy,* May 1979.
19 See *China Reconstructs,* issues of Mar. 1974 and Oct. 1975.
20 See G.B. Ng: 'The operation of the workpoint system in the Chinese People's communes', Rural Employment Policies Branch (Geneva, ILO, Nov. 1978; mimeographed World Employment Programme Research Working Paper).
21 ibid.
22 ibid.
23 For details on records of floods and droughts in pre-liberation China, see *China tames her rivers* (Peking, Foreign Language Press, 1972); and Ho Chin: *Harm into benefit: Taming the Haiho River* (Peking, Foreign Language Press, 1975).
24 See P. Chen: 'China's population programme at the grassroot level' in *Studies in Family Planning* (Population Planning, New York), August 1973, pp. 219–27; L.A. Orlean: 'China's population growth: Another perspective' in *Current Scene,* Developments in mainland China (Hong Kong), Feb.–Mar. 1978 pp. 1 – 24; and W.C. Chun, op. cit.
25 *Ten great years* op. cit., p. 10; L.A. Orlean, op. cit., p. 22; and W.C. Chun: 'How China conducts birth control' in *China towards modernisation: Collected essays for the fifth China week,* the Hong Kong Federation of Students (Hong Kong, 1977), p. 142.
26 *People's Daily,* 15 March 1977.
27 The rate of attendance of female labour force of Nankun county of Hopeh Province, which is famous for its achievement in birth control, was 93 per cent in 1975 as compared with that of 60 per cent in the early 1970s – *People's Daily,* 14 Apr. 1975.
28 ILO: *Employment, growth and basic needs: A one-world problem* (Geneva, 1978).
29 *Guanming Daily,* 8 October 1977.
30 ibid., 5 Aug. 1978; and D. Perkins: *Agriculture in the People's Republic of China,* Report on a conference held 21–26 Feb. 1975 at the National Academy of Science, Washington, D.C. (Washington, 1976), p. 10.
31 For details on China's health care system, see 'WHO visits China' *World Health,* Sept. 1974; S.V. Rifkin and R. Kaplinsky: 'Health strategy and development planning: Lessons for the People's Republic of China' *Journal of Development Studies,* vol. XI, no. 2, 1973; S. Akhtar (ed.): *Health care in the People's Republic of China: A bibliography with abstracts,* International Development Research Centre (Ottawa, Southam Communication, Ltd., 1975); and D.M. Lampton: 'Development and health care: Is China's medical programme exportable?' *World Development,* vol. 6, 1978, pp. 621–30.
32 See H.F. Hsu and S.Y. Li: 'Historical development, present status and future prospect of living vaccine against schistosomiasis' *China Towards Modernisation,* op. cit., pp. 411–24.
33 'Barefoot doctors' first appeared in China in 1968 when an initial group of 28 took up duty at the Chiangchen People's Commune of Chuansha County in the Shangai municipality. The most salient feature of the system is that this type of medical personnel are trained within a relatively short period of time, compared to that required for formal doctors, to perform such duties as providing treatment for common illnesses, propagating personal hygiene and environmental sanitation, promoting family planning, mobilising the masses for collecting medicinal herbs and running co-operative medical services. Barefoot doctors are also engaged in collective farming as members of communes and receive incomes like other members; this approach promotes their integration with the peasants as well as

contributes to greater self-reliance in the provision of health care facilities at the local level. Barefoot doctors now exist throughout the rural areas of China and their total number was estimated at 1.3 million in 1975. For details see 'The barefoot doctor system grows in strength' in *New China's first quarter-century* (Peking, Foreign Language Press, 1975), pp. 199–209.

34 The Yuetian Production Brigade of Yueyang County in Hunan Province offers a good example on this point. Before the establishment of the co-operative medical service, 610 out of the Brigade's total labour force of 780 caught a cold and could not go to work. This badly affected the harvest of that year. The Brigade set up its own co-operative medical service in June 1970 and by 1973 it had two barefoot doctors, 20 health aides and their own pharmacy. As a consequence, a similar outbreak of colds in 1973 did not result in any large-scale absenteeism and production was not in any way affected; *People's Daily*, 24 Dec. 1973.

35 United Nations General Assembly Resolution 2626 (XXV) of 24 Oct. 1970, paras. 78 and 84.

36 Mao Tse-tung: *Selected works of Mao Tse-tung*, volume 5 (Peking, Foreign Language Press, 1965), pp. 292–4.

37 An agricultural plan covers most socio-economic activities of collectives such as the production of foodgrains and major cash crops, education and the development of rural industries, handicrafts, forestry, fishery and husbandry. It fixes the targets on cultivated acreage, per *mou* output, gross output and procurement quotas of foodgrain and major cash crops. The plan also includes such items as forestation, investment and loans, and infrastructural development projects. See *Economic Research* no. 5, 1965.

38 For example, in 1975 the actual planting acreage of sugar cane in Hainan Prefecture was 42 per cent higher than the target fixed by the state plan. Also, the rapid expansion of sugar beet planting acreage in southern provinces in 1975 is mainly attributed to the use of idle winter-land and the introduction of inter-cropping with sugar cane. See *People's Daily*, 24 May 1977.

39 In Hopei province, for example, 3.5 billion tons of subterranean water was needed per annum for irrigating its farm land. This target was not reached in 1973 as the total pumping capacity was only 2 billion tons of water per annum. Drought in spring and waterlogged land in autumn were the main obstacles to raising farm output. As a result of launching a mass campaign in the manufacturing sector, the output of diesel engines in 1974 increased by 50 per cent and water pumps by 31 per cent as compared with 1973. Consequently, Hopei province managed to achieve self-sufficiency in foodgrain. For details see 'Three former grain deficient provinces show surpluses' in *New China's first quarter-century*, op. cit., pp. 180–9.

40 For example, see the discussions in the earlier section on the delivery of medical and health services and the network of scientific experimentation in rural areas.

41 Mao Tse-tung (ed.): *Socialist upsurge in China's countryside* (Peking, Foreign Language Press, 1957).

42 For details on this see V. Subramaniam: 'Representative bureaucracy: A reassessment' *American Political Science Review*, Dec. 1967.

43 For details see: *Peking Review* (Peking, China Publications Centre), no. 20, 1976, p. 9.

44 See: *China Reconstructs*, July 1974.

45 Ankang is the abbreviation of the Anshan Iron and Steel Company in Northeast China. The 'Ankang Charter', which emphasised mass participation in decision making and democratic management, contrasts with the 'Ma-an Charter' of the early 1950s which was renowned for its authoritarian style of industrial management.

46 Tachai County in Shansi Province became famous on account of its production brigade which achieved great success in meeting production targets and promoting

rural development, through educating and mobilising the masses to initiate actions for solving fundamental problems of production. As a consequence, the authorities launched a mass campaign on the theme of 'In agriculture, learn from Tachai' to publicise the impressive performance of this brigade which should serve as a model for others. For details, see K.F. Hua: *Let the whole party mobilise for a vast effort to develop agriculture and build Tachai-type counties throughout the country* (Peking, Foreign Language Press, 1975), pp. 9–10; G.B. Ng: 'Inequalities and the commune system in rural China', op. cit.; N. Maxwell: 'Learning from Tachai' *World Development*, vol. 3, nos. 7 and 8, 1975.

47 For details see G.B. Ng: *The incentive policy in Chinese agriculture: An overview* (ILO, Geneva, mimeographed, 1978); G.B. Ng: *The operation of the workpoint system in Chinese people's communes* (Geneva, ILO, mimeographed, Nov. 1978).

48 *People's Pictorial* no. 11, 1977, p. 31.

49 For details see G.B. Ng: *The incentive policy in Chinese agriculture: An overview*, op. cit.

50 See G.B. Ng: *Operation and control of individual economic activities in collective agriculture: The case of China* (Geneva, ILO, mimeographed; World Employment Programme Research Working Paper, WEP 10–16/WP19, 1978).

51 For details see Chai Piea: *A glance at China's culture* (Peking, Foreign Language Press, 1975), pp. 23–5.

52 See *People's Daily,* 7 May 1978 and *Guanming Daily,* 18 Aug. 1978.

53 *Constitution of the People's Republic of China,* Article 17, see *Peking Review* (Peking, China Publications Centre), no. 11, 1978.

5 Popular Participation and Administrative Decentralisation in a Basic Needs-Oriented Planning Framework: The Case of The United Republic of Tanzania

David H. Freedman

Since the promulgation of the Arusha Declaration in 1967, popular participation in public decision making at various levels of government has been an important feature of the political ideology as well as the administrative structure of the Tanzanian system. People's participation in the planning and implementation of the social, economic and political activities that affect their livelihood is viewed not only as an effective means to achieve the country's articulated development objectives (which emphasise satisfaction of people's basic needs), but also as a right or an end in itself. Therefore, since 1967, considerable effort has been invested in restructuring socio-economic and political institutions towards the end of greater popular participation in the development process. Given that President Nyerere's choice of a development path for the United Republic of Tanzania, in which notions of mass participation were to have a vital role to play, predated by nine years the proclamation in the ILO World Employment Conference Programme of Action that 'a basic needs-oriented policy implies the participation of the people in making the decisions which affect them through organisations of their own choice', the Tanzanian experience is of special interest for this volume.

In this chapter we look at popular participation in the context of the United Republic of Tanzania's socialist transformation. The purpose is two-fold: (a) to examine the adequacy of the administrative framework or machinery created to promote popular participation in development; and (b) to assess the contributory role of popular participation in meeting basic needs.

THE ADMINISTRATIVE FRAMEWORK

Administrative Capacity: The Missing Link in Formal Planning

Critically speaking, the development plans of many Third World countries constitute little more than laudable statements of intent and aspiration linked to popular objectives of development such as rapid economic growth, reduction in inequalities and poverty and so on. Even when such plans include specific goals and targets in concrete terms, these sometimes are ambitious and unrealistic projections with hardly any hope of being achieved during the plan period. Overall, these weaknesses in development planning may be traced to the lack of suitable and workable organisational framework and procedures for policy formulation and the selection of programmes and projects and, perhaps most importantly, the absence of an appropriate administrative machinery as required for effective plan implementation.[1] Too often development planners have tended to overlook the vital requirement of building into the planning process an efficient administrative machinery for plan implementation and monitoring, even though there are indications of growing awareness of this need with the changing conceptualisation of development over the past two decades.

Development administration, and the related school of institution building, emerged in the development scene in the 1960s as development scholars and practitioners sought to address administrative and institutional weaknesses that impinge on the efficacy of planned development. But development objectives then were related to the growth-oriented approach that left largely unspecified and untackled the problems of inequality and poverty. It was not until the very end of the 1960s and the early 1970s that equity issues and concerns about directing developmental resources to the poorest segments of society assumed some prominence as the development spotlight came to be focused more directly on the well-being of deprived and disadvantaged groups, such as landless peasants and the working poor in urban areas. The basic needs approach (BNA) emerged as a natural evolution of development thinking in this direction, building upon and seeking to increase the potential impact of existing strategies that advocated the 'redistribution with growth', anti-poverty or employment-oriented approaches to development.[2] Significantly, the BNA identifies and emphasises the effective participation of the broad mass of a country's population in the development process as an important and necessary condition for meeting basic needs. In this connection, the BNA specifically advocates the organisation of the poor, and the building and strengthening of institutions for their participation, as a desirable feature of the planning process.

Strangely enough, while development objectives and policy were becoming increasingly people-centred and equity-oriented, the process of planning, at least initially, remained a fairly mechanical exercise involving the counting, costing and allocation of resources to implement planned activities and programmes aimed at meeting basic needs. That is to say limited attention was given to the adequacy of administrative structures and institutional arrangements for implementing basic needs-oriented development plans and programmes.

In its attempt to give operational significance to the BNA, especially with respect to the promotion of broad-based participation in the development process, the ILO has now begun to examine the potentials of local-level planning as a viable means of fulfilling basic needs and employment-related objectives. Yet, there has been little or no attempt to date to examine specifically, at the individual country level, the requirements and operation of an appropriate administrative framework established for ensuring popular participation in the making and implementing of key planning decisions. Such a framework underlies the machinery for identifying priorities, allocating resources, selecting projects and implementing development activities. The United Republic of Tanzania, with the Arusha Declaration and, even more particularly, since the adoption of the policy of 'Decentralisation of Government Administration' in July 1972, provides a useful framework for examining and assessing the administrative capability of the planning system with reference to meeting basic needs. Moreover, this case study is focused on a country whose leadership is committed to a people-centred approach to development, based on the principle of self-reliance, which coincides with the main concerns of the BNA.

The United Republic of Tanzania's Institutional and Administrative Framework

Since the policy of 'Decentralisation of Government Administration' was adopted in 1972 a fairly complex administrative system of decision making has evolved, which is only summarised here.[3] While, in practice, the administrative structures set up have resulted in more 'top-down' control than perhaps was originally intended, it is reported that reforms aimed at establishing greater autonomy and a more solid foundation for decision making at local levels are about to be introduced.

The main features of the present system are: a series of administrative and direct and indirect representational links that run from the village up through district and regional levels to the Prime Minister's Office, which co-ordinates regional programmes at the centre; and a complex set of relationships between the government administration and the country's single political party, the CCM, which involves a combination of independent and overlapping responsibilities at each level of the aforementioned hierarchy.

Key actors and institutions at the village level are: the Village Council consisting of 25 elected members; the Village Assembly made up of all village members who are 18 years and over; five functional committees; and the Village Party Chairman and Secretary who are elected by the Party members in the village and automatically serve in those capacities in the Village Council. The Village Assembly is the main policy-making body at the village level and is required to ratify all major decisions taken by the village leaders or the other organs of the village authority.

The higher institutional level of decision making is the district. The key actors and institutions at this level are: the District Development Council, consisting mainly of popularly elected councillors representing each of the district's wards; the District Development and Planning Committee, which is a committee of the Council; and relevant government functionaries at the district level. The district is the basic unit for purposes of formal planning, although inputs to the plan at this level are largely based on programme and project proposals emanating from the villages. Following an appraisal of the technical feasibility of programme and project proposals from the village level and an assessment of their financial requirements in relation to available resources, some proposals may be dropped at the district level. Eventually a draft programme, following the approval of the Party organ at the district level, is sent to the regional level for further consideration in relation to other district plans. The regional administration is the Central Government's representative and the main co-ordinator of both central and local government activities in the region. Before regional budgets are finally approved, plan proposals from the regions are submitted to the Prime Minister's Office for review of their consistency in terms of national objectives, priorities, technical and financial feasibility.

A parallel structure for decision making exists at the work place. The United Republic of Tanzania established in 1970 a system of workers' councils in public corporations employing ten or more workers. Simply stated, the workers' council advises the corporation's Board of Directors through what is called the Executive Committee. The Executive Committee, on which workers are represented, scrutinises the recommendations of the workers' council before making its own recommendations to the General Manager and the Board of Directors.

Thus to the extent that the workers' council itself is conceived as an advisory body this role is performed through the intermediate body of the Executive Committee and not directly. The Executive Committee can accept, modify or reject advice coming from the workers' council. This chapter later examines what is termed workers' participation in the Tanzanian context.

Generally speaking then, the political and administrative framework and associated institutions of a country constitute the foundation for translating development goals and aspirations into basic needs-oriented programmes, projects and activities. Yet whether or not the desired

130

development action is achieved very much depends on or is conditioned by the availability or the presence, when and where needed, of certain resources or inputs. For the purpose of the analysis to follow, five sets of necessary inputs can be identified.[4]

1 Skilled manpower, including the technicians, managers, planners and administrators needed at the various levels of government.
2 Financial resources, including public revenues and foreign exchange for development and recurrent expenditure.
3 Physical resources: the supply of such development inputs as raw materials, machinery and spare parts including their movement, storage and distribution.
4 Information: the timely flow of data, decisions, guidelines, suggestions and reactions between different government agencies and different levels of government, as well as between government and the public; and
5 Leadership: at both local and national levels capable of effectively guiding and gaining people's confidence and co-operation in carrying out development decisions.

Shortfalls and deficiencies in the above inputs can, on the one hand, act as constraints on popular participation, which itself is an input to the development process; on the other hand, effective popular participation can serve to compensate for certain shortcomings or bottle-necks with respect to these inputs. The range of required inputs listed above suggests that popular participation is not a smooth, easy to accomplish, once and for all process. Efforts to introduce mass participation at local levels may, in fact, produce countervailing tendencies which in turn may necessitate higher-level interventions – though not always with successful outcome – aimed at restoring or enhancing broader-based participation.

POPULAR PARTICIPATION AND BASIC NEEDS SATISFACTION: APPLYING A DECENTRALISED ADMINISTRATIVE FRAMEWORK TO DEVELOPMENT PLANNING

In this section an attempt is made to assess the impact of popular participation on the development process in the United Republic of Tanzania, as practised within the overall framework of decentralised administration and development planning, on basic needs-oriented goals and objectives.

Broadly speaking, one can distinguish at least five ways in which popular participation can contribute to the satisfaction of basic needs.[5] These are:

1 Playing a part in identification of basic needs and the selection of basic needs projects. In the Tanzanian case, this also may be viewed as the degree of influence at the village and the district levels on the basic needs decisions.
2 Mobilising and efficiently utilising local resources for the provision of essential public services and, generally speaking, for more self-reliant forms of development.
3 Ensuring that the benefits of development reach the poor. This includes the distribution of basic needs goods, services and inputs, which in turn involves the operation of efficient delivery systems and adequate access to basic needs services.
4 Serving as a vehicle for psychological satisfaction and motivation of the individual. In this regard participation may be related to such intangible requirements of well-being as social justice, self-confidence and self-respect. This aim of participation fits well with the socialist transformation that the United Republic of Tanzania is trying to carry out.
5 Providing a training ground for more enlightened participation, and future leadership roles in political and economic institutions. In the United Republic of Tanzania, where development is regarded equally as the concern of both the Party and the Government structures, this acquires special meaning.

An examination of each of the above-mentioned roles of popular participation, against the background of the administrative structure described in the previous section, constitutes an appropriate analytical framework for assessing how well popular participation has worked in the United Republic of Tanzania in relation to the fulfilment of basic needs-oriented development objectives. Although what follows will inevitably highlight constraints and problems impeding the fuller realisation of those objectives, it is, however, not intended to minimise the efforts and the achievements of the United Republic of Tanzania in the areas of decentralised planning and promotion of popular participation in the development process. The purpose, instead, is to draw attention to obstacles to effective popular participation for meeting basic needs, with a view to identifying feasible ways and means of overcoming such obstacles.

Identification of Basic Needs and Selection of Basic Needs Projects

Clean water, primary education and health care, together with increased domestic production of food crops, have been expressed as national priority areas for basic needs satisfaction. If one were to add transportation to this list, there is little reason to believe that there would be

132

major variations in the identification of basic needs priorities at sub-national levels, allowing of course, for some areas having progressed much further than others in meeting certain basic needs. What is more relevant, however, is the process by which general expressions of basic needs priorities are translated into specific proposals and the likelihood of funds subsequently being provided for their implementation. Once the problem is put in these terms, it becomes necessary to look more closely at what exactly has been decentralised.

Most scholars of decentralisation in the United Republic of Tanzania argue that the form that it has taken up to the present is more that of 'deconcentration', i.e., the transfer of administrative authority lower down the hierarchy, than of 'devolution', i.e., the power to make policy decisions at local levels.[6] While the bureaucracy has been greatly expanded and decentralised in the former sense, control over decision making is limited due to deficiencies in all five development input areas outlined earlier. In this regard, particular mention should be made of financial resources, information and skilled manpower.

Together with introducing a decentralised administrative structure, the Government, guided by what were then strong development and equity considerations, took away the taxing powers of the former local authorities. With taxing powers centralised, each level of government became dependent on the Central Government for resource allocations. Therefore, villages had to operate with a very limited revenue base of their own. As a result, the villages took a 'shopping list' approach by submitting ideas for far more projects than they knew they would receive funding.[7] District officials once estimated that during the initial stages of implementing the decentralisation policy, budgetary constraints led to the dropping of as many as 60 per cent or more of the proposals originating from the villages and wards upon their reaching the district or regional level.[8] Over time this could only lead to disillusionment and act as a brake on popular participation. In recognition of the seriousness of this problem there is now a move afoot to introduce greater revenue-earning capacity at district and village levels.

Information comes into play, because clearly the circumstances require that the villagers have some understanding of what level of resources they can reasonably expect to receive. Related to this, the villagers must be given a clear understanding of how their priorities relate to national objectives and priorities and the types of projects for which they are most likely to receive development funds and other types of government assistance. Sometimes requests made by villages correspond closely to national priorities but still have to be turned down due to the fact that the overall number of requests reaching the district or regional level for, say, a dispensary or a school, far exceeds the availability of complementary skilled manpower and material inputs at a given time.

The absence of skilled manpower, particularly in the fields of planning and administration, is another strong constraint on village-level decision making. Generally speaking, low levels of education have impeded villagers in putting across their ideas of what they want for their villages. Given that villagers' proposals generally take the form of long lists of projects wished for, with no technical detail or priority rating, it has been suggested that projects proposed by officials with more technical knowledge and communication skills have a much greater chance of implementation.[9]

It was in response to the shortages of skilled planners and administrators that the Government moved in 1978 to begin appointing a village manager for each village. The managers were drawn from a pool of officials, with professional qualifications, already employed by the government in ministries, parastatals and other government organisations. The managers have widely divergent backgrounds in terms of their education and training but often little or no practical experience in local-level planning. Many were new graduates who were posted to villages almost immediately after their studies. Therefore, in addition to their own adjustment problems, they often experienced, as paid outside employees of government, difficulties in gaining acceptance by the villagers. It has been suggested that many villagers would prefer to see these managers recruited from within the local community.[10] In fact, it can be argued that the presence of a centrally appointed and paid functionary from outside, ironically, may create dependence on the part of the villagers, if the manager is somewhat effective. Apart from stifling local initiatives for self-reliance, there is also the danger that the departure of a good village administrator could lead to the demise of useful on-going projects. In other cases where there are conflicts between the manager and the local community, the former may find it difficult, if not impossible, to fulfil his advisory role to the Village Chairman or the Village Council. Nevertheless, some village managers are reported to have already achieved good results, but others are said to have been ineffective.

While assistance from outside has a useful role to play, the true essence of popular participation remains with individuals influencing decisions on problems and issues that concern them. This includes the formulation and implementation of plans as well as evaluation of projects that have been carried out. In order to avoid the imposition of decisions from above, it is necessary to ensure (a) that the local people are really conscious and knowledgeable about their actual needs and (b) that they are involved with technocrats and planners in formulating and implementing local development programmes and projects. This again draws attention to the importance of mass education for raising the understanding of local people to the necessary level. It also brings us back to the fundamental question of who in fact participates. Do the poor participate? Do women participate to any meaningful extent? Or is participation largely by those who, by virtue of wealth, position or superior status, control the levers of power?

The question is partly answered by the observation that, in the Tanzanian context, in spite of the mechanisms established to ensure that initiatives for the selection of local-level development projects come from the masses in response to their felt needs, in reality the influence of the technocrats continues to be greater than that of the people in determining important decisions.[11] A real shift in power can be expected only when there is increased technical sophistication among the masses and especially among their representatives.[12] The Tanzanian experience, therefore, shows that even where clearly defined and elaborate organisational structures for popular participation exist, participation is not necessarily guaranteed. Village Councils can be democratically elected and yet the authority of the masses not exercised effectively. This goes to show that the effectiveness of participation does not depend only on how it is organised, but, more importantly, by whom, i.e., the people who truly believe in participation on the one hand, or those seeking to use the organisational structures to facilitate their own control over decision making on the other.[13]

Similar questions can be raised as well about workers' participation, to which reference was made earlier. It is said that a common complaint heard from workers is that, in preparing the agenda of Workers' Council meetings, their representatives do not always consult them and, therefore, the decisions taken do not necessarily represent broad or popular views. Perhaps an even more serious allegation is that the minutes of Workers' Council meetings are often stamped 'confidential' and thereby are not readily accessible to all workers in the enterprise.[14]

What also is apparent is that workers' participation as practised in the United Republic of Tanzania is directed at the overall running of the enterprise rather than participation in shop-floor level decisions, which might be assumed to be of greater day to day concern to many workers. It also is evident that participation in essentially company-wide policy matters requires, if anything, more sophistication and understanding on the part of those involved. Workers' education becomes all the more important.

Mobilisation of Local Resources and Greater Self-Reliance in Development

Related to establishing priorities and selecting basic needs projects is the question of how resources are allocated to regions, districts and villages. It appears as if there are no explicit standard criteria for taking decisions regarding allocation of resources, although such broad considerations as equity or balanced development between and within regions; development potential, and past performance or capacity utilisation all appear, to

135

varying degrees, to be taken into account. While an equity criterion would tend to favour the poorer areas of the country, one based on development potential or past performance could easily favour those which are most well off. Such a vague approach to resource allocation, however, might be regarded as pragmatic, leaving sufficient flexibility for case by case decisions; but the absence of more clearly established, universally applied criteria also can lead to arbitrary decisions and, at a minimum, contribute to the confusion about what is required to obtain necessary resources from higher level government authorities.

It is recognised, of course, that resource allocation becomes even more difficult when a poor country like the United Republic of Tanzania finds itself in the throes of a mounting economic crisis which not only impedes well-intentioned efforts to raise living standards, but threatens past achievements in fulfilling people's basic needs. Faced with an acute shortage of foreign exchange and a serious insufficiency of funds for development and recurrent expenditures, one might look to the effective mobilisation and utilisation of local resources as a way of easing economic and financial constraints.

On the face of it, a country like the United Republic of Tanzania, where the espousal of self-reliance is firmly embodied in the Arusha Declaration and where the 1972 Decentralisation Policy and the 1975 Villages and Ujamaa Villages Act transferred at least some measure of decision making to local levels, should be well poised for self-help and community development schemes that involve broad-based popular participation and aim at generating additional resources. Yet ten years after the Arusha Declaration, President Nyerere himself was arguing that at the root of the country's development problem was the failure to understand and to apply properly the concept of self-reliance. He observed, 'We do not approach a problem by asking how we can solve it by our efforts, with the resources which we have in front of us' but 'in terms of. . . what we can afford and what we can do ourselves'.[15]

In this and the following section an attempt is made to delve into *where* and *why* local self-reliance has fallen short of expectations. At the outset, however, it will be useful to dispose of a definitional problem with respect to the notion of self-help. There is little disagreement that self-help implies the mobilisation of local resources, including available under-utilised manpower, for use in productive activities or to provide essential services of benefit to a significant portion of the community if not the community as a whole. Some argument seems to arise, however, over the question of remuneration, with many maintaining that anything beyond token direct payment to the individuals supplying labour would automatically remove a community development activity from the category of self-help. Yet in the United Republic of Tanzania, where the peasantry still appears to be very much motivated by direct benefits and becomes disillusioned when benefits from communal activities accrue disproportionately to those who

136

are better off, this should be of less concern. What seems more relevant is to ensure that self-help schemes are designed and financed in ways that guarantee that those who contribute to labour reap their share of direct and/or indirect benefits. The financial implications of this are examined in the next section.

In fact, the nature and level of remuneration and the extent to which it is collected by the village, paid to the individual or credited towards his contribution to communal activity appear to vary greatly from village to village and project to project. Regardless of the arrangement, however, villagers generally are expected to contribute either in time or on a piece-rate basis a certain proportion of each working week to a communal activity.

What our examination has shown is that there is a much greater willingness to contribute labour at a reasonably high level of productivity to the provision of public facilities and services than to communal agricultural plots, being that the perceived benefits from the latter tend to be not as great as those from, say, the construction of a dispensary, a school house or an irrigation channel.

The importance of self-help schemes in one of the United Republic of Tanzania's national priority areas, that of water, has been documented elsewhere.[16] Popular involvement in the development of water projects has always been encouraged and is called for in the five-year development plans. There are numerous examples of local people having dug wells or built dams in their communities on a self-help basis.

Still popular participation has always fallen short of the type of public involvement implied in both Government and Party policy. Generally people's participation in self-help activities has taken the form of doing such unskilled jobs as digging trenches for pipelines or collecting building materials. People seldom have been involved in the actual planning of projects or in running and maintaining them. Ideally, popular partici-pation in planning should take the form of generating information about local needs, priorities and potential, followed by direct involvement of the people in the decision-making process. For example, participation in construction and maintenance of a project become feasible when the technology used is simple, locally based, and produces satisfactory results at a low cost.[17] That popular participation along these lines is not practised more frequently is another reflection of technical bias and what often is perceived to be an inherent conflict between the goal of participation and that of efficiency.

Institutional Arrangements for Mass Mobilisation

Any discussion of mobilisation of resources in the context of popular participation in the United Republic of Tanzania would be incomplete without mention of the five mass organisations or special groups affiliated

137

with the Party. These mass organisations are: the Workers' Organisation (JUWATA), the Women's Organisation (UWT), the Youth Organisation (VIJANA), the Parents' Organisation (WAZAZI), and the Union of Cooperative Societies (WASHIRIKA). Besides providing special services to their members, these organisations are intended to mobilise the masses (Party and non-Party members alike) for effective participation in the activities of their special groups as well as to help shape attitudes in line with the Party's ideology of socialism and self-reliance. The organisational structures of each of these special groups is supposed to reach down to the village level. These mass organisations are institutionally linked to the Party organs at all levels. It appears that all these mass organisations face serious problems of inadequacy of resources for carrying out their activities. The UWT, in particular, appears to be further handicapped by low levels of education and leadership training among women and limitations imposed by the multiple roles performed by women in Tanzanian rural society. After women have completed their farming for the day, fetched water and fed and cared for the family (all activities associated with daily living, if not survival), there is little time left over for popular participation activities for which the potential gains may be much less readily apparent.

Ensuring that the Benefits of Development Reach the Poor

As already observed, poor Tanzanian villagers are concerned about and responsive to the distribution of communally produced goods and services. Given the guiding philosophy of their country, they have more than enough reason to be. Yet, even where it is the genuine intention of governments that public services should benefit the poor, the incidence of the costs and benefits of public services can be as uneven between different income groups as the overall distribution of income and wealth.[18]

As also pointed out, a strong case can now be made for returning a considerable measure of revenue collection power to local levels of government. The objective is to provide decision-making authorities at the village level with the means and the capacity for fulfilling their obligations to the local population with respect to the provision of a range of essential services and facilities. Furthermore, a system of revenue collection at the local level should include provisions whereby those who benefit more from communal services pay back part of those benefits in order to have funds available for providing additional services or for maintaining existing facilities. What follows is illustrative of how such a system might operate in practice.[19]

A self-help irrigation project constructed by mainly labour inputs from less well-to-do villagers, but with disproportionately greater potential benefits for rich farmers who stand to realise higher yields and, hence,

138

incomes from their larger and now more fertile plots of land, might usefully be associated with a water levy or some type of land tax on users. This would serve to recapture some of the benefits from the project for the improvement of the larger community.

However, if it is the poorer segments of the community that stand to benefit substantially from a self-help irrigation project, through increased access to irrigated land, they too might pay back part of the benefits they derive. Their payments could take the form of an unrecompensed contribution of labour to other communal projects. Viewed as a tax, such a payment would be easier to assess than an actual levy on earned income. But from an equity standpoint, contributions of this nature from the poor would have to be complemented by user payments or taxes coming from the wealthier segment of the community, although in this context payments in the form of materials or even privately held land might also be envisaged. Proceeds from the sale of communal output, of course, would remain a potentially sizeable source of development funds. At the same time, in order to avoid the introduction of further incentives to shift away from communal towards private production, especially in agriculture, some share of what is produced and marketed privately would have to be taxed.[20] Moreover, this could introduce a progressive element into taxation, in addition to providing additional revenues for essential services.

There are other ways of channelling additional resources to local levels that might also be explored. One such possibility is through matching grants whereby the central Government, or any higher level of government for that matter, rewarded local revenue earning efforts with some measure of matching support. Such an approach could be structured in a way that enabled the Government also to pursue the objective of balanced development. For instance, a sliding scale formula could be adopted whereby the Government would contribute a proportion of between 20 per cent in a rich area to 80 per cent in a very poor area, of total resources raised locally for development purposes. Thus, without in any way penalising rich areas, the Government would provide incentives for poor areas to do as well as they can in the mobilisation of local resources.

Quite apart, it should be recognised that the Government can always intervene to transfer resources to rural areas through its price policies rather than depending entirely on administrative mechanisms and tax policy. By raising the relative prices of agricultural products, the Government can effect a transfer of funds to rural areas, irrespective of the type of revenue collection and disbursement machinery it has established.

The basic needs approach to development is concerned as much, if not more, with the distribution of goods and services, as with their production. This introduces special problems of access and the associated need to develop delivery systems that can both efficiently and effectively channel basic needs inputs as well as outputs to those whose needs are greatest. Popular participation has a role to play in the design and efficient operation of delivery systems. In the case of the United Republic of Tanzania, a reorganised co-operative system may offer an especially worthwhile instrument for efficient delivery of basic needs goods and services.

In May 1976, the Government dissolved the 1300 primary marketing co-operatives and their umbrella organisations, the 16 Regional Co-operative Unions. The old co-operatives were generally characterised as both corrupt and inefficient. With the dissociation of the old co-operative movement, the functions directly related to crop cultivation were transferred to the Crop Authorities. But, before long the Crop Authorities were rivalling the co-operatives in mismanagement and malpractices.[21] Moreover, the virtually unassailable power position of the Crop Authorities removed participation and effective control further away from the people. The villagers lost practically all control over marketing operations.

Yet when properly managed a production and marketing co-operative can be turned into a true grass-roots participatory institution with development potential. Under the 1975 Villages and Ujamaa Act, the villages were conceived as multi-purpose co-operative societies. Of course, they also were to function as autonomous administrative entities, which as already shown, too often operate more in a 'top-down' than in a 'bottom-up' manner.

Under the proposed reforms for reconstituting the co-operative movement, regional and district co-operative unions would be made up of primary co-operative societies established within the region or district. The unions would be expected to pull together the production, marketing and other activities of the primary co-operative societies. If self-help could be encouraged on a broader scale, some villages might be able to handle the processing of certain crops, with greater income going to the community. Yet where this was found not to be feasible because of economies of scale, the district or regional co-operative unions could process various outputs coming from the villages, while also serving as a channel for certain production inputs that could then be purchased more cheaply at bulk rate. Mobilisation of savings and distribution of credits are other functions of co-operatives that might have to involve a higher level of organisation than the individual village unit. Still it would seem that an underlying goal of the revived co-operatives should be to encourage mass involvement in various economic activities and stages of production, processing and marketing, with the maximum amount of self-reliance possible at the village level, while at the same time ensuring that a maximum of profits are retained by or ploughed back to the village itself. Clearly one consideration of importance to the future success of the revived co-operatives will be the size of the surplus generated and whether a sizeable portion can be controlled by the villages themselves. The ultimate aim, however, should be to make the individual villages more economically viable and self-reliant.

Serving as a Vehicle for Psychological Satisfaction and Motivation of the Individual

Following from what has already been said, it perhaps is appropriate to view self-reliance as a process whereby people undertake to solve problems and provide for themselves through their own efforts and depending essentially, though not entirely, on their own resources. Government can enhance the spirit and practice of self-reliance by providing the necessary support structures, but if people are to be placed more in control of their own destiny, they have to be allowed to influence key decisions that relate to and affect their well-being. It has been established that genuine participation increases confidence of individuals and groups in their ability to initiate action to defend and promote their interests. In this sense popular participation may be regarded as a psychological stimulant towards greater motivation and effort and, hence, higher levels of productivity and earnings.[22]

It could be argued that the United Republic of Tanzania through its villagisation programme already has introduced a firmer institutional foundation for community-oriented basic needs efforts than is to be found in most other developing societies. Through a combination of persuasion, inducement and some compulsion peasants have been brought together to live in villages. It has been contended, however, that there is a need to distinguish between the implementation requirements of getting people to work together as distinct from getting them to live together. Implementation of the working together aspect, it is argued, was hampered by confusion over the meaning of 'Ujamaa'. By the mid 1970s, few villagers identified villagisation with working together and sharing of proceeds from collective production, although according to most policy pronouncements such communal production was the principal factor distinguishing an ordinary village from an Ujamaa village. It is suggested that the discrepancies between official policy and the peasant conception of 'Ujamaa' may be accounted for in part by the combination of their unpleasant experiences with communal farming and the desire not to oppose what public officials support.[23] By way of contrast, as already pointed out, working together at such tasks as the construction of schools, dispensaries, irrigation and water supply facilities has gone on much more successfully.

It is against this background that we view the periodic exhortations and occasional decrees aimed at stimulating greater communal food production. For instance, in October 1981 the Party decreed that village governments must put under Ujamaa farming at least 100 hectares of food and cash crops during the 1981/82 season in an effort to generate surplus for the rehabilitation of the Tanzanian economy. It is well known that co-ordinated planning in agricultural production, and target-setting in crop output for different production levels are major features of a socialist economic system. Nevertheless, the United Republic of Tanzania's past experience with communal production, and our own central argument that work and higher levels of output follow more naturally from popularly determined decisions coupled with readily perceived benefits, suggest that the call for greater communal production should neither be issued as uniform decrees nor should targets be set on the basis of the number of hectares cultivated; rather it should make allowance for the ecological variations in the country, including availability of adequate land and output potential.

If grass-roots participation is to have meaning and the peasants are to be properly motivated, they must feel free to express their needs, put forward their ideas and contribute to the decision-making process. Psychological satisfaction, as an aim of participation, can only be realised when the people are placed more in control of their own lives and livelihood. Maximal participation in decision making at the village level, as it has been observed in one village study, appears to be greatest, (a) where the village leadership effectively uses the villages' participatory machinery, that is the Village Assembly, Council and sub-committees, ensuring that they meet regularly and perform the functions expected of them; (b) when previous experiences with participation have had positive results; and (c) when economically-oriented collective undertakings produce a high return, and a substantial amount of the surplus generated, as well as the services provided are used to benefit the participants.[24] The role and qualities of leadership are therefore crucial in determining the degree as well as the effectiveness of popular participation at the village level.

Providing a Training Ground for More Enlightened Participation and Future Leadership Roles

Any discussion of popular participation in the United Republic of Tanzania would be incomplete without further comment on CCM (the Revolutionary Party), the nation's single mass party. This stems not only from its leading role in shaping the ideological framework on which the country's move towards socialism and self-reliance is based, but its influence on public policy as well. In an earlier section, we traced the

142

parallel and hierarchical structure of Government and Party with respect to planning. The final approval of all development plans at the various organisational levels rests with the Party, and the major role of the Party here is to review programme proposals in terms of their broad policy implications. Given the supreme mobilisation and leadership role of the Party within the country's political system the question of leadership capacity of the Party becomes of great importance.

A major weakness of the Party in the past appears to have been centred on the limited ability of the Party to exercise its leadership functions effectively due to the limited technical and administrative competence of many of the people involved in the decision-making process.[25] The Party needs to be able to draw upon expertise, experience, skills and other technical inputs if it is to have the capacity to acquire, interpret and utilise the information which is essential for rational decision making.[26] It seems that the Party is well aware of this problem. It now has a technical wing, through which it hopes to create its own technical capacity. Still, on the face of it, it would seem that the Party and its affiliates could do much more in the area of training for leadership at the local levels.

From the standpoint of participation, the question of leadership assumes its greatest importance at the village level. Leaders, after all, can influence the setting of priorities and the formulation of development proposals within the village, and the very nature of their positions ensures that they come into greater contact with district and higher level officials, i.e. those who subsequently take decisions on requests originating at village level.

While it is not apposite to discuss the qualities of good local leaders here, there is little doubt that almost all village leaders, whether elected by the Party or appointed by the Government, can benefit from further training. Levels of education and the technical knowledge base are probably much lower at the village than at higher levels. Until the overall platform of knowledge and understanding – on which the ultimate success of true popular participation, grass-roots development and bottom-up planning must to a large degree be pegged – has been raised substantially, the need to provide adequate training cannot be overly stressed.

The fact that the village manager too often is ineffective today, results from a combination of political and technical factors. It does not help that his status as an outsider deprives him of a local support base and makes it difficult for him to become an integral part of village leadership. Yet the technical deficiencies of village managers should not be minimised either. Village managers, irrespective of their backgrounds, should at a minimum be equipped with planning and administrative skills. Over time, as Universal Primary Education (UPE) begins to bear fruit, efforts could be made to begin to recruit managers from within their own villages.

Knowledge and understanding are also prerequisites for effective workers' participation. Workers' participation, therefore, cannot be discussed separately from workers' education, because only by increasing workers' awareness and understanding of the development process to which they are supposed to be contributing can workers' participation be meaningfully pursued. Through a combination of mass political and public education by the Party – based on mass media and speeches at public rallies and at the work place – and with specialised seminars and courses for workers organised by the Ministry of Labour and JUWATA, workers' education now seems to be making some headway.

Enterprises themselves at present offer or make possible two types of workers' education: (a) skill upgrading courses offered in-house or outside; and (b) secondary education programmes offered on the premises to workers who seek advancement by achieving higher education levels. The University of Dar-es-Salaam, for instance, has both the former and the latter types of programmes for its employees. In fact, every public institution is expected to set aside funds for a staff development programme for its workers.

Overall then, some progress is being made in preparing individuals for effective mass participation in the villages or at their work places. Still, institutions must be further strengthened for this role as well as for the development of capable and competent leadership at all levels.

CONCLUSIONS

The United Republic of Tanzania already has gone further in the direction of popular participation in development and decentralisation of public decision making than the great majority of countries in the Third World. In fact, it could be argued that the Tanzanian model, despite its weaknesses, in many ways provides useful guidelines for establishing the basis of a people-centred pattern of development. This could be relevant to the situation in many other African countries, where the prevailing levels and forms of popular participation in development are much more limited.

The approach followed in this chapter, however, has been to examine the Tanzanian performance in relation to the aspirations of its leadership and the expectations and felt needs of its own people. While this inevitably has resulted in a more critical assessment of national experience, the intention has been constructively to highlight problems and constraints to the fuller realisation of development objectives at the grass-roots level in the United Republic of Tanzania. It is felt that the conclusions reached are of somewhat wider applicability, in the sense that they constitute useful lessons for guiding other developing countries regarding pitfalls to be avoided in the pursuit of popular participation in development.

The Tanzanian experience clearly demonstrates the link between decentralisation and effective participation. Through its shortcomings and successes, it has been found that a form of decentralisation wherein local authorities are given much more say with respect to policy decisions pertaining to their own development could in fact enhance the role and value of popular participation. Within such a framework, development planning could almost inevitably become more 'bottom-up' oriented and decisions based to a greater extent on local needs and conditions. Conversely, the decentralisation of administration without the transfer of decision-making powers and resources to local levels has been seen as a major obstacle to the realisation of effective popular participation in the development process.

This study of the United Republic of Tanzania also has shown the importance of better motivating and preparing people to participate in communal activity. It has been argued, with respect to the former, that popular participation can best be encouraged through meaningful forms of involvement and by establishing, wherever possible, greater correspondence between people's contributions to self-help activities and benefits actually obtained from participation in such activities. As a corollary, the return of a considerable measure of revenue collection power to local authorities has been suggested, with the proviso that the incidence of payments, generally speaking, should bear some relationship to the benefits received in terms of greater or improved communal services.

Moreover, the Tanzanian experience has shown the extent to which participation is conditioned by the presence or absence of certain vital inputs. In addition to financial resources these include physical resources, skilled manpower, the timely flow of relevant information, and effective leadership at all levels. What also emerges from this study of the United Republic of Tanzania is the important role of education in relation to the last three inputs mentioned above and, in turn, to the promotion of effective popular participation itself. For in the end, it is the understanding, knowledge and willing co-operation of the people themselves that translate popular participation from a slogan to an operationally sound approach for meeting basic needs and reducing poverty in society.

NOTES

1 Donald C. Stone: 'Removing administrative and planning constraints to development' *Journal of Administration Overseas*, London, Jan. 1973, p. 5.
2 See, for instance, Paul Streeten: 'The distinctive features of a basic-needs approach to development' *International Development Review*, 1977/3, p. 8; F. Lisk, 'Conventional development strategies and basic-needs fulfilment: A reassessment of objectives and policies' *International Labour Review* (Geneva, ILO), vol. 115, no. 2, Mar./Apr. 1977.
3 The most extensive treatment of decentralisation policy in the United Republic of

Tanzania is to be found in Justin H.J. Maeda: 'Popular participation control and development (A case study of the nature and role of popular participation in Tanzania's rural development)', an unpublished Ph.D. dissertation presented to the Faculty of the Graduate School of Yale University, Dec. 1976. Shorter pieces by Maeda on the subject include *National structure for implementing people-centred agrarian development* (Dar-Es-Salaam, Institute of Development Studies, University of Dar-Es-Salaam, Jan. 1979) and *Decentralisation of government administration* (Dar-Es-Salaam, Institute of Development Studies, University of Dar-Es-Salaam, Nov. 1980).

4 This draws upon but then somewhat modifies the presentation in a chapter on 'Meeting technical needs' in Saul M. Katz: *Guide to modernising administration for national development* (Pittsburgh, Graduate School of Public and International Affairs, University of Pittsburgh, 1965), pp. 7–28.

5 The treatment here of the first four roles of public participation is derived from Franklyn A.N. Lisk: 'Popular participation in basic-needs oriented development planning' *Labour and Society* (Geneva, International Institute for Labour Studies), vol. 6, no. 1, Jan.–Mar. 1981, pp. 8–12.

6 For a fuller discussion of these terms, see Paul Collins: 'The working of Tanzania's Rural Development Fund: A problem in decentralisation' *East African Journal of Rural Development*, vol. 5, nos. 1 and 2, pp. 141–2. The government appears to be conscious of the limitations of the more restricted deconcentration approach to decentralisation and is thinking seriously of ways of moving further in the direction of devolution.

7 As Maeda (1980), op. cit., p. 17, points out, over time as the villagers came to learn that if they asked for ten projects they might get five, they therefore ask for twenty in the hope of getting ten.

8 Maeda (1976), op. cit., p. 292.

9 Frances Moore Lappe and Adele Beccar-Varela: *Mozambique and Tanzania: Asking the big questions* (San Francisco, Institute for Food and Development Policy, 1980), p. 94.

10 Koenraad Verhagen: 'Changes in Tanzanian rural development policy 1975–1978' *Development and Change*, London, vol. 11, no. 2, Apr. 1980, p. 294.

11 Maeda (1980), op. cit., p. 17.

12 ibid.

13 Lappe and Beccar-Varela, op. cit., p. 95.

14 Wilfred Philip Ochieng Olum: *Workers' participation in Tanzania. What is wrong with the system?* A thesis submitted in partial fulfilment of the requirements for the Labour Studies Diploma at Ruskin College, Oxford, 1981.

15 Julius K. Nyerere: *The Arusha Declaration ten years after* (Dar-Es-Salaam, 1977), pp.28–9.

16 See M.R. Muhwahuzi: 'Popular participation: The Tanzanian case in water supply' in Leonard Berry and Robert W. Kates (eds): *Making the most of the least alternative ways to development* (New York, Holmes and Meier Publishers, Inc., 1980), pp. 176–81.

17 ibid., pp. 178–9.

18 Paul Streeten and Shahid Javed Burki: 'Basic needs: Some issues' *World Development*, vol. 6, no. 3, 1978, p. 415.

19 Clearly it is not intended that such principles should be applied indiscriminately to all groups, in order to avoid poor villagers having to pay for such services as health care and education for themselves and their families.

20 Of course, it then becomes necessary to guard against the risks of extensive output being held off the market or smuggled.

21 See Verhagen, op. cit., p. 293.
22 Lisk (1981), op. cit., p. 12.
23 Dean E. McHenry, Jr.: *Tanzania's Ujamaa villages. The implementation of a rural development strategy* (Berkeley, University of California, Institute of International Studies, 1979), p. 209.
24 Maeda (1976), op. cit., pp. 358–9.
25 Bismark U. Mwansasu: 'The changing role of the Tanganyika African National Union' in B.U. Mwansasu and Cranford Pratt (eds): *Towards Socialism in Tanzania* (Dar-Es-Salaam, Tanzania Publishing House, 1979), p. 187.
26 ibid.

6 Popular Participation and Access to Basic Needs in Kenya

W. Ouma Oyugi

This case study surveys different forms of popular participation in the development process in Kenya since independence. The main aim is to investigate the effectiveness of each type with specific reference to actual and potential contribution to basic needs satisfaction among the broad mass of the population. In this regard, the role of popular participation is also examined in relation to opportunities for productive and adequately remunerating employment and access to essential services and facilities, especially for the poorer segments of the population. The operational framework for popular participation in the specific context of this case study is the overall planning system, although, for obvious reasons, emphasis is placed on development planning at the local level where popular involvement in the making and implementation of key decisions has been found to be crucial to improvements in living standards for the broad mass of the population.

This approach is consistent with the observation in Kenya (and many other developing countries) that poverty and shortfalls from basic needs are more discernible at the local level and closely related to the lack of effective participation of all concerned in the development process. Furthermore, lack of popular participation at the local level is inextricably linked to weaknesses in national development planning pertaining to desirable decentralisation of decision-making power and resources: too often decisions taken at the centre do not adequately reflect local needs and aspirations, mainly because of insufficient local influence on national decision making, which in turn may be due to inadequate representation of diverse interests in local administration and decision-making bodies. The case study, therefore, looks as well at the relationships between national and local level decision-making bodies within the planning system.

The information and data for the study are derived from both primary and secondary sources. In the case of the former, this author undertook field investigations in ten districts widely dispersed throughout Kenya to supplement and up-date available information on the subject. Although these investigations were restricted mainly to the district level, admittedly without the benefit of contacts at the grass roots, this cannot be considered a major drawback since the district is still the basic unit for planning purposes at the local level in Kenya. In practice, all important decisions pertaining to the formulation and implementation of local-level development programmes and projects, including self-help projects, are made or scrutinised by district-level authorities and institutions. Additional information on popular participation at the village level referred to in this study has come mainly from this author's own appreciation and documentation of local-level planning based on previous field research undertaken in recent years.

BACKGROUND

Since Kenya became an independent state some two decades ago, the Government has at various times emphasised popular participation in the development process as a strategy for attaining the broadly stated development objective of rapid economic growth with social equity. Indeed, the concept of popular participation has more or less come to be regarded as a necessary condition for spreading the benefits of development widely among all groups in society.

Right from the start of nationhood, the new Government adopted the *Harambee* philosophy of self-help development as a key feature of development planning aimed at meeting the needs and expectations of the hitherto disadvantaged indigenous population. Although official support which the *Harambee* movement enjoyed from its earliest beginning could be linked with the desire of government to promote popular participation in the development process at the local level, it should also be seen in terms of an attempt by government to pre-empt and, accordingly, reduce the burden of numerous local claims for development assistance, that would otherwise overstretch its own limited resources. In general, the self-help approach to development involves some cost-sharing between government and the local community. More specifically in the case of Kenya, government financial support for Harambee projects is usually provided to activities *already* started on the basis of local efforts – in compliance with the official view that help will be given only to those communities or groups that have in the first instance taken the initiative to

149

help themselves. As we shall see later, this in effect means that poorer local communities which cannot afford the cost of starting a development project on their own can hardly qualify for government assistance, while, on the other hand, the more prosperous communities with resources to embark on development projects can in fact pre-empt official assistance and thereby distort the rational allocation of developmental resources. This form of 'pre-emptive planning' in Kenya may have contributed to increasing regional inequalities in the distribution of development resources and benefits.

The national development plans of Kenya since independence have all stressed the important role of popular participation in the development process as a means of promoting development and spreading its benefits more widely and evenly among different socio-economic groups. Hence, over time the need for increased participation has been variously linked to the attainment of objectives such as rapid economic growth, equitable distribution of income, employment promotion, poverty alleviation and basic needs satisfaction. Official pronouncements and restatements of the concept strongly support the view that popular participation is a prerequisite for economic development and social progress. Consider, for example, the following statements from the latest development plan:

All Kenyans are expected to participate in the development process. Increasing and dispersing opportunities for such participation is a major aim of development strategy;[1]

and

An essential ingredient of successful rural development is increased participation in decision making process. . .[2]

In this chapter an attempt is made to examine critically the validity of official claims about the potential contribution of popular participation to improvements in well-being among the broad mass of the Kenyan population. Based on the experience of Kenya since independence, the modalities and practices of participatory development at both local and national levels are reviewed in the light of stated goals and objectives and against the background of the political structure, the socio-economic framework, and the institutional arrangements established to promote popular participation. Such a review should help in identifying conditions both favourable and adverse to the realisation of genuine popular participation in the development process at all levels of decision making and planning.

THE NEED FOR POPULAR PARTICIPATION IN KENYA

It seems desirable at this stage to enquire into the need for popular participation in the specific context of Kenya. At the time of independence, greater participation by Africans in the economic and social life of the country was widely acknowledged as a natural follow-up to the transfer of political power to a nationalist government. This meant that the colonial structure which determined distribution and access to productive resources and socio-economic opportunities, mainly in favour of Europeans, had to be dismantled and re-organised to support greater participation by Africans in the development process and the distribution of benefits therefrom. This was largely achieved within the framework of policies and programmes adopted in the first two national development plans. At the same time, however, it became increasingly obvious that while development in the immediate post-independence period was characterised by impressive growth performance, this was accompanied by increasing inequalities between different socio-economic groups within the indigenous population. Participation of the broad mass of the population in the development process may therefore be seen as desirable to arrest this trend which, in itself, threatened the overall development objectives of government.

Yet the broad strand of official development policies pursued in the late sixties and early seventies did not, on the whole, suggest a particular awareness of the need for broad-based participation at the local level in order to tackle the problem of inequality.[3] By the early seventies the Provincial Administration had come to assume a dominant role in the planning and implementation of local-level development; administrative decision-making power was progressively delegated by the central government to the civil bureaucracy rather than being decentralised to local representative bodies as is required for the promotion of effective popular participation at the local level. At the best, this dominance of the bureaucracy over local-level bodies and institutions fostered a paternalistic relationship between the authorities and the people; at worst, it prevented local people or their representatives from having a direct say in the making and implementation of decisions which affect their livelihood as well as, perhaps, stifled initiatives towards local self-reliance even though this was an important component of government development policy.

Being deprived of effective participation in formal decision making and of the opportunity to influence externally-induced development, it is, perhaps, not surprising that local communities resorted to the *Harambee* movement as an alternative means to respond to their 'felt' needs. In fact such was the extent of local response to the *Harambee* movement that the Government's own development programme was being distorted by the uncoordinated growth of local self-help projects throughout the country.

Local political leaders and aspirant politicians found the movement a convenient mechanism for promoting their own self interests, while at the same time using it as a means of mobilising their people to benefit from the pre-emptive planning, implicit in government's commitment to fund only on-going projects based on local initiatives. The result was that numerous local communities were identifying and implementing development projects whose nature and method of implementation were sometimes inconsistent with the development priorities of government. In addition, the rapid growth of local self-help projects posed a serious threat to the capacity of government to provide matching funds for construction and other forms of assistance, including recurrent and maintenance costs, as it was now expected to do. Government, therefore, at an early stage had to introduce guidelines and regulations for controlling the planning and implementation of local self-help activities:

> Self-help projects must be fitted into the plan and self-help efforts must be guided into useful channels. Self-help is an integral part of planned development and must be subject to the same discipline as other parts of the development effort.[4]

Similarly, the current plan makes the point that 'local projects will be registered in each district to prevent overlapping and waste of scarce resources'.[5]

What the *Harambee* experience goes to show in general is that the need for participation is linked to the desire of local people to organise themselves for the purpose of initiating actions aimed at improving their living conditions as well as for exerting some influence on externally determined decision making pertaining to their livelihood. In the *Harambee* movement local communities and their leaders found an inspiration for mobilising local resources for meeting certain felt needs as well as a means for attracting government development funds, which might otherwise not have been available to them. In addition, the scope which self-help projects offer for some degree of participation by local people in the decision-making process could well be regarded as an additional motive for people to associate themselves with local self-help projects. This in fact leads to the notion that popular participation, in addition to being a means for attaining development objectives, is an end in itself in terms of the innate satisfaction that people may derive from influencing decisions that affect their lives.[6]

THE POLITICAL STRUCTURE

Normally in a one-party state like Kenya the dominant ideology and the development orientation of the ruling party and its government should have the greatest influence on the modalities and practices of popular

152

participation within the entire system. The civil bureaucracy and related administrative organs of government at all levels will then play the role mainly of an executing agency responsible for implementing policies and programmes designed by the party to achieve the forms of popular participation consistent with its ideology and its perception of the type of society it seeks to build; the civil bureaucracy, or more precisely the technocrats, may to varying degrees provide advice to the Party and government on policy issues and programme and project implementation.

The extension of government's decision-making power to non-political bodies in a one-party system is often not automatic, and will depend on the circumstances prevailing within the political system as regards the extent to which the administrative structure and its institutions are relied upon by government to advise on or influence key policy decisions. Although Kenya can be considered a *de facto* one-party state since about 1969 when the main opposition party, the Kenya People's Union (KPU), was proscribed and the ruling party, the Kenya African National Union (KANU), effectively became about the only channel for political participation, the situation that has evolved as regards the relationship between the party/government and the civil bureaucracy in the decision-making process clearly deviates from the norm as summarised above.[7]

More recently, KANU has been identified as a 'mass party' through which all Kenyans are expected to participate in the development process, yet when it comes to influence on decision making pertaining to the actual practice of participation the Party assumes a subordinate role to the civil bureaucracy. This is largely the outcome of the policy and system of *bureaucratic decentralisation* adopted by the government since independence to promote development at the local level. A key feature of this system, which distinguishes the Kenyan situation from the single mass party system of China or even the neighbouring United Republic of Tanzania, is that the Party tends to be strongly influenced by the bureaucracy rather than the other way round. More so at the local level, key decisions pertaining to development planning are usually made by the bureaucracy, since it is the policy of government to delegate administrative decision-making power to civil servants. Furthermore, to the extent that KANU as a mass party represents the people at the local level, the subordinate role of the Party in the development process leaves very little scope for popular influence on decision making. A combination of bureaucratic decentralisation and an elitist system at the local level ensures that effective participation takes place mainly within the framework of formal administrative institutions or others recognised and approved for this purpose by the Provincial Administration.[8]

The dominance of the bureaucracy over the Party and popular representative bodies at the local level has indeed served to reinforce the paternalistic relationship between administrative authorities and the people. This also means, as is shown later, that the formal institutions for participation in public decision making are not broad-based and, therefore, the scope for mass involvement in the development process in a way becomes extremely limited. The usually crucial role of the mass party in the process of mass mobilisation at the grass-roots level is also significantly diminished in the Kenyan context as a result of the subordinate status of KANU vis-à-vis the bureaucracy. Similarly, initiatives for the promotion and enhancement of local self-reliance, as advocated by the Party and Government, may have been discouraged and stifled, ironically, by the official policy of bureaucratic decentralisation which allows the bureaucracy a high degree of control over the planning and implementation of local self-help projects.[9]

THE INSTITUTIONAL FRAMEWORK

In a given context, popular participation in the development process may take place within an institutional framework that can be either formal or informal, or some contribution of both. The nature of the institutional framework itself will, to a great extent, determine the form that participation takes and, more importantly, the effectiveness of partici-pation for meeting basic needs. In other words, the scope for popular influence on decision making concerning development options and priorities and the distribution of benefits from development depends on the extent to which the institutional framework is amenable to genuine participatory practices. Within a formal planning system, the institutional framework may be closely related to or even determined by the existing political structure and socio-economic system. Outside the formal system, the institutional framework will be crucially influenced by the degree of awareness and need in the community for popular organisations to promote and defend specific local interests.

In the case of Kenya, the formal institutional framework for promoting popular participation in the development process is predominantly administrative in nature. As already noted, the scope for popular participation within the administrative structure at the local level is rather limited; this is because the related institutional arrangement in practice emphasises the role of the bureaucracy and the elites in decision making, while at the same time ignoring that of the broad mass of the population and their own chosen representatives. As far as informal popular organisations are concerned, it may be said that the institutional framework for participation is significant only to the extent that such organisations are willing to be managed and controlled by the bureaucrats and representatives of government at the local level – instead of by the people themselves or their own representatives. This is evident today in Kenya in the form that popular participation takes outside the formal

154

system: organisations or institutions such as rural workers' organisations, women and youth groups, mutual aid societies and the self-help movement, though falling outside the formal administrative structure of central or local government, are nevertheless strongly influenced, or in some cases even effectively controlled, by the bureaucracy at all levels of decision making. The following review of different participatory institutions in Kenya is intended to provide some insights into the critical issue of the scope and extent of genuine popular participation in the development process in Kenya since independence.

PARTICIPATORY INSTITUTIONS

Broadly, these are taken to include all forms of participatory practices, whether based on a formal institution or on an informal arrangement, and both within and outside the administrative structures of government at all levels. For the purpose of this study, the distinction is made between *public institutions*, on the one hand, and *popular institutions*, on the other. The former refer strictly to formal government bodies that have participatory-oriented functions or potentials including the system of local government throughout the country. The latter cover relevant 'non-official' organisations and institutions supposedly based on popular initiatives or specific group interests which may or may not enjoy official sponsorship and support.

Public Institutions

Government Ministries and Departments

In the Fourth National Development Plan, 1979–83, it is estimated that about K£30 million or about 10 per cent of the total national development budget will be on account of *Harambee* self-help projects at the local level. Part of this amount is attributable to grants to be provided by the Community Development Division of the Social Services ministry to local self-help committees to support the implementation and operation of *Harambee* projects and related training activities. Similarly, other central government operating ministries (for example, health, education, water development, work) have budgetary allocations that are earmarked for local-level development projects. Therefore, leaving aside the Provincial Administration which has strong influence on local-level development planning, central government operating ministries and departments assume a key role in the planning and implementation of local self-help and other development projects. This being so, to what extent then do the existing institutional arrangements within the administrative structure allow for effective popular participation in the decision-making process as related to local-level development planning?

As far as popular influence on decisions pertaining to projects partially or fully funded directly by central ministries is concerned, there appears to be very little scope within the existing formal institutions to support this goal. Almost without exception, decision making is the responsibility of relevant operating ministries and departments which in turn delegate some of their planning functions to local-level government officials as may be appropriate. However, in most cases the locally based staff of central ministries do not have the necessary authority to make even routine decisions without first referring to Nairobi for clearance or endorsement; and Nairobi will not always give its approval to proposals and tentative decisions emanating from the field structure. This means in effect that even if there were adequate consultations between local civil servants and the people, with a view to reflecting popular opinions in public decisions pertaining to local-level development, popular influence on final decisions could not be guaranteed since this depends more on the views of bureaucrats who are often out of touch with local opinions. At any rate, there is little evidence to suggest that any meaningful consultation takes place between local civil servants and the people or their own representatives.

As is argued below, the specific institutions that have been established to ensure popular participation in public decision making at the local level are far from effective in this regard. With the possible exception of the Department of Agriculture which tries to co-opt local farmers or their representatives into district development committees, most government departments and agencies have no structures or arrangements for involving local people in public decision making on matters that directly affect their living conditions.

Local-Level Development Committees

The decision by government in 1966 partially to decentralise the planning system was followed by the establishment of *Provincial and District Development Committees* (PDCs and DDCs). These committees which were established between 1968 and 1970 draw their membership mainly from among civil servants of operating ministries and government departments directly involved in development planning at the local level. In addition, and, ostensibly, as a way of involving local people in the planning process, parallel *advisory committees* with local representation were created respectively at the provincial and district levels. The composition of these advisory bodies usually includes senior representatives of the Provincial Administration, local MPs, administrative heads of local government authorities, district Chairmen of KANU, and a few 'prominent citizens' nominated by the Provincial or District Commissioner. Thus, even with this arrangement participation of local people in the decision-making process can be secured only *indirectly* and mainly through government representatives or their nominees. The need for popular participation through the *bona fide* representatives of the people is thus scarcely being fulfilled, contrary to the objective of decentralised planning as stated by the government:

> The coordination and stimulation of development at the local level by involving in the planning process, not only the government officials but also the people through their representatives, are also to be a major instrument in plan implementation.[10]

The very narrow interpretation given to 'people's representatives' in constituting the local-level development and advisory committees has also meant that there is very little interest on the part of the membership to support effective participatory organisations at the local level. But even when judged within this limited scope for indirect participation, it is clear that the system of decentralised planning (through local-level development and advisory committees) has not operated as was intended in terms of involving local people in the planning process. Certain factors can be identified as relevant to the failure of the local development committees to promote popular participation in development.

The first important reason is that right from the beginning there were difficulties in constituting and getting these committees off the ground. In many districts the development and advisory committees took a long time – in some cases over five years – to become fully operational. Even after then, there were initial problems concerning the definition of their actual functions in the planning process. As far as the advisory committees were concerned, many became highly dependent on the goodwill and patronage of the Provincial Administration which itself often looked to civil servants rather than local bodies or groups for guidance; therefore, local initiative was strikingly absent from the discussions and conclusions of the advisory committees. Secondly, the local planning officers attached to the development committees were either new recruits or mostly civil servants recently redeployed from Nairobi and, as such, not sufficiently familiar with local conditions and the issues they were supposed to deal with. Furthermore, by operating from the provincial and district levels, they were in some cases effectively cut off from the village level.

Observers of the system have noted that for various reasons the local MPs and prominent citizens on the committees, who were supposed to represent local interests, seldom attended committee meetings; as a result, key decisions were often taken mainly by the civil servants. It was also observed that in many districts, popularly recognised local leaders were even never appointed to sit on the advisory committees in the first instance.[11] On reflection it can be said that the practice of appointing local representatives from among 'absentee' national politicians and party bosses, rather than from among locally-based citizens, was a major weakness of the system. With the initial failure of the local development and advisory committees to bring about popular involvement in development planning at the local level, the only avenue for some expression of popular opinion on matters of local interest was the local self-help group until the launching of the Special Rural Development Programme (SRDP) in 1970.

The Special Rural Development Programme. The launching of the SRDP somehow led to a reactivation of many local development committees in the direction of popular participation, since the programme was, among other things, designed to facilitate rural development in close co-operation with local-level bodies. To support the effective implementation of the SRDP, the district development committees were further decentralised to the divisional level (i.e. the project level). This move, however, did not improve the situation in terms of involving local people in the planning process. First, the composition of the divisional development committee was similar to that of the district development committee – i.e. dominated by civil servants and national or district level politicians – which meant little or no *direct* representation of local interests. Secondly, as in the case of the DDCs, indirect representation turned out to be ineffective as a means of articulating popular views and demands. This author attended several divisional committee meetings as an observer between 1970 and 1976 and concludes, accordingly, that the so-called representatives of the people were sometimes either unaware of genuine local needs or mainly interested in promoting those projects which served to benefit only a small, and usually better-off, segment of the local population. Here again, the experience is that the decentralisation of planning to the local level has not led to greater popular participation or influence on decision making.

The implementation of the SRDP at the divisional level also revealed that it is not just sufficient to decentralise planning responsibilities without a corresponding decentralisation of resources to the local level. Some viable SRDP projects of potential benefits to the local community could in the end not be implemented due to lack of funds which were expected to come from the central ministries concerned. The experience of the SRDP in fact suggests that financial approval from Nairobi, for the allocation of funds from the programme budget, was more readily given in the case of those local projects wherein the local representatives of central ministries had maintained regular consultations with their superiors at headquarters throughout the project planning and appraisal phase. There is the inherent danger in this procedure that district and divisional officials might be more inclined to favour projects that correspond to Nairobi's understanding or perceptions of local needs, which may not be consistent with the felt needs of the local people. Popular influence on project identification therefore becomes subordinate to bureaucratic concerns regarding financial approval and the related desire of local officials to meet spending targets irrespective of what they are being spent on and their relevance to local development needs.

District Development Planning. Similar institutional weaknesses are largely responsible for the relative ineffectiveness of district level planning to promote popular participation in the development process at the local level. Following the recommendation of a government-appointed commission, a new institutional arrangement for development planning at the district level was introduced in 1972 with the aim of strengthening the *district* as the basic unit for planning and plan implementation in the country. This new arrangement provided for the preparation of individual district development plans which should reflect more closely the actual needs of local communities. More specifically, it was officially stated that 'district planning will be concerned with the spatial distribution of government services such as schools, health centres and also with identifying in detail the development resources available in each district which remain unexploited'.[12] In this connection, the District Development Committee was given a new and key role to play: it was expected to spearhead the mobilisation of local resources which can then be directed to the implementation of development projects based on local priorities and initiatives and for the benefit of the community as a whole. Accordingly, District Development Officers (DDOs) were appointed and assigned to work directly with the DDCs.

The first set of district plans prepared under this new arrangement came out in 1976, and this author, who had monitored very keenly the process by which some of them (especially those in poorer districts) were prepared, comes to the conclusion that there had been virtually no popular participation in their preparation. For example in the case of two provinces, all of the district plans were prepared almost independently by expatriate planning advisers attached to the Provincial Planning Office. In one of those districts, the minutes of a DDC meeting had recorded that:

> The [provincial] planning team intends to visit government officers at divisional level and also any interested persons in Machakos [District]. This exercise is to make the team acquainted with the local needs and resources and also to see for themselves the area for which they intend to plan.[13]

Yet some time later when this author visited the same district headquarters, he was able to ascertain that hardly any such consultations had taken place at the local level, and that the plan had in fact gone to Nairobi in its final form without being fully discussed by the District Development Committee.

In several other instances, district development plans were prepared either by Provincial Planning Officers (PPOs) or by the newly appointed District Development Officers (DDOs) in consultation with District Commissioners but not the people. Such was the pressure to have these plans out as early as possible that the officers preparing them, even if they wished, had no opportunity to hold meaningful consultations with the local people. Similarly, the preparation of the 1974–78 National Development Plan, a year after the policy of district planning had been adopted, was undertaken with hardly any account being taken of the views of the district planners, let alone those of local people or their representatives on the DDCs. This author's investigation indicates again that most of the current district development plans published in 1980 have been prepared mainly by the DDOs without the effective participation of local people in the decision-making process.[14]

Therefore, notwithstanding the official policy to promote popular participation in development planning through the institution of the local development committees, in practice very little seems to have been achieved. This appears to have been the case even for those projects over which the district development committees have allocative authority, as a critical evaluation of the performance of Rural Development Fund (RDF) projects would reveal.

The Rural Development Fund. The RDF is made up of two separate components: the District Development Grant Fund which was established in 1971/72, and the Rural Works Programme Fund set up in 1974 on the recommendation of the 1972 ILO Comprehensive Employment Mission.[15] District development grants were originally intended to 'stimulate the initiative of DDCs and to encourage them to take increasingly active interest in planned local development', while funds provided under the Rural Works Programme were, among other things, aimed at increasing cash incomes of the rural landless and small-holders through the provision of supplementary off-farm rural employment opportunities during the slack periods. In this latter context, emphasis was placed on the implementation of labour-intensive public work projects directly linked to the provision of vital infrastructure, public services and facilities in rural areas.

Although the RDF gives the local development committees some authority over the allocation of resources, in practice the scope for making operational the decentralisation of resources to the local level is somewhat limited. The DDCs can only allocate resources from their RDF budgets to those projects which have been approved in Nairobi; their power to spend is therefore not supported by the authority to select projects in accordance with local preferences and needs. The final selection of projects to be funded from the RDF is made by the Ministry responsible for economic planning, following the identification of local projects by the DDCs and rigorous scrutiny at the provincial level by

PPOs. In what corresponds to a 'bottom-up' process of planning, local-level views and priorities emanating from the DDCs are passed on to the top (i.e. the central planning ministry) – through the provincial level – where the actual decision making takes place.

Regarding how these decisions are made, available evidence suggests that the selection of projects to be financed by the RDF is often influenced by the value and preference of 'influential' people at the district, provincial and national levels. A study of the operation of the RDF in three districts in Eastern and Central Provinces (i.e. Machakos, Meru, and Muranga) revealed that in many cases the views and interventions of leading national politicians with local connections were more important than the recommendations of local development committees.[16] Often, these politicians may not even have participated in relevant DDC meetings at the local level. Equally as important in the final selection process are the views of wealthy local businessmen and senior civil servants. The same study reported that, in general, if the District Commissioner proposed or supported any project it was highly likely to be selected for funding regardless of its merits. On the other hand, it was found that projects proposed by the advisory committees or those originating from sub-district level committees had little or no chance of getting the support of the DDCs for submission to Nairobi. Thus, the author of the above-mentioned study observed that 'the fact that the DDC could ignore proposals from the divisions and substitute others with impunity shows that members did not take the idea of grass-roots participation seriously.'[17] In a like manner, one District Development Officer more recently, somewhat regrettably, told this author that:

> There is the tendency by the more powerful members (of the DDC) to have more projects from their areas passed. This works against the principle of balanced growth.[18]

Participation of local people in RDF projects has some significance only at the implementation stage when district development grants may be made available as government contributions to local self-help projects. But then local involvement has to be officially sanctioned, and takes the form mainly of people's contribution in cash and labour to project implementation. It is therefore not surprising that there have been reported cases of 'poor mobilisation of local resources' stemming from the initial reluctance of local people to contribute their labour or cash to projects with which they cannot easily identify in terms of their felt needs, priorities or benefits.

Local Government Authorities

Based on the British model, local government authorities were estab-lished in Kenya during the colonial period, ostensibly, as a means of taking government closer to the people.[19] From this standpoint, local government should then be seen as an institutional arrangement potentially useful for involving local people in the decision-making process. Furthermore, by being based at the local level, such authorities are better placed (than the central government) to understand local problems and needs. Thus, local government is generally regarded as more amenable to broad-based participation in the overall development process than other forms of public institutions. In addition, to the extent that local authorities are responsible for the provision of essential public services, such as health, education, water supply, they can play a critical role in the satisfaction of basic needs. Yet, it has been observed that the importance of this role may be limited by the extent to which such bodies:

1 actually represent diverse views and interests in the community as a whole;
2 control resources;
3 enjoy real discretion in decision making; and
4 have access to information and qualified personnel required for effective planning.[20]

These factors can be taken as relevant criteria against which to evaluate the performance of local authorities in Kenya.

The structure of local government inherited at independence was made up of municipal councils (for the large urban areas); county councils (for the rural districts); and area councils (for towns within the rural districts). Right from their inception in the mid-twenties, local authorities in Kenya were charged with the responsibility of providing basic public services in their areas of jurisdiction. In carrying out these functions they have faced a number of difficulties, although the problems of the rural county councils seem to have been more acute than those of the municipalities. On the whole, however, they have all shared the fundamental weakness of failing to promote genuine popular participation in the decision-making process. The main reasons for this weakness can be found from an evaluation of the system in Kenya, according to the four criteria identified above.

The Degree to which Local Authorities are Truly Representative of Diverse Local Interests. Given that popular participation in public decision making at the level of local government is indirectly fulfilled through representatives of the people, the effectiveness of participation through this institution will largely depend on the extent to which local councils truly represent the wide spectrum of local interests and opinions in the community. A major problem of indirect participation through elected or appointed representatives is that representation in the first instance may be such that it does not reflect popular views. While the idea of people participating in public decision making through their elected

162

representatives is a widely accepted principle of democracy, it can nevertheless also be the basis of much abuse in a situation where representation, for various reasons, is not based on free and popular elections, and where there is no regular accountability of elected representatives to the people. Popular elections imply that different interest groups in society can, either on their own or in alliance with formal political parties, seek and be able to influence public decision making through their elected representatives. At the local level where electoral issues are likely to be more narrowly parochial than broadly national, the opportunity should even be greater for specific local interests to be represented in the decision-making process.

In general, on the basis of available evidence, the poorest groups at the local level in Kenya have so far failed to achieve adequate representation in local government institutions even where elections may be free and fair. It would seem that such disadvantaged groups, for a number of socio-economic and politically-related reasons, have not been able to come together and use their potential numerical strength to ensure adequate representation of their interests in decision-making bodies. What obtains then is a sort of vicious circle wherein the relative disadvantage of poorer groups in society further serves to prevent them from articulating their interests and demands in a manner that could be meaningful in terms of adequate representation in elected bodies.

In Kenya there is also the long established tradition of *nominated* councillors in the local government system which further serves to weaken the influence of elected representatives in the decision-making process within local authorities. In most cases, the central government is empowered to appoint fixed numbers of representatives to local government bodies. While the intention is to ensure that 'special interests' in a given local context are represented in decision making, the practice has usually been for government to nominate persons (for example big businessmen, commercial farmers) whose interests are sometimes far removed from those of the broad mass of the local population and especially the poor. As a matter of fact, the appointment of nominated councillors to local authorities in Kenya can be regarded as a means of strengthening the representation of the 'better-off' groups in the decision-making process. There is also the tendency for the nominated representatives of special interests to define their functions in terms of only those interests to the exclusion of all others: hence, they are often insensitive to the wider needs of the community as a whole. Furthermore, by being nominees of the central government they are usually more sympathetic to the views of government officials at the local level than to those of the local people. Thus, it is not unusual for District Commissioners to use nominated councillors to support or defend official positions in local government decision making even when these are known to be clearly at variance with popular views and demands.

Largely because of the inadequacy of local government in Kenya to be truly representative, it has not been possible for this institution to act as an effective means of promoting and enhancing popular participation in public decision making. Of more serious concern is the consequence of this state of affairs: the views of disadvantaged groups are seldom if ever reflected in policy making or taken into account in the planning and implementation of local development projects which are critical to the satisfaction of basic needs.

Control of Resources Needed to Meet Basic Needs. In Kenya local authorities in common are highly dependent on the central government for financial resources required to cover their development and recurrent expenditures, since they usually have limited and unreliable sources of revenue at their disposal. As is to be expected, the situation is much more serious for rural councils than for urban municipalities which have a larger and relatively more reliable revenue base. In the case of the former, their financial status deteriorated to such an extent in the late sixties that the central government was left with no option but to take over their responsibilities for the provision of health, primary education and secondary roads.[21] But even the municipalities have experienced serious financial problems in recent years leading to difficulties in fulfilling their obligation to provide essential public services. On several occasions the central grovernment has had to come to the rescue of these authorities through either the provision of additional grants or the provision of guarantees on loans from the banking system.[22]

While poor and inefficient internal management may be blamed for the financial problems of local government authorities, it is certainly not the major cause of the ineffectiveness of local authorities to fulfil their statutory obligations to the community. Apart from the fact that funds provided by the central government to local authorities in Kenya may be insufficient for the tasks they are expected to carry out, the dependence of local authorities on government for the bulk of their finance together with the lack of control over the allocation and spending of such funds is a hindrance to local initiatives on matters of development. As it is, local authorities are obliged to submit most expenditure proposals and development projects and programmes to the central government for prior approval and funding.

In summary, local government in Kenya has very little control over resources required for the provision of essential services: local taxes and levies collected and controlled by local authorities account for only a small fraction of their total budgetary requirements and they therefore have to rely on funds provided and controlled by government to make up deficits. A greater decentralisation of resources to the local level would be a practical way of giving local authorities more control over decision making on essentially local issues. If indeed representation at the local level is to reflect the wide range of community interests in the decision-making process, then the decentralisation of planning responsibilities to the local level should significantly include greater control over requisite resources. This is not to say that the central government should abrogate its authority and control over public spending at the local level, especially in view of certain recent cases of financial mismanagement by local councils; this function can still be fulfilled by government within a more flexible arrangement that leaves local authorities with adequate control over allocation and spending of development funds for intended purposes. An effective machinery for monitoring and evaluation of local-level development projects can be built into the overall planning system precisely to minimise the risk of mismanagement of local government funds, while at the same time steps could be taken to make local authorities more accountable to popular scrutiny through broader-based representation of local interests. This in itself will enhance popular participation in the development process at the local level.

The Degree of Discretion Enjoyed by Local Authorities in Decision Making. Besides central government control over local government spending, overall decision-making powers by local authorities in Kenya are very limited. In theory, as well as in practice, there is no decision of any substance that a local authority can make and implement without the approval of the Minister for local government. The Local Government Regulations of 1963 give the Minister wide-ranging and discretionary power to control the affairs of local authorities. Any council that violates the stipulations of the regulations and related directives can be penalised or even be dissolved by the Minister, as shown by the recent dissolution of Mombassa, Kisumu, Nyeri and Kiambu councils.

The tight control that the central Government exercises over local authorities in principle renders the latter incapable of immediately and directly making decisions in response to emergencies and unforeseen needs of the local community. However, given the serious doubt that exists about the ability and willingness of many local authorities in Kenya to effectively fulfil their obligations to the broad mass of the population, especially the most disadvantaged groups, central government control over key decisions should not entirely be regarded as a negative feature of the system. There have been times when central government intervention has served the interest of the majority of local people with regard to the actual provision of essential public services. Until local authorities in general display a more responsible attitude towards the discharge of their functions – a factor which itself depends on more broadly based representation – it may be necessary for the central government to intervene from time to time. Whether or not control by the central government is inimical to the promotion of popular participation at the local level then becomes a secondary issue in the light of existing shortcomings of the local government system to fulfil its statutory obligations independently.

The Quality of Information and Personnel Available to Local Authorities in Performing their Functions. Since local authorities exist to serve the interests of the local people, councillors and officials of such bodies must, of necessity, be familiar with the needs of the people. This familiarity has been found to be lacking in several instances in the Kenyan context, mainly as a result of inadequate contacts between local authorities and the people. Where representation is not sufficiently broad-based, and the administrative and technical staff of local authorities are mainly 'outsiders' who are not very knowledgeable about local conditions nor adaptable to grass-roots organisation and planning, it becomes extremely difficult to make decisions in the wide interest of the community as a whole. In general, local authorities in Kenya do not appear to be able to attract the most competent and capable staff as compared with private sector enterprises or even the civil service. This itself might be due to the relatively inferior conditions of service and career prospects associated with local government employment. As a consequence, the efficiency of these authorities is impaired. In addition, there is the now familiar conflict between local councillors and the administrative and technical staff which again serves to impede effective planning and co-ordination of local development programmes.

The 'distance' between local councillors and officials, on the one hand, and the people, on the other, is indeed an obstacle to popular participation, since it is likely to lead to the making and execution of decisions that may not enjoy popular support as required for motivating people to participate in the development process. The existence of an 'information gap' between local authorities and the people means that, far from reflecting popular demands, local decisions are made in a vacuum that is shut off from the real life situation. As a consequence, even well-intentioned efforts of local authorities to provide basic services to the people could end up being ineffective due to lack of adequate consultation and understanding between all concerned.

Overall, the nature and structure of the system of local government and the related decision-making process are not conducive to the promotion of broad-based local participation in the development process. The system as it exists is equally not amenable to the enhancement of local self-reliance as a viable strategy for promoting development at the grass-roots level.

Popular Institutions

In Kenya, there are a number of participatory organisations and related institutions which fall outside the formal administrative structures, but are

166

nevertheless potentially useful for mobilising local human and material resources to support local-level development. By definition, such organisations should be relatively freer from government control and intervention than public institutions and, therefore, more amenable to the promotion of popular participation. Yet, the experience so far is that these organisations can equally be subjected to 'outside' influence and control which detract from their participation potential.

Harambee Self-Help Movement and Committees

As a development ideology, the *Harambee* movement implies the 'pulling together' of resources by government and local people to support development goals and objectives. More importantly, the ideology advocates the self-reliance doctrine in so far as it is supposed to encourage local people to take initiatives on matters pertaining to their own well-being. To this end, an institutional framework was established in the form of self-help committees made up of local leaders and locally-based government administrators and technicians. What follows is an attempt to assess the effectiveness of the *Harambee* self-help movement in terms of its contribution to the promotion of popular participation as is claimed to be necessary for achieving stated development objectives at the local level.

Self-Help as a Participatory Strategy. The idea of local people initiating their own development projects implies some decentralisation of decision-making powers. In the early years of the *Harambee* movement, the local initiators of self-help projects enjoyed considerable freedom in the identification and planning of projects. Although local initiators were mainly from the leadership of the community, decisions pertaining to the selection and actual implementation of projects were often made in consultation with local people at public meetings. In those earlier days, it was thus possible for key, or seemingly controversial decisions to be made on the basis of wide consultations with various interest groups in the community. Such a situation might involve a choice of project between, say, a health centre and a Chief's *baraza* hall or community centre with distinctly different benefits to the community. Also in the early days of the movement, it was usual for the local committee to be entirely responsible for organising and implementing each self-help project agreed upon by the community.

However, the situation today is quite different. The independence from outside control which the movement enjoyed in the sixties is now conspicuously absent. Self-help committees are now effectively 'sub-committees' of the government development committees, and no project can be started without the written approval of the District Development Committee (DDC). This change, as earlier noted, was found to be necessary for ensuring that self-help activities are consistent with the goals and priorities of national development:

> In order to make the maximum contribution to the nation's effort for more rapid economic and social development, the growing self-help activities must be planned and directed. . . they must be planned and coordinated so that they are consistent with the National Development Plan.[23]

However, this requirement also made it possible for popular views to be overlooked or even ignored in the planning and implementation of local-level projects in the name of national development. The probability of a concurrence of national concerns and local priorities may not be sufficiently high to avoid conflicts of interests in project selection and implementation. At any rate, in the event of such conflicts the DDC can use its veto power to overrule popular demands. Today, the role of the State is no longer limited to encouraging and supporting local initiatives, but extends to effective control over the actual selection, planning and organisation of self-help activities.

This new role of government in its relationship with the *Harambee* movement has accordingly reduced the scope for popular participation in the development process at the local level. Local 'participation' is now confined to contribution of the people to the mobilisation of financial and human resources required for the implementation of projects on which they may not have been consulted as regards planning, organisation and distribution of benefits. It is not surprising, therefore, that the enthusiasm which characterised the *Harambee* movement in the sixties has been dampened especially with the growing tendency of the local representatives of the Provincial Administration (nominated chiefs and their assistants) to extract contributions from local people forcibly.

Self-Help and Access to Basic Needs. It is generally accepted that voluntary participation in local self-help projects will depend on people's perception of individual and collective benefits to be derived from the facilities or services being provided. By this reasoning, popular participation in self-help projects should lead to improved access of the poor – who are often in the majority in the community – to basic needs goods and services. To what extent then has this been true in the experience of Kenya?

Increased employment opportunities in local communities should no doubt contribute to the satisfaction of private consumption needs through higher levels of household income. However, the *direct* and immediate employment and income benefits of self-help projects are generally negligible in so far as implementation is often based on voluntary labour. While it may be possible to realise *indirect* employment benefits from self-help projects through, say, the use of locally-produced and purchased materials in construction (for example, mud bricks and blocks, timber doors and window frames, furniture), in practice most infrastructural projects are undertaken with heavy reliance on externally-produced material inputs with the result that potential local employment opportunities are lost. Furthermore, even the possibility of some permanent employment benefits linked to the operation and maintenance of self-help communal facilities and services is unlikely, since completed projects such as health centres are often run by personnel brought in from 'outside' the community.

The provision or availability of a public service or facility in the community by itself does not guarantee access for all in terms of usage. There are other factors which affect access that have to be taken into account in planning and operating self-help projects. In this regard, the quality of the service provided has to be considered, especially in the case of health and educational facilities. If people perceive that they can obtain a better service by going to a district hospital or by sending their children to government schools in towns, they may well bypass available, but inferior, local facilities and do so in spite of the hardship and costs involved. When this happens 'accessibility' is severely reduced. As it is, many self-help provided facilities in Kenya are either of inferior quality, compared to alternative conventionally provided ones, or soon fall into serious state of disrepair due to lack of adequate maintenance. Health centres in several localities visited by this author were found to be inoperative by any standard and the same can be said about many self-help built roads and water supplies in several districts.

Access chances are also affected by cost to the user of a public facility or service. Where the poor have been called upon to contribute their labour and time to a local self-help project and are then required to pay a service charge for use of the facility beyond what they can reasonably afford, access is effectively restricted. The fact that the poor, accordingly, cannot benefit from projects to which they made some contribution is also socially unjust. In one self-help constructed cattle dip visited by this author in Central Alego of Siayo district (Kaluo-Komolo dip along the Ndere-Rangala road) it was found that most farmers cannot afford to use the facility because of the charges involved in doing so.

Self-Help and Domestic Capital Formation. Since independence self-help activities have made an increasing contribution to domestic capital formation in Kenya. From an estimated total value of K£0.6 million in 1964, the value of self-help projects rose steadily to K£2m in 1968, K£3.1m in 1972 and to an annual average of K£7m during the 1974/78 plan period.[24] The annual average for the plan period, 1979/83, is estimated at K£7.25m.[25] Through local self-help efforts many health centres, schools, community centres, cattle dips, recreational facilities, rural roads, and so on, have been built throughout the country in recent years.

Although some of these projects, as they exist today, are not operating efficiently due to poor maintenance or lack of equipment, they are nevertheless a visible manifestation of the efforts of local people themselves to cater for their fundamental needs. There is, therefore, an urgent need to strengthen the operational and maintenance aspects of local self-help projects if they are to play a major role in meeting basic needs at the local level. There are those who feel that increased financial support from government would improve the situation, yet there is the likelihood that this might be accompanied by even greater involvement of government in self-help activities at the local level. Experience has shown that this involvement could further reduce the scope for genuine popular participation in the decision-making process.

Self-Help and Equity. The issue of equity in the specific context of self-help projects should be looked at from the points of view of:

1 the distribution of benefits from projects (in relation to inputs) among different socio-economic groups, and
2 the spatial distribution of essential public services within the country as a whole.

Also of importance is the related question of equalisation of socio-economic opportunities between different groups as a result of the implementation and operation of self-help projects.

As regards the distribution of benefits from self-help projects, the Kenyan experience so far does not offer any concrete evidence of equity. Many projects are planned and implemented without any prior consideration of distribution according to the needs or an acceptable formula that relates expected benefits to inputs.In general, contributions to self-help projects by individuals and groups take the form of cash and labour which are supposed to be donated voluntarily, although levies or work tasks may be imposed by local leaders and project organisers in consultation with the community or the local self-help committee. People's perception of benefits to be derived from a specific project would normally influence their attitudes towards voluntary contribution in the absence of coercion. In theory, this should ensure that contributions are somehow linked to expected benefits even when these are not clearly defined as such. In practice contributions are usually expected from both the rich and poor alike, but where a project stands to benefit the richer segments of the population more than the rest of the community the notion of equity may be lost. This could be so in the case of projects which by their very nature benefit mainly large commercial farmers as against peasant smallholders and the landless or export producers as against food crop and subsistence producers. Even when the project has a wider community appeal, such as a health centre or community hall, access for certain groups may be restricted by distance or service charges on the use of the facility, thereby distorting the equitable distribution of benefits.

It has been claimed that to the extent that the richer members of the community contribute proportionately more cash to self-help projects than the poor there is a redistributive effect in support of equity. Leaving aside the fact that such contributions by the rich may in the first instance be motivated by personal ambitions linked to political benefits as in the case of MPs and aspirant politicians, redistribution will only take place if the poor constitute the principal beneficiaries of self-help projects: there is no firm evidence to support this on a wide scale in Kenya. Second, in terms of percentage of disposable income, the cash or labour contributions of the poor to self-help projects are likely to be much higher than those of the rich, which implies greater sacrifice by the poor than the rich. In fact, the claim that the self-help movement allows for a redistribution from richer groups to the poor – through differential contributions – can hardly be supported by what seems to be an increasingly common practice for local organisers of self-help projects to impose a fixed levy on individuals or families irrespective of income levels or ability to contribute. When this happens, contributions to self-help projects represent a form of indirect taxation and a regressive one for that matter. This could in fact result in increasing inequalities within the community.

An examination of the spatial distribution of self-help projects already completed and being undertaken in Kenya is likely to reveal a skewed pattern. This somehow contradicts the view that the *Harambee* movement is contributing to a more equitable pattern of regional development within the country. The experience so far in this regard is that self-help projects tend to be highly concentrated in certain districts (for example, those in the Central and Coast Provinces) which are better endowed in terms of financial resources for starting such projects or have more influential and dynamic representatives in national and local politics to promote their interests and take initiatives to organise and implement self-help development projects. In contrast, poorer districts (for example, those in the remote North Eastern Province which is mainly arid or semi-arid) with relatively less resources and little influence in national politics are inherently disadvantaged in terms of embarking on self-help projects.

Given the policy of the government to provide financial assistance to local self-help projects on the basis of initiatives already taken by the local community, those districts which are capable of initiating several projects naturally stand to benefit more from government support (for example, matching funds and recurrent costs) than those which have fewer or no projects on which to base their claims for government support. Thus, the form of pre-emptive planning which characterises the *Harambee* movement works to the advantage of richer local communities and against the interests and needs of poorer areas. While it is true to some extent that richer districts are more heavily populated than poorer ones in Kenya – and therefore the distribution of public resources to support self-help projects in this manner may not be grossly inequitable – the fact still remains that the latter have always had less access to essential services and facilities and that the balance cannot be redressed without a deliberate bias in the allocation of public resources in their favour. As it is, the main criterion for government support to *Harambee* projects does not represent an appropriate formula for redressing the balance; poorer communities are not likely ever to match the dynamism and effectiveness of richer areas in *Harambee* fund-raising activities and will therefore continue to benefit less from public funds earmarked for self-help projects.

There is also the claim at the global level that the *Harambee* movement has helped to reduce urban–rural inequalities by attracting more funds from government for rural development than would otherwise be the case. Again this claim should be examined in the light of the historical evidence that the movement was originally sponsored by government, *inter alia*, as a strategy for getting local communities to share the cost of development while at the same time giving them a greater say in the selection, planning and implementation of projects. According to available evidence, it would appear that this cost-sharing arrangement has worked more to the advantage of government than the local communities: it is estimated that for the period 1970–74, government's contributions to all self-help projects amounted to K£444 000 as compared with about K£8.5 million contributed in cash and kind by local communities; similarly, total government contribution to self-help projects during the 1974–78 plan period was estimated at only about 8 per cent of total people's contribution.[26] This leaves much doubt about the importance of the *Harambee* movement as a strategy for redistributing developmental resources in favour of rural areas at a time when government spending on services and facilities in the major urban centres has increased rapidly.

Improving Self-Help as a Basic Needs-Oriented Development Strategy.
The challenge now facing the *Harambee* movement is how to render itself more relevant and useful to the felt needs and expectations of the local people, especially the poorer segments of the population. This clearly implies a need for changes in the institutional arrangements for planning and implementing self-help projects.

First, it is necessary to increase popular influence and control over the decision-making process within the *Harambee* movement. The present dominance of the bureaucracy and powerful political elites in local self-help committees should give way to greater control by local leadership which is more likely to be in close contact with the people. This should be supported by appropriate arrangements to broaden the base of represen-tation on local-level development committees to reflect diverse interests and concerns within the community. In this regard, it may be useful overall to restructure local participatory institutions on the basis of the traditional system that operated so well in the past to support broad-based participation in decision making but has since become more or less defunct. For example, traditional institutions such as the *Baraza*, which is essentially a village assembly open to everyone in the community, should be revived and strengthened to become the locus of key decision making at the village level. People are likely to become more interested in local affairs only when they believe and have confidence in the institutions that have been established to solicit and act on popular demands. The role of the bureaucracy and politicians could then be limited to that of an 'enlightened catalyst' working in close co-operation with local people or their representatives and institutions to support local initiatives on development matters.

Secondly, the policy of government to decentralise planning responsibilities to the local level should effectively be extended to activities within the framework of the *Harambee* movement. This is particularly relevant in the context of resource allocation and control over spending. While recognising the obvious need for central control over the use of public resources by local self-help committees, it is at the same time necessary to have a more flexible system that will give local leadership greater scope for directing resources to popular projects than at present is the case. People are likely to have more confidence in decisions taken by their own leaders within the community, than those emanating from or forced upon them by 'outsiders' whose interests may not coincide with theirs. The confidence of local people in their own leaders can be created and boosted only if those leaders are seen as having the authority and means for responding to popular demands.

Thirdly, the present criterion for obtaining government financial assistance for local self-help projects should be reviewed and, if necessary, replaced by one which is not biased against poorer communities unable to afford the cost of starting such projects. A criterion based on actual needs, rather than pre-emptive capacity to attract public resources, could be more useful for reducing regional inequalities. Financial, technical and administrative support from government should be readily made available to disadvantaged areas in cases where viable self-help projects have been identified by local people but funds are lacking for starting such projects. Local contribution mainly in the form of labour could then be mobilised to supplement public resources in the implementation of self-help projects. Assurance of official support for project proposals designed to meet their fundamental needs would greatly contribute to the creation of confidence among local people in their own ability to take initiatives for improving their well-being.

The official policy of the Government of Kenya as regards the role of the co-operative movement in national development clearly recognises the importance of co-operatives as a means for promoting popular participation:

> The co-operative movement is an important instrument for achieving mass participation in national development and for providing a means of raising the living standard of the participants and of those who would otherwise not have access to inputs and services necessary for them to achieve a better standard of living.[27]

Furthermore, the movement is officially regarded as 'an organisational tool for promoting rural development generally and income earning opportunities in both rural and urban areas'.[28] This implies a direct link between the benefits of co-operatives and the satisfaction of basic needs at the local level. The extent to which the co-operative movement in Kenya contributes to basic needs satisfaction will, to a large extent, depend on its coverage among the poor and the degree of participation of the broad membership in the decision-making process within the movement.

Membership of the Movement. Although formal co-operatives have been in existence in Kenya for well over half a century, it was not until after the Second World War that the movement became accessible to African peasant producers. However, in contrast to the established and more organised co-operative societies serving the interests of European large-scale commercial farmers, the few officially sanctioned African societies in the post-war years were characterised by poor organisation and management while at the same time rigidly controlled and restricted by the colonial administration. There was also a high rate of failure and liquidation among African societies during this initial phase. Furthermore, scepticism and suspicion among peasant producers about the real motive of the colonial administration in organising them into this form of co-operation – in opposition to their own traditional mutual self-help societies – kept membership at a very low level.

However, this trend was reversed in the immediate pre-independence period when it was realised by nationalist leaders that co-operatives could be a viable means of securing and consolidating the rights of Africans to own and farm land in former European areas after independence. Thus between 1960 and 1963 many African co-operative societies, with a political orientation, were established throughout the country. Indeed, after independence these societies became the main means through which African peasant producers were able to pool together their resources for buying and operating former European commercial farms.

The establishment of a Ministry of Co-operatives soon after independence was also instrumental in promoting and funding the development of primary co-operative societies among African agricultural producers. According to official figures, the number of registered and active co-operative societies in Kenya rose from about 900 in 1968 to 1060 in 1974 and then to 1437 in 1977. By 1980, it was estimated that there were nearly 1600 societies with a total membership of over a million throughout the country. Most of these are agricultural marketing societies dominated by smallholder producers of both export and domestic produce. In addition to producer and marketing co-operatives there are farm purchase societies, consumer societies, housing co-operatives, credit and saving societies, and so on.

Institutionally, these grass-roots societies are grouped on a district basis under the umbrella of 39 district co-operative unions. The district organisations are in turn affiliated to a single national body, the Kenya National Federation of Co-operatives (KNFC), which is a sort of apex organisation to the co-operative movement. The KNFC receives direct financial assistance from the government to support the development of the movement and the fulfilment of its official role as adviser to the government on co-operative matters.

Co-operatives and Popular Participation. It has been claimed that co-operatives generally represent a democratic institution through which their members participate directly in the decision-making process, and that, collectively, co-operatives contribute to the promotion of broad-based participation in the overall development process. Consider, for example, the following remark by one observer of the movement in Kenya:

> Co-operatives involve members directly in the operation of their business and orient their awareness on the national level. The members participate in the decision-making process. Democracy becomes rooted in (the member's) thinking. He helps formulate the co-operative's policy. More basically this means that the member himself decides what values are to be held. He sets the fundamental value system of the co-operative.[29]

As a participatory institution, the functions of modern co-operatives in Kenya are, however, mainly economic in nature, and their performance is usually judged by how efficiently they can provide goods and services to their members. Hardly ever is the issue of popular participation in decision making *per se* regarded as necessary to the efficient operation of co-operatives. In fact, the Ministry of Co-operative Development, which oversees the activities of co-operatives, exercises strict control and supervision over co-operatives exclusively to ensure that individual societies fulfil their financial and other material obligations to their members.[30] Whether this is achieved with or without effective popular participation in the running of the affairs of societies seems to be of little or no concern to the ministry.

The extent of government involvement in the decision-making process of the movement could be seen from the provisions of the Co-operative Societies Act of 1967 (and as revised in 1972) which gives the Commissioner for Co-operative Development – a civil servant – wide powers including the right to dissolve popularly elected committees and replace them on a temporary basis by ones established by himself. The commissioner can also enforce amalgamation of primary societies and demand compulsory affiliation to district unions.

Accordingly, it is extremely difficult for co-operative societies to take any major decision without reference to and the approval of the Commissioner or his field representatives acting on his behalf. Therefore, even if members manage to influence or even dominate discussion in society meetings at the grass-roots level, the need to secure official approval on most issues effectively limits their role in the decision-making process. Admittedly, as in the case of the local government system, there appears to be a need for some degree of government control over the affairs of co-operatives in Kenya – if for no other reason but to protect the interests of the rank and file membership against malpractices and abuses by elected officers. But, at the same time, the nature and extent of this external control today are such that societies are left with very little authority and control over their own affairs.

Even at the basic level of the primary societies, the views of the ordinary members can be heard only indirectly through elected management committee members; it is only on major issues involving procedural and organisational changes that all members are balloted. Overall, the structure of the movement is fairly hierarchical and representation at higher levels is indirect which again may reduce the extent of popular influence over decision making. For example, grass-roots participation even at the primary society level is through elected representation and further up, at the district level, the selection of union representatives is often based on nominations rather than elections, from the society level. Hence, rank and file views can easily be overlooked or disregarded in key decision making, through inadequate representation of the broad membership, at both the society and district levels. Evidence shows that, on the whole, indirect participation in decision making through representatives does not constitute an adequate basis for achieving popular influence on the policies and activities of the co-operative movement in Kenya.

From the standpoint of a participatory institution, it can therefore be concluded that the co-operative movement does not offer much opportunity for broad-based participation in decision making. There is also the fact that the coverage of the movement does not extend to all socio-economic groups in rural areas, such as landless labourers and

176

many subsistence producers. Another relevant point is that the increasing intervention of government in recent years has consequently diminished the independence of the movement to such an extent that it now exists and operates as just another type of public institution. Just as the *Harambee* self-help movement has all but in name become an integral part of the Department of Social Services, the co-operative movement is now more or less run by the Ministry of Co-operative Development. In both cases, the basic issue seems to concern the lack of confidence or suspicion on the part of the government in the ability of local people to organise themselves to promote and defend their interests.

Co-operatives and Access to Basic Needs. From the onset, co-operatives have been regarded by government as an important instrument for improving access of 'co-operators' to essential inputs and services for production activities. This has favourable implications for the satisfaction of basic needs through higher levels of income among members. The experience of the co-operative movement in Kenya so far suggests that the issue of access to productive resources is one that has become embroiled by partisan and class conflicts. There are many known cases of group rivalries and struggles within individual societies which often result in those members belonging to powerful or triumphant factions benefiting more than others in terms of access to resources. Furthermore, since the leadership of co-operative societies is usually made up of the better-off 'co-operators' and the local elites, the criterion of need or relative deprivation is seldom taken into account in the distribution of additional benefits such as access to credits and extension services.

Weaknesses of the Co-operative Movement. In addition to institutional shortcomings mentioned above, there are also built-in structural weaknesses that impair the effectiveness of co-operative societies and similar economic welfare institutions to contribute to basic needs satisfaction. From this author's own observation of the activities of the co-operative movement in the ten districts investigated for this study, the following weaknesses can be highlighted:

1 *Financial:* poor book-keeping and auditing and inefficient financial management, with instances of outright embezzlement; lack of capital to enable societies to operate effectively.
2 *Political:* leadership struggles and patronage often resulting in the election of committee members with little commitment to the goals and obligations of co-operative societies; frequent interference by government in decision making.
3 *Organisational:* excessively high handling fees which discourage poorer farmers from joining societies; lack of experience in marketing techniques; delays in payment to members; inability of

societies to provide adequate services with respect to storage and delivery systems; the 'smallness' of some societies to be economically viable.

4 *Socio-economic:* resistance to change and innovation by some farmers; ignorance about the purpose of co-operation leading to reluctance to honour debt obligations; dominance by local elites and lack of control by ordinary members who are often less inclined to challenge their leaders.

These weaknesses have combined to reduce significantly the impact of co-operative societies in Kenya as an economic welfare institution with respect to improvement of access to basic needs goods and services. Some of these weaknesses, as we have seen, are closely linked to the lack of popular participation in policy-making and operational activities, and, therefore, any attempt at improving the performance of co-operatives must revolve around the need to make the movement as a whole a more genuine popular institution.

Improving Popular Participation in Co-operatives. Co-operatives have the potential to involve a fairly large percentage of the rural population in the development process. Whether or not people participate actively in the movement will largely depend on their perception of individual and collective benefits of co-operation. So far, the performance of co-operative societies in Kenya has, on the contrary, contributed to the decline of the movement. For example, lack of prompt payments for produce delivered has forced members to withdraw from societies and find alternative marketing outlets. It appears therefore that an important way to broaden the base of the movement is to improve the efficiency of co-operative societies. Training programmes for officials and 'co-operators' should be expanded and intensified as a way of increasing efficiency.

At the same time, steps should be taken to give ordinary 'co-operators' more control over the affairs of their societies, including a say in the determination of producer prices. This implies that the popular influence should be effective both in terms of internal decision making, currently monopolised by the management committees, and of external control which is now a prerogative of the Commissioner of Co-operatives. Internally, more broad-based representation on the management committees reflecting diverse interests would be an improvement on the present situation. External control should be exercised mainly to protect popular interests, rather than to force political decisions on societies or defend minority interests. Greater awareness among people at the grassroots level about the purpose and benefits of co-operation would also help to eliminate the practice whereby many co-operative societies depend mainly on the support and patronage of local elites and political agencies for their existence.

178

Although women account for about two-thirds of Kenya's rural population and play an important role in agricultural production and related activities – a fact which is seldom highlighted in the context of national development[31] – the level of their participation in the decision-making process is extremely low. Similarly, access to socio-economic opportunities for women in the modern economy can still be regarded as inadequate when compared with the situation of male members of society. While part of the reason for this state of affairs is due to traditional biases against women, it has much to do with the inadequate representation of women – relative to their numerical strength – in important decision-making bodies in both public and private life and at all levels. Therefore, any attempt to promote genuine popular participation in the development process will be meaningless if it does not first recognise the present disadvantaged situation of women and, accordingly, include specific measures to improve the socio-economic status of women in society.

However, specific measures designed to improve the participation rate of women in existing decision-making institutions within the formal administrative structure and in popular organisations may have to be carefully worked out and effectively implemented to have any impact. Furthermore, in a situation where decision making is male dominated, it may be rather difficult to obtain the necessary support among decision makers for changes required to ensure that women are adequately and effectively represented in central government, local authorities, self-help committees and other participatory institutions in the country. Clearly a fundamental change in attitudes and perceptions will be required in the society as a whole before the notion of women's equality will enjoy widespread support where it matters – and this might take a long time in coming.

A more practical and feasible approach would be to increase awareness among women about their present situation, and thereby provide a motivation for them to form gender-specific organisations for defending their specific interests. If women, as a presently disadvantaged group, become more conscious of their situation and, accordingly, take action themselves to influence decisions in their favour, they may even find sympathisers and allies from among male members of society. Consciousness would also provide the foundation for transforming women's groups into viable gender-specific organisations that can contribute significantly to improvements in living and working conditions of women at all levels. Already the nucleus of such organisations exists in Kenya in the form of both traditional mutual aid women's groups and more modern types of women's welfare societies.

The existence of mutual aid work groups amongst women was a common phenomenon in traditional Kenyan societies. In many communities today these groups have survived though in somewhat modified forms. For example, traditional women's groups have formed themselves as labour 'teams' for hiring out their services as manual workers on construction projects as a way of supplementing household incomes. However, it has been observed that the employment and income-earning potentials of these labour teams are limited due to constraints on members' time arising from the necessity to fulfil other duties at home and on the farm. Furthermore, the current scarcity of wage employment opportunities in general, combined with inherent sexual biases, put women at a disadvantage in terms of securing adequately remunerating employment. Female employment tends to be regarded as a residual element in the labour market or an alternative form of cheap labour.

Since independence, several women's groups have emerged throughout the country. According to the current National Development Plan, there are about 5000 of such gender-specific groups with a total membership of more than 250 000. However, this is a very small fraction of the estimated total adult female population in the country. Furthermore, given that a significant proportion of this total membership is attributable to urban-based organisations, the coverage of women at the grass-roots level must be extremely small.

The mode of participation of women in the development process through membership of these groups is, in many respects, similar throughout the country. Starting initially as mutual aid groups, their functions usually cover both social welfare and commercial activities. Social welfare-oriented activities are mainly concerned with improvement in the living conditions of women in the home, as well as with facilitating access to basic community services such as nursery schools and pre- and post-natal clinics. Commercial activities, on the other hand, involve the establishment of income-generating ventures such as small retail businesses, poultry rearing, production and sale of handicrafts, and so on. The performance of these ventures in Kenya has ranged from dismal failures and success stories, but according to observations by this author the more successful ones are in common characterised by a high degree of group commitment and a good knowledge of market conditions.

The Nyakinywa Mabati* Women's Group of Nyeri district provides a good example of a success story.[32] The formation of the group, which was purely on the initiative of the women themselves, has its roots in the situation created by the *Mau Mau* emergency of the fifties when the absence of husbands meant that the women had to fend for themselves. Initially, the women organised themselves into a mutual aid society and contributed money – approximately 2–4 shillings per week – towards the cost of roofing members' houses on a rotating basis. Of importance was

*Swahili word for corrugated iron sheet.

the criterion used for determining one's place in the queue: the most deprived got their *mabati* first. By 1971 there were about 570 such groups in the district with a total membership of 48 685 or roughly one-seventh of the total population of the district. Such was the impact of the movement that it caught the attention of the government which in turn provided some financial assistance to support its activities. The successful experience of the Nyeri movement had a demonstration effect in the other Kikuyu districts with the result that the Nyakinywa movement was transferred into an ethnic mutual aid movement which by the mid-seventies was capable of purchasing and farming large tracts of land on a co-operative basis.

As has been the fate of other popular institutions in Kenya, government intervention has crept into the operation of the women's mutual aid movement in recent years with adverse consequences. Worse still is the fact that official intervention has not been accompanied by any significant increase in the participation of women in public decision making. The creation of a Division of Women's Affairs within the Ministry of Social Services in 1975 has ironically contributed to the diminishing of initiatives among local women to help themselves and to defend their interests. Charged with the responsibility for 'formulating relevant programmes to meet the needs of women and co-ordinating all women's programmes in the country', the Division has tended to take and implement decisions on the basis of extremely limited consultations with those who will be affected by such decisions. As a result, local women's organisations today find themselves increasingly under the control of the Division which has so far done very little to decentralise decision-making powers to popular women's organisations at the local level.

CONCLUSIONS

Current economic circumstances in Kenya are difficult and the prospect of achieving economic growth and balanced development on a sustainable basis is seriously threatened by adverse external factors. Therefore it is all the more necessary to strengthen the mechanism for popular participation in the development process as a way of enhancing the mobilisation of local resources for development purposes. Popular participation is also desirable in order to achieve a more even distribution of the benefits of development within the country. This view is linked to the possibility that participation in the decision-making process would result in a better national allocation of developmental resources according to a need criterion at the global level and progress towards the equalisations of socio-economic opportunities at the local level.

It is important to recall the often declared policy of the government to involve the mass of the population actively in the development process through their effective participation in decision making at all levels of administration. It becomes clear from this study, however, that there are certain inherent weaknesses in the political structure and the socio-economic system in Kenya that limit the scope for broad-based participation in the decision-making process. Among these, ironically, the modalities employed by the government to implement its own declared policy to promote popular participation can be singled out. In general, by actively involving itself in the organisation and supervision of the main channels for promoting popular participation in the development process the government has at the same time, perhaps inadvertently, created institutions and conditions which are not very conducive to this objective. More specifically, the tendency for the civil bureaucracy at all levels to dominate decision making in both public and popular institutions has effectively served to discourage the mass of the population from actively supporting government initiated programmes designed to promote mass participation in the development process. As a result of past experience of government involvement and intervention in local-level development initiatives, motivation and enthusiasm have been replaced by frustration and indifference among local people. These and other obstacles identified in this study have made it difficult to achieve genuine popular participation in the development process in Kenya. This being the case, it seems desirable, by way of a conclusion, to consider some ways of improving the situation overall.

The institutional basis of promoting popular participation in Kenya, as we have seen, is inappropriate with reference to that objective. In addition to institutional weaknesses, there are more fundamental issues – some of a structural nature – that should be addressed in order to realise the full potential of popular participation for meeting basic needs.

First, given that past and current policies have unfortunately not achieved much in terms of the declared objective of government to reduce inequalities in support of poverty alleviation, there is a need to review the situation overall and to adopt appropriate policies for spreading the benefits of development more widely than is the case at present. This would imply important changes in the distributive mechanism including the allocation of public resources and access to socio-economic opportunities. A more egalitarian framework for distributing income and productive assets seems necessary for motivating people to participate actively in government sponsored participatory development projects at the local level. Needless to say, the institutions created for this type of co-operation between government and the local people would have to be conducive to popular participation in the decision-making process.

Second, a change in official attitudes with regard to the desirability of popular influence on decision making, backed by effective measures to ensure more broad-based representation of local interests on decision-making bodies, would by itself contribute to greater willingness of local people and their organisations to support development efforts through increased mobilisation of resources. In turn, a proven capacity among local organisations and self-help groups to take initiatives on development matters would influence government to have more confidence in the ability of local people to run their own affairs as is consistent with the policy of decentralised planning. This should help to eliminate the need for undue government intervention in local-level development planning which has been found to be a major obstacle to the enhancement of popular participation.

Another fundamental issue involves the elimination of the 'culture of dependence' which tends to stifle initiatives for self-reliant styles of development at the local level. The mobilisation of local resources for meeting basic needs at the local level can be enhanced only if those resources are directed at projects and activities that benefit the broad mass of the population. This again implies popular influence on local-level decision making. Once people realise and experience the benefits of collective self-reliance, they are more likely to become motivated and favourably disposed to participation in communal development projects based on their own initiative and resources. With greater confidence in their own ability, local people would become less dependent on the government for planning and implementing their own development programmes and projects.

The experience of the past seems to have left most Kenyans believing that their development efforts cannot bear fruits without government supervision and support. If participatory institutions, such as the development committees, the self-help and co-operative movements, are to become more effective for meeting essentially local needs, they should be seen as institutions that are capable of acting independently of outside influence or patronage for the common good. There is, therefore, an urgent need to restructure local-level public popular institutions along lines that would make them more suitable for responding to local needs. An important requirement in this regard concerns the decision-making process, which should be amenable to popular influence and control.

In conclusion, it should be recognised that there are indeed problems involved in the promotion of popular participation in Kenya. So far, the experience has been more symbolic and less effective in practical terms. The attitude of the government, on the one hand, and the apparent lack of consciousness on the part of the participants, on the other, have combined to hinder progress. A viable solution, therefore, will depend on how realistically these two obstacles can be successfully overcome in the context of Kenya's political system and the current difficult socio-economic circumstances of the country.

NOTES

1 Republic of Kenya: *Development Plan, 1979–83* (Government Printer, Nairobi, 1979), p. 1.
2 ibid., p. 15.
3 See ILO: *Employment, income and inequalities: A strategy for improving productive employment in Kenya* (Geneva, 1972); C.T. Leys: *Underemployment in Kenya: The political economy of neo-colonialism* (London, 1975); A Hazelwood: *The economy of Kenya: The Kenyatta era* (Oxford, 1979); and Dharam Ghai, *et al.: Planning for basic-needs in Kenya: Performance, policies and prospects* (Geneva, ILO, 1979).
4 Republic of Kenya, Sessional Paper No. 10 of 1965 on *African socialism and its application to planning in Kenya* (Nairobi, Government Printer, 1965), p. 36.
5 Republic of Kenya, *Development Plan, 1979–83* (Nairobi, Government Printer, 1965), p. 36.
6 See E.L.H. Lee: 'Some normative aspects of a basic-needs strategy' in D.P. Ghai, *et al.: The basic-needs approach to development: Some issues regarding concepts and methodology* (Geneva, ILO, 1977); and Franklyn Lisk: 'Popular participation in basic-needs oriented development and planning' *Labour and Society*, vol. 6, no. 1, Geneva, Jan.–Mar. 1981, pp. 1–14.
7 For the historical development of this situation, see J.J. Okumu: 'The socio-political setting' in Goran Hyden, *et al.: Development administration: The Kenyan experience* (Nairobi, East African Literature Bureau, 1970).
8 See this author's 'Participation in development planning at the local level' in D.K. Leonard: *Rural administration in Kenya* (Nairobi, East African Literature Bureau, 1973), pp. 53–75.
9 See this author's 'Assessing administrative capacity for development purposes' *African Review*, vol. 5, no. 3, 1975.
10 Republic of Kenya, *Development Plan, 1966–70* (Nairobi, Government Printer), p. 8.
11 See this author's *Participation in development planning at the local level*, op. cit.
12 Republic of Kenya, *Development Plan, 1974–78* (Nairobi, Government Printer), p. 112.
13 Machakos District Development Committee minutes for the meeting held on 11 June 1973.
14 Personal interviews with several District Development Officers, Aug. and Oct. 1980. This author also investigated in great detail the background to the preparation of District Development Plans produced in 1980 for Siaya, Kisumu (in Nyanza Province); Bungoma and Kakamega (in Western Province); Muranga and Nyeri (in Central Province); Nandi and Kericho (in Rift Valley Province); Kilifi and Kwale (in Coast Province); and Kitui and Embu (in Eastern Province).
15 See ILO: *Employment, incomes and inequalities*, op. cit., and Republic of Kenya, *Development Plan*, 1974–78, pp. 110–111.
16 Njage Nthiga: *The management of rural development fund in Kenya*, unpublished M.A. Thesis, University of Nairobi, 1978.
17 ibid., p. 140.
18 Personal communication with the Bungoma District Development Officer, Aug. 1980.
19 For the articulation of this view with reference to the British model, see H. Maddick: *Democracy, decentralisation and development* (Bombay, Asia Publishing House, 1963).
20 See Donald Curtis, *et al.: Popular participation in decision-making and the basic-needs approach to development: Methods, issues and experiences*, World Employment Programme research working paper 2-32/WP 12 (Geneva, ILO, June 1978), p. 15.

21 For details see H.K. Colebatch: *Local services in the Governmental process in Kenya*, unpublished PhD. Thesis, University of Sussex, 1974; idem., 'Local councils and local services' in IDS, Sussex, *Bulletin*, vol. 6, no. 1, Sept. 1974, pp. 13–24; and this author's 'Local government and development in Kenya' in IDS, Sussex, *Discussion Paper* no. 131, Apr. 1978.

22 Republic of Kenya, *Development Plan, 1979–83*, p. 454.

23 Republic of Kenya, *Development Plan, 1966–70*, p. 324.

24 Republic of Kenya, *Development Plan, 1970–74*, p. 58–59.

25 Republic of Kenya, *Development Plan, 1979–84*, p. 185.

26 Republic of Kenya, *Development Plan, 1974–78*, p. 482.

27 Republic of Kenya, *Development Plan, 1979–83*, p. 309.

28 ibid.; also Arthur Durbin: 'The role of agrarian co-operatives in the development of Kenya' *Studies in Comparative International Development* (Rutgers University), vol. V, no. 6, 1969–70.

29 Durbin, op. cit., p. 112.

30 For details see G. Hyden: *Efficiency versus distribution in East African co-operatives: A study of organisation conflict* (Nairobi, East African Literature Bureau, 1973).

31 See Achola D. Pala: *The changing economic position of women in rural areas: Case studies from Kisumu District, Kenya*, IDS, University of Nairobi, *Working Paper* no. 156, Apr. 1974.

32 See G.C.M. Mutiso: 'Rural women in socio-political change' in Mutiso (ed.): *Kenya, politics, policy and society* (Nairobi, East African Literature Bureau, 1975).

PART III

PARTICIPATORY PRACTICE: LOCAL-LEVEL EXPERIENCES

7 Peasant Participation in Latin America in Historical Perspective: Experience and Lessons

Gerrit Huizer

In order to improve understanding and suggest viable ways of promoting popular participation in the development process, the types of obstacles to effective broad-based participation in development at the local level must also be considered. Nowhere, perhaps, can this be more true than in Latin America where the history of popular participation has, broadly speaking, been one of continuing conflicts of interests and, consequently, attempts to resolve conflicts.

Societal Conflicts and the Need for Popular Participation in Development

Until about the 1960s the analysis of social conflict and tension in social science literature was sparse, but since then there has been an increasing interest among researchers to venture into this area.[1] There is now growing awareness that conflicts of interests, rather than being something to be avoided at all costs, can even be a positive factor in promoting needed structural changes to support effective participation in the development process. It is also increasingly recognised that conflict and change are interrelated in the sense that the resolution of conflicts often leads to change: 'To plan for social change very often means to anticipate social conflict and devise programmes for meeting the problems which arise out of such conflict'.[2]

An important prerequisite for successfully implementing a conflict-resolution type development strategy is the existence within the political system of a machinery for identifying the nature and the causes of societal conflicts in the first instance. Generally speaking, these may be traced to particular structural and institutional weaknesses which underlie inequalities and distortions in the distribution of the benefits of development. Thus, with specific reference to rural communities, a better understanding of local problems requires some familiarity with the peasants' perception of their own situation vis-à-vis the rest of society, this being the so-called 'view from below'.[3] This approach has revealed that, in general, peasants and other disadvantaged groups view their present deprivation and frustration in a historical perspective, whereas development planners from the 'outside' tend to take the existing *status quo* as the most logical point of departure for drafting plans and designing development projects aimed at ameliorating the living conditions of the underprivileged. It is not unusual, therefore, for peasants to view such efforts as inadequate to their 'felt' needs, or even as retrogressive when compared with their present situation. For example, the strongest felt needs of a peasant community may not be in terms of merely new inputs of communal services but, in addition, more opportunities for productive employment and incomes as the means of access to such services. This in turn might imply and require a restoration of peasants' rights and status regarding land ownership and adequate access to other factors of production and socio-economic opportunities.

One of the main justifications for advocating broad-based local participation is that local people themselves are in a much better position, than 'outside' administrators and planners, to assess their own situation and identify their basic needs. In the absence of effective popular participation in decision making, efforts from above could well end up worsening their situation or leave them with less opportunity for improvement, as may be the case when prevailing economic and social forces combine to sustain inequitable production and distribution systems. A meaningful conflict-resolution development strategy should, therefore, include measures to bring about requisite structural and institutional changes simultaneously with concrete action programmes aimed at satisfying the basic needs of the poor. In all of these the effective participation of the people themselves is crucial.

The application of an appropriate conflict-resolution strategy to development planning should take account of the people's perception of their needs, both material and non-material, and, in so doing, will have a strongly motivational effect on the population. Moreover, as advocated by scholars of conflict sociology, the very organisation of people to defend their interests and strengthen their representation in decision-making bodies provides that extra commitment and motivation required to sustain popular participation.[4]

A useful approach to finding out how best deprived groups can strengthen their participatory role within the development process is to examine specific examples of how the poor have successfully organised themselves to increase their share of the benefits of development with the aid of appropriate conflict-resolution development strategies,[5] and to discuss objectively the possible implications of such interventions. Accordingly, this chapter focuses on some of the methods used by poor peasants in Latin America to organise themselves in defence of their legitimate rights and interest.

Evolution of Peasant Movements: A Response to the Need for Participation

An abundance of evidence exists in Latin American history to show that acute frustration and disillusionment, stemming from rapid deterioration of living standards and unfair land tenure conditions, had been instrumental in prompting apparently passive and traditionally-minded peasants to organise effectively and mobilise their ranks to defend their interests.[6] As is to be expected, in view of the importance of land as the key factor of production in rural areas, such mobilisation has occurred mainly in areas where land has been alienated from traditional communities for the introduction of cash crops or other forms of commercial agriculture by outside interests. When this happens, the often precarious livelihood of poor peasants is thrown into disequilibrium and, with their very survival threatened, they more or less spontaneously take action to defend their interests, even to the extent of reacting violently at times. In the past many such protest movements, as a result of being spontaneous, localised and not systematically organised on a broad scale, were often ineffective especially where the authorities were opposed to any form of participatory development. These early experiences of failure to promote popular participation at the local level explains, to a large extent, the very long period of inactivity as regards grass-roots mobilisation in most of rural Latin America.

The repressive measures that had been adopted by some authorities to contain peasant movements in the past underlie the proverbial distrust of peasants towards participating in local development schemes, however well-intentioned these may be. This distrust was most evident in the failure to arouse popular interest in development programmes and projects in the region in the early 1960s. As a result, the United Nations, in a major report on land reform, concluded that only a restoration of more egalitarian land tenure conditions, through the redistribution of large estates, would ensure the success of well-intentioned rural development programmes. Furthermore, the same report observed that 'legal provisions pertaining to land reform would remain a dead letter if there were no organised peasantry to counter-balance strongly organised vested interests opposed to land redistribution'.[7]

Today, the potential of organised peasantry to instigate, support and sustain agrarian reform to the lasting benefit of the majority of the poor peasants has been realised in several Latin American countries. In a number of cases land reform came about largely as a result of well co-ordinated organised actions by the peasants themselves as, for example, in Mexico and Cuba. In the case of Mexico, organised pressure from peasants played a crucial part in prompting and supporting a progressive government to take up the challenge to promulgate and implement land reform legislation against the wishes of vested interests.[8] In Cuba, oppression had forced the organised peasantry to go underground, thus motivating them to support a violent revolution only after which an effective land reform could be carried out.[9]

Conflict Resolution Development Strategies

The historical lessons from the Latin American experience, as will be presented below, suggest that development planners and administrators should give more serious consideration to constructive conflict-resolution development strategies in their thinking and activities. Consciously or not, many development planners are probably so much identified with the elitist biases that they cannot objectively perceive the nature and causes of deterioration in the living standards of the masses, to say nothing of their appreciation of a 'view from below'. They adopt popular slogans, such as more resources for the 'poorest of the poor', but hardly back these up with concrete proposals for any fundamental structural changes in the existing development pattern which may itself be the cause of sharp polarisation between the few rich and the many poor.

The rapid increase in the members of the latter group and their worsening poverty is making it even more difficult to find meaningful solutions in conventional and 'neo-conventional' strategies. Rather than continue to search for solutions in traditional development strategies, which hardly touch on causal factors, development efforts should be oriented to focus on social and institutional changes which would rapidly reverse the present polarisation trend through allowing for the effective participation of the masses in decision making. This may call for radical changes to the social and political structures, but as Raùl Prebisch, the then Director of the United Nations Economic Commission for Latin America, stated almost two decades ago, this could be done in a peaceful and orderly fashion. The conflict of interests between the few rich and the many poor in numerous developing countries today should be recognised, analysed and dealt with by appropriate forms of conflict-resolution development strategies, rather than be ignored. Genuine participation of the masses in decision making and in the overall development process can be an important means of implementing such strategies. Drawing on a variety of experiences in Latin America over the last few decades, an attempt is made in this chapter to analyse major aspects of participatory-oriented, conflict-resolution type development strategies.

THE ORGANISATION OF PEASANTS FOR EFFECTIVE PARTICIPATION IN THE DEVELOPMENT PROCESS

A noteworthy feature of the Latin American rural scene today is the presence of a growing number of well organised peasant movements which exist primarily to promote and defend the rights and interests of their members. The trend itself is the direct result of modernisation and development in the countries of the region over the last three decades. In general, as more isolated rural areas become integrated into the national economy, through improvements in communications and the spread of commercial agriculture and related agro-based industrial activities and mining operations, the peasants in those areas become more aware of their situation of relative deprivation and acquire rising expectations with respect to their share of the benefits of development. These two factors, increasing consciousness and higher levels of expectation, together with the gradual spread of education in the rural areas have combined to strengthen the participatory potential of peasants to the degree where this can be translated into reality. Once peasants become aware of the potential of their numbers to influence decision making, they are likely to have more confidence in their own ability to organise themselves into an effective force within the development process. In this section, some of the main factors behind the growth of strong peasant organisations in Latin America are identified and analysed with reference to their role in promoting and sustaining effective popular participation in socio-economic decision making.

'Organisability' of Peasants

For reasons summarised above, strong peasant organisations in Latin America have evolved in areas experiencing relatively rapid economic development. Yet, in many of these areas, the peasantry as a whole tends to be more the victim and less the beneficiary of modernisation. They may lose their lands to large-scale commercial and state entrepreneurs, often with inadequate or even no compensation, and, as a consequence, they may be forced to seek a livelihood from less fertile lands. Their traditional way of life and institutions may be upset as modernisation, from which they stand to benefit very little, catches up with them. Historically, such indeed was the fate of peasants in the states of Morelos and Sonora and the Laguna region in Mexico, the Cochabamba Department in Bolivia, the state of Pernambuco in Brazil, the Convención Valley in Peru, the states of Aragua and Carabobo in Venezuela and the sugar areas in Cuba. But, as already noted, the spread of modernisation into the rural areas has also resulted in close links with the more advanced sectors of the economy, through various forms of infrastructural development and the spread of literacy and vocational training programmes.

These all are factors which have had a positive effect on the 'organisability' of the peasants in the areas affected, especially in the context of modernisation programmes and activities that hold out little promise or expectations of substantial direct benefits for the local population itself. Benefits from modernisation may in fact be confined to exploitative forms of manual employment (in mines, agricultural estates and construction projects), characterised by poor working conditions and extremely low levels of wages which may not even compensate for loss of foregone subsistence household production, thus leading to further immiseration and poverty. In such a situation, the peasantry becomes easily frustrated and aroused, and seeks to improve its situation through its collective strength, usually leading to the organisation of peasants into mass movements and occupational associations to further and defend their interests.

In Latin America, as in other developing regions, the emphasis on rapid economic growth has in the past resulted in the adoption of development strategies that seek to maximise output through the deliberate bias of investment resources towards key, or 'progressive', sectors where growth potential was believed to be greatest. It was further assumed that social and economic development in the low-growth potential rural areas can best be promoted by the creation and support for an entrepreneurial class which is better able to provide the impetus for rapid growth and, thereby, spread the benefits of development to the rural masses via the so-called 'trickle-down' process and demonstration effects. Thus, for example, to support widespread commercialisation of agricultural production in Mexico, large-scale irrigation schemes were set up in the north-western part of the country, but these were directed mainly towards the larger and, apparently, more progressive farmers. Far from spreading the benefits of development to the peasants through a trickle-down process, the result was deterioration in their living standards as they were transformed from once viable subsistence producers to lowly-paid agricultural wage-earners. This and other similar experiences in the region provide concrete evidence to question the validity of the 'trickle-down' assumption.[10] But at the same time, by further alienating the peasantry from the mainstream and benefits of development, the implementation of these types of growth-oriented development strategies have led to the raising of consciousness among peasants and encouraged them to form effective rural organisations to defend their interests.

Largely as a result of the state of affairs in the past and the realisation by the authorities that the pattern of development itself provided a favourable climate for more radical forms of peasant organisations and activities, there is now increasing recognition by governments in the region that modernisation and rural development programmes must be designed to benefit all groups proportionately as exemplified by the recent policy in Mexico favouring the collective cultivation of the expropriable 'haciendas'. However, there is still the danger inherent in such a conflict-resolution development strategy if marketing and producer co-operatives or collective farming ventures become too dependent on 'outside' multinational corporations or agro-business interests for their survival, as indeed was happening on an increasing scale in the region.[11] There is a considerable body of evidence indicating that, in general, the forms of socio-economic planning that support mass participation and widespread distribution of benefits often cannot cope sufficiently with pressures from those with vested interests (both of internal and external origin) who may feel that their privileged position is threatened by a more egalitarian type of development strategy, and may therefore be ready to make use of effective power at their disposal to ward off such threats. Indeed, there have been instances where, due to strong pressures from powerful interest groups, governments committed to egalitarian styles of participatory development have had to manipulate even well-intentioned rural development programmes more in favour of the needs of privileged groups, thereby leading to a polarisation between the rich and the poor in the rural areas.[12]

This trend of increasing polarisation between the rich and the poor in rural areas has made the peasantry, as a group, generally more willing to organise its ranks for radical action, than its urban working-class counterpart. While the problems and grievances of urban workers may be solved by adaptations and improvements within the existing socio-economic system, such as wage increases and more fringe benefits, the most strongly felt needs of the peasantry – landless labourers dependent on employment in the large commercial 'haciendas' for a living, as well as small farmers who have lost land to the powerful interests – are more likely to be met through a more fundamental change in the existing socio-political structure in many cases. The rigid opposition of powerful rural elites to desirable structural changes, and the inability of governments to adopt and effectively implement desirable social reform programmes, could only serve to exacerbate rather than solve the problem of polarisation. In the long run, the failure to implement needed social reforms and to establish appropriate institutions for promoting broad-based local participation could lead to the peasants themselves taking the initiative to bring about a change in the social structure, such as through organised action and even radical activities if necessary.

Interest in the organisational potential of the peasantry has grown in recent times as a result of successes achieved by certain peasant movements. The most spectacular case of organised peasant protest in Latin America in the post-Second World War period is, perhaps, that of the peasant syndicates in the Cochabamba Valley in Bolivia in 1962 which resulted eventually in the implementation of some measures of agrarian reform. The Bolivian peasants became strongly aroused after their traditional isolation from modernisation was broken by the Chaco

War; awareness of their state of relative deprivation and, hence, the need for radical changes in the system, was significantly raised as a result of injustices suffered under the repressive military regime between 1946 and 1952.

Throughout Latin America the spread of economic development programmes to remote rural areas and the consequent integration of isolated areas into the modern economy have contributed much to the growth of critical awareness and consciousness among peasants. This, indeed, is evidence to support the claim that 'conscientisation' is a *conditio sine qua non* for mass organisation in support of more effective participation and influence in the development process as a whole.

Growth of Awareness Through Raising of Consciousness about Relative Deprivation

The so-called 'resistance to change' hypothesis is often presented in social science literature as one of the major obstacles to the effective mobilisation of peasants, as well as a causal factor underlying the apathy of the local population that is associated with rural societies in the Third World. Yet resistance to change, or apathy on the part of peasants, is frequently a natural reaction to what they themselves consider to be inequitable and unjust forms of socio-economic development. Worse still, as a disadvantaged group, peasants usually have little or no influence or control over decision making in order to bring about desirable changes. Over time they tend to become very suspicious and even lose confidence in those who take decisions on their behalf, however well-intentioned those decisions might be. Non-participation by peasants in social institutions imposed on them without prior consultations, and the making of decisions by 'outsiders' on their behalf, could be seen not so much as an obstacle to participation in development, but rather as a form of self-protection of interests by those who already benefit most from development. This resistance syndrome can be – and at times has been – instrumental in triggering off forms of popular participation that are favourable to the interests of underprivileged groups in society.

The formation and establishment of dynamic peasant organisations can be regarded as an evolutionary process. First, and most important, is the creation of consciousness among the peasants about their present situation and a transformation of this into an awareness of needs in terms of specific demands around which effective participatory groups can be formed. Yet, it is important that consciousness of social injustice and of absolute and relative deprivation should be seen not only as a specific problem to be solved but as a symptom of the need to change the prevailing socio-economic structure as a whole. Growing awareness among peasants that their deprivations and needs coincide with the requirement for structural changes in the system as a whole is the next important step in

196

the formation of effective and large-scale peasant participatory organisations.

Some action programmes aimed at organising peasants at the local or regional level have used the 'creation of awareness' method as a crucial step towards that objective. In the state of Rio Grande do Norte in Brazil, the Serviço de Asistença Rural started a church-sponsored peasant organisation programme with a campaign of 'creation of awareness' ('concientização') in 1960. The objective of this and a related 'basic education' programme was to make the peasants become more aware of the situation in which they live and to promote creativity in direct opposition to their fatalistic philosophy of life. One technique used was Paolo Freire's 'conscientisation' method based on literacy teaching, which is designed to make people become more aware of their situation and status in the society as a whole through acquiring the ability to read and write and to participate in group discussions.[13] As part of the process of 'conscientisation', the organisers of the programme made special efforts to explain complicated issues, such as those pertaining to ownership of land, in simple terms which can be understood by the peasants themselves. Through an understanding of critical issues that determine and affect their situation, the peasants became more aware of their rights and needs and were motivated to organise themselves to defend their interests.

Since the late sixties, progressive church groups in Latin America have increasingly taken up such awareness-creation methods to help the poor in rural areas and urban slums to have a greater say in their own development. However, such passive efforts at organising the poor have sometimes encountered opposition from the authorities, thereby leading in some cases to the adoption of more radical forms of protest which were then denounced as 'revolutionary'. Opposition to participatory initiatives has sometimes led to the increasing 'radicalisation' of the Church as, for example, in Brazil where much inspiration for effective popular participation has come from Dom Helder Camara, Archbishop of Recife. There has indeed been a considerable change in the attitude of the Church in Latin America as a whole towards the need for popular mobilisation in support of social justice. At the Latin America Bishops Conference (CELAM) in Medellin, Colombia, in 1968 this need was strongly emphasised, and over the years many more priests have become active in efforts to promote popular participation. This change of attitude led to the emergence of the 'theology of liberation' as an alternative to the traditional passive role of the Church in development matters.[14]

Leadership and Outside Support

While awareness creation is undoubtedly an important condition for motivating peasants towards collective action, the availability of able local leaders to organise and 'educate' peasants about their rights is equally as important for promoting popular participation. Able leadership is also needed to transform the more or less spontaneous mobilisation of local people into a cohesive and organised participatory institution that is capable of initiating appropriate action in support of popular demands and sustaining its potential over time. In Latin America a number of spontaneous local protest movements or pressure groups gained organisational strength and became established broad-based participatory organisations mainly due to the ability and commitment of their local leaders. In this connection one could cite as examples the powerful peasant union of Ucureña in Bolivia, the peasant movement in La Convención in Peru, the peasant leagues in north-eastern Brazil, and those in the eastern part of Cuba.

There is considerable evidence, however, that help from sympathetic 'outsiders', such as school teachers, lawyers, priests, students and urban labour leaders, is important for the success of peasant participatory movements. This is probably one of the reasons why the more successful peasant organisations in Latin America have emerged in areas which are relatively close to urban centres. Proximity to urban centres also makes it easier for the peasantry to be exposed to the organisational methods of their urban-based allies; as a result, peasant groups in those areas have produced from among their ranks individuals capable of taking up leadership roles in new participatory organisations.

Urban-based catalytic agents who have experienced actual conditions in rural communities through living and working in those areas (for example, priests and school teachers) are generally more sympathetic to the problems, and understand better the needs of peasants. On a number of occasions in recent times, sympathetic 'outsiders' have played an active role in providing support and encouragement for emergent peasant organisations or have even been directly involved in non-violent protest actions of such organisations including peaceful land invasions. But 'outsiders' who offer their assistance to peasant organisations need proper training and orientation in the intricacies of peasant livelihood if they are to be really effective. Furthermore, their role should be restricted to that of 'promoters' or 'catalysts', so as to encourage the emergence of a truly local peasant leadership and enhance the practice of self-reliance among the peasants themselves.

An important factor which contributed to the success of some smaller peasant movements in Latin America was the fact that they were amalgamated and organised on a regional basis and adapted to the particular situation of one homogeneous area. In some Latin American countries, federations of local peasant organisations have been able to maintain their independence while at the same time increasing their bargaining power substantially to defend their members' interests. The regional level seems to be a particularly suitable one from which peasant organisations can extend their activities to political participation. Frequent contacts between the rank and file and the top leadership is also still possible at that level. Furthermore, since the interests represented at the regional level are likely to be more or less homogeneous, it is therefore possible for the membership to be mobilised around specific political issues, as and when necessary. However, it is more difficult to organise peasant groups nationally, since at that level local interests tend to get lost in the wider issues of national and international concerns. Overall, the grouping of local peasant organisations into regional federations seems to be a useful and practical way of guaranteeing effective broad-based participation in decision making, but again the success of this approach will depend on the quality of local leadership as well as on the sincerity of outside catalytic agents.

Peasant organisations generally need enlightened but sympathetic outside support, particularly when local movements extend their activities to the regional and national levels. However, at those levels, most of the allies and supporters of peasant organisations may belong to other more sophisticated organisations, some of which are concerned with objectives and activities that may not be consistent with the goals of the peasantry. This implies the need for caution on the part of peasant groups in forming alliance with outside organisations. This having been said, there are many examples of genuine support provided by outside organisations to peasant groups in Latin America. In both Mexico and Bolivia, teachers' unions have encouraged their members and advised them on how to help peasant groups to form regional peasant federations. Elsewhere in the region, student groups of one kind or another have been engaged in similar activities. More common has been help from leaders of organised labour in urban areas, sometimes under the banner of a specific labour-based political party. The spread of the Bolivian peasant federation all over the country in 1953 and the growth of the Federación Campesina de Venezuela after 1958 illustrate the important role of a sincere and sympathetic urban political ally – provided in this case respectively by the populist government in Bolivia (through its Ministry of Peasant Affairs) and the Acción Democrática Party in Venezuela – in promoting peasant participation in development even at the highest level.

Urban Labour Support

In a number of countries in Latin America urban workers, out of a sense of solidarity and, in some cases, perceived self-interest, have felt obliged to help rural workers organise themselves into labour unions. From the standpoint of the interest of urban labour, better living conditions in rural areas would relieve the pressure on the labour market in urban areas which is mainly the result of massive influx of unemployed rural workers into urban centres. Also improvement in the income levels in rural areas would considerably expand the domestic market for urban manufactured products with significant employment implications in urban areas. This latter reasoning has even encouraged some industrial entrepreneurs in certain Latin American countries to support rural workers' organisations. For example, industrialists in São Paulo have at certain periods of economic down-swing given their support to the Ligas Camponesas in the north-east of Brazil, which, together with other rural unions, won considerable benefits in 1963–64 as a result of such outside support.

Several cases are known where miners and urban labourers with organising experience have directly helped rural workers to create viable peasant organisations. In the early 1950s miners in Bolivia were instrumental in organising peasants leading to the creation of the Confederación de Trabajadores Campesinos de Bolivia. During the Cardenas regime in Mexico in the 1930s urban labour organisers working in the Laguna area helped to create a strong rural workers' organisation which successfully obtained important land concessions and improvements in working conditions for its members.

Special training courses designed to help urban labour organisers to understand better the problems of rural workers have been introduced by urban unions so as to increase the effectiveness of the support given to peasant organisations. For example, many of the cadres of the Federación Campesina de Venezuela were originally urban labour organisers who became actively involved in peasant organisations mainly through such in-service training. Urban workers' organisations now frequently extend their leadership training programmes to include participants from rural workers' organisations or even run special courses for rural workers' leaders at the local level. International workers' organisations and similar bodies have supported such efforts in various ways, including the provision of training, money, equipment and personnel.

Nevertheless, there are still ways by which urban unions can contribute further to the development of rural workers' organisations. A particularly important contribution could be made by providing the growing number of rural organisations in Latin America with certain services which they are not able to provide themselves but which are highly desirable for their membership. It is a well-known strategy of rural development that people are better motivated to join interest and occupational groups when they believe that membership would facilitate the fulfilment of their most strongly-felt needs. One such need, acutely felt by peasants of various kinds in Latin America, is security of land tenure and legal protection. Peasants in many areas still suffer from illegal usurpation of their lands by powerful interests. Therefore, one of the most important services urban labour unions and other sympathetic groups could render to peasant organisations is to make available to them legal advisers with respect to defending their civil and other rights which, though guaranteed by law, are not always recognised by long established local practice. Legal defence is more effective when it is directed at cases of widespread violations of existing laws, rather than isolated single offences, such as those relating to minimum wages regulations, protection of tenancy, rent regulations, freedom of association, and so on. This implies the need for legal representation at the regional and national levels which itself implies a need for local rural workers' organisations from the outset to be integrated into stronger regional or national federations. Since most existing urban labour organisations already operate at those higher levels, it should be easier for them to put their legal facilities at the disposal of aggrieved peasant organisations. This in fact has happened in a few cases in Latin America, the most well-known example being that of the peasant federation in La Convención, Peru, which won some important litigations in the 1960s with the aid of legal support provided by the urban labour movement.[15]

As to be expected, urban unions with strong branches in outlying provincial towns are better adapted to assist in the organisation of peasants than those concentrated in the capital. The presence of mining activities in rural areas has proved to be a positive factor for the creation of rural workers' organisations. Not only is there direct contact between the mining centres and surrounding villages, but many mine workers after spending several years on their jobs retire to their villages of origin nearby. Their experience of wage employment becomes extremely valuable for the formation of rural workers' organisations in their localities. Hence, some of the more effective peasant organisations in Bolivia, Peru and Chile have emerged in areas around important mining centres. However, one must not lose sight of the danger that the urban workers may dominate peasant organisations and utilise them for motives which serve urban labour's interests and its political objective, rather than those of the peasantry.

FAVOURABLE FACTORS AND OBSTACLES TO PEASANT PARTICIPATION

The Legitimacy of Peasant Organisations

Judging from past experiences, it would appear that peasant organisations in Latin America are potentially capable of defending the interests of their members, even in the face of opposition from vested interests (both local and foreign), if the authorities provide the requisite legal and institutional support. Naturally, the enactment and enforcement of favourable legislation would enhance the effectiveness of peasant organisations in terms of influence over decision making and participation in development. But it seems more rational and desirable, particularly in the context of emergent peasant organisations, initially to exploit favourable provisions in existing legislation and press for their effective implementation, rather than to demand the immediate enactment of new laws that relate exclusively to the well-being of the peasants as a separate group in society. Such a 'moderate' approach has the advantage of appealing to and winning the support of those groups in society which are relatively neutral regarding the need to bring about necessary structural changes. Their support could be vital as a countervailing force to possible opposition from extremists who are against the participation of peasants and other disadvantaged groups in decision making. Even more conservative interest groups might be less opposed to implementation of existing laws than to the enactment of new ones of a similar nature. On the whole, the precise content of laws relating to peasant organisations and rural living and working conditions seems to be relatively of lesser importance than how effectively such laws are implemented and the spirit in which this is done.

Nevertheless, there are instances where existing laws regarding peasant organisations are more of an obstacle to their meaningful existence. Can strong and effective peasant organisations emerge in such a climate? In theory, if the legal basis of their very existence is inadequate or not guaranteed, peasant organisations may find it extremely hard to survive. But such a situation itself could serve to strengthen the will and determination of peasant groups and their leaders to promote their interests and defend what they believe to be their rights when faced with the challenge. For example, the peasant leagues in Brazil during the late 1950s were successful in gaining widespread recognition and eventually became an effective channel for defending the interests of peasants even though these organisations were not enjoying official patronage and the protection of the law.

In Latin America as a whole, many effective peasant organisations have existed without any legal recognition at all. The best example of this is, perhaps, the Unión General de Obreros y Campesinos de México which, though not legally recognised, was an important force behind the implementation of an agrarian reform programme after 1958 mainly as a result of its real political bargaining power. But it would be misleading to downplay the absence of a legal basis and guarantees for the existence of peasant and similar organisations as an obstacle to genuine popular participation. It is not sufficient only to include such basic civil rights as freedom of association and speech in the constitution, but, more important, there must be official recognition and tolerance of legal provisions which are intended to promote and guarantee the existence of occupational interest groups. This point is important since there have been instances, not only in Latin America, where powerful interests flouted basic constitutional rights pertaining to freedom of association, sometimes even with the open or covert support of the authorities. Even today in Latin America, there are cases of big landowners preventing

202

workers in their employment from forming associations to represent and defend their interests; if they try to do so they may lose their jobs and be dislodged or evicted from the estate. Although the International Labour Organisation, when presented with complaints of infringements of trade union rights, has been able to intervene successfully in some of the more publicised cases of violation, it is probable that many infractions of these rights, especially at the local level, still take place. This underlies the importance of the need for more effective enforcement of relevant constitutional provisions and international conventions and labour standards.

Opposition and Repression by Powerful Elites

It is well known that the history of peasant movements in Latin America has not followed a very smooth path. Attempts to promote peasant organisations and their effective participation in decision making have in some cases resulted in more violent forms of mobilisation and protest activities. When this happens it is often a reaction of the peasants to opposition and repression by powerful vested interests in both private and government sectors. Thus, peasant groups, which initially sought to defend the interests of their members by orderly and peaceful means, but suddenly found themselves confronted with obstacles that took the form of extremes of repression by elites and dominant groups, have out of frustration and despair resorted to similar acts of violence and lawlessness in order to protect themselves.[16] In situations where the oppressors enjoy the support of the authorities, for one reason or another, the full force of the law may even be brought to bear on the peasants ostensibly in the name of law and order. When the situation is analysed objectively, as has been done by some international agencies, it becomes clear that violent clashes and struggles between the elites and the peasants, sometimes with fatal consequences, could in fact have been avoided if a conflict-resolution type of rural development strategy had been adopted and implemented by the authorities.

It would, however, be misleading to generalise that there is widespread repression against those engaged in the promotion and running of representative rural organisations in Latin America as a whole. There is considerable variation from country to country, and between regions within a given country, depending on the orientation of national or local authorities and the attitude of the rural elites. While, according to reports by Amnesty International, opposition to rural mobilisation seems to have been more significant in parts of Brazil, Guatemala, El Salvador, Chile, Argentina and Nicaragua (before 1979),[17] the situation elsewhere is, by many accounts, satisfactory; in certain countries in the region peasant organisations have never encountered repression and violence.

The kind of self-defence adopted by peasant organisations in response to opposition and repression tends to vary depending on the local circumstances. In cases such as in the north-western development region of Mexico, where the authorities have used less repressive measures to counter peasant demands and organised actions, peasant organisations have adopted a strategy that on the whole is conspicuously non-violent. In other cases, usually in more isolated rural areas where the local elites openly flout constitutional and other legal provisions and the population suffers from, more or less, a permanent state of repression, the response from peasant groups has taken more violent forms. Thus, in areas where landowners, in violation of the law, have sponsored vigilanté groups which intimidate the peasantry, the people have felt a strong need to organise themselves into self-defence groups for reasons of personal security. At times it had even been necessary for the Government to help peasant communities to form armed militia groups for the purpose of defending themselves against the aggression of landowning elites who were opposed to the implementation of land reform measures, as happened in Mexico in the 1930s and Bolivia in 1952.

While the taking up of arms by peasants cannot generally be condoned, this line of self-defence should be seen in relation to the nature and magnitude of aggression directed at them by the land-owning elites in defiance and violation of the law. In the extreme examples cited above, it is doubtful whether any less violent forms of protest by the peasants would have been effective to neutralise the violent opposition of land-owning elites to the implementation of land reform as stipulated by law. However, under more normal conditions, differences and conflicts between rural elites and the masses can be resolved through non-violent means. In some Latin American countries, the dominant local elites in certain rural areas have been influenced by changing attitudes of higher-level authorities and elite groups, or forced by the threat of mass revolt from below, to adopt a more tolerant attitude towards broad-based participation in the development process. In effect they came to a *modus vivendi* with the new and more progressive forces in society including those which represented peasant interests. In this type of climate, agrarian reform could be carried out with the minimum of violence and peasant organisations themselves can evolve into viable and responsible political institutions and agents of development.

The Quality of Peasant Leadership

However, there is the danger that such a *modus vivendi* between the old elites and new progressive forces could lead to new problems and obstacles if representative peasant organisations became increasingly influenced and controlled by the new elites. Peasant organisations which had succeeded in restoring the rights of their members with the help of progressive elements could later be easily neutralised and kept in a state of tranquillity by the strategic granting of a minimum of limited benefits by their new allies or patrons when the latter succeed to government. Peasant leaders can also be easily bought in such a situation. For example, the leadership of the National Peasant Confederation (CNC) in Mexico in the late 1930s became increasingly less effective as the protector of peasants' interests and even corrupt following its alliance with the then ruling party (PRI) and its involvement in official decision making. As a consequence, alternative and more dynamic organisations with closer links to the masses emerged – for example the Union of Peasants and Workers (UGOCM) in 1946, the Independent Peasant Federation (CCI) in the early 1960s and several smaller local organisations.[18]

In some instances, younger elements from among the land-owning elite have broken with their class and become leaders of peasant groups. Francisco Madero during the Mexican revolution, Francisco Juliao's involvement with the Brazilian peasant leagues and Fidel Castro in Cuba are outstanding examples. This tendency gives much support to the view that the formation of strong peasant organisations could be facilitated through efforts to raise the social consciousness of the more progressive elements among the traditional elite, especially young people, who tend to be more concerned about issues of social justice and equity and, hence, more willing to forego their privileged status and accept constructive roles in the promotion of a more egalitarian pattern of development.

Official Intervention and Support for Peasant Organisations

More recently, some conservative military regimes in Latin America, which had in the past employed strong measures against peasant movements in their struggles with rural elites, have abandoned repression and adopted instead a more conciliatory strategy by which representative peasant organisations are given legal recognition under official guidance. For example, the Peruvian 'revolutionary' military government of Juan Velasco Alvarado which came to power in 1968 soon recognised and established contacts with existing peasant organisations leading to the implementation of some measures of land reform which these organis-ations had been demanding.[19] In addition, that same government made use of the National System for Social Mobilisation (SINAMOS) to bring together local peasant leagues all over the country under a National Peasant Confederation (CNA). By adopting such a conflict-resolution strategy, the regime was able to neutralise existing contradictions and conflicts between rich and poor in the rural areas and to utilise constructively this new and unprecedented rapport between both groups to build a strong popular movement between 1969 and 1975. Such official support can be explained partly in terms of the necessity to keep a potentially powerful social group under constant surveillance and partly in terms of political expediency on the part of a new regime seeking to legitimise its existence and to win broad-based popular support so as to ensure its survival. However, there are also indications that official support for peasant movements has come from a genuine desire to redress past injustices. But whatever may be the reason behind official support for peasant organisations, it does emphasise the need for the government to take the risk of alienating itself from powerful vested interests – for example the traditional elites – in order to resolve existing contradictions and conflicts.

In Colombia, a similar effort to organise peasants under official guidance through the Association of Colombian Peasants (ANUC) was undertaken by the Lleras Restrepo Government at about the same time. But, unlike Peru, the Government did very little to implement effectively promised land reform measures which had been demanded by the peasant groups. Consequently, and out of frustration and disappointment, the ANUC broke with the Government, became radicalised and organised land invasions in disputed areas on a large scale. The Government reacted with strong measures aimed at weakening the movement, though not very successfully. This experience suggests that a strategy of conflict-resolution can only be successful if it is accompanied by positive changes within the system that would lead to improvement in the living conditions of those previously disadvantaged.

One danger related to official support for peasant movement is the co-opting of leaders into the ruling elite once their organisations have become established within the system. The already-mentioned practice of 'buying' leaders with political favours has been found by some governments to be an effective means of neutralising potentially strong representative groups that constitute a threat or challenge to their authority or survival. Peasant organisations can also be enticed or deceived into allying with a political party which in reality is less progressive than its manifesto indicates for election purposes. Once such parties succeed to government, sometimes mainly as a result of the support of peasant groups, they may abandon commitments to agrarian and social reform programmes and turn their attention instead to the needs of more privileged groups. Sometimes it is the dire need for financial aid to support their activities that forces peasant organisations to seek alliance with outside organisations, both national and international, with the risk of losing their identity and original purpose. Thus peasant organisations may be threatened with the withdrawal of financial support by their sponsors if they become too radical. This seems to have been the case in Ecuador where a strong peasant and labour organisation of Christian socialist origin, CEDOC, enjoyed financial and other support from the Latin American Labour Confederation (CLAT) to which it was affiliated; this support was threatened and eventually stopped when CEDOC adopted a more radical policy and began to undertake joint activities with leftist-oriented trade unions in the country.

One way then by which peasant organisations can maintain their identity and original aims, particularly when they ally themselves with 'outside' institutions, is by being financially independent. The best example of this approach in Latin America is provided by the Unión Central de Sociedades de Crédito Colectivo Ejidal of the Laguna region in Mexico. This peasant organisation was able on many occasions to protest effectively against abuses and violations of its members' rights largely due to its financial independence and non-reliance for aid from powerful outside patronage and sponsorship. Since its inception in 1940 this union has relied on membership contributions as its major source of finance, an approach which has had the additional benefit of giving the rank and file effective control over the leadership. To supplement this source of finance the organisation also imposes a one per cent levy on the sales of agricultural produce by its members which is marketed on a co-operative basis.

It would appear then, that a proper combination of co-operative economic ventures with collective or trade union activities could enhance the financial status of peasant organisations. Financial independence is of much importance with regard to the need to promote effective peasant organisations that will not become susceptible to political favours and financial inducements from powerful outsiders.

THE NATURE AND EFFECTIVENESS OF PEASANTS' PARTICIPATION

Land Demands by Peasant Groups

Generally in Latin America as a whole peasant organisations were originally formed as a result of demands pertaining to land rights and improved tenancy conditions, broadly defined to include wages and working conditions. Experience in the region suggests though that it is apparently easier to organise peasants around specific and concrete grievances that they experience daily and feel very strongly about than, say, around wider issues such as a general agrarian reform programme. Furthermore, when, as a result of collective action over a particular local grievance, peasant groups win some benefits and concessions they tend to become more confident in their own organisational ability and are motivated towards more effective forms of organisations with interest sometimes extending beyond purely local issues. At times it is the reluctance of local landowners to negotiate or give in to moderate demands by peasant groups that provides the impetus for the formation of stronger and more radical peasant organisations.

Usually the first types of demands made by emergent peasant organisations are those relating to the payment of legal minimum wages and the abolition of unpaid services in the large landholdings or 'haciendas' where peasants are engaged as agricultural labourers. One result of success by peasant organisations, with respect to demands for higher wages, is that 'haciendas' which were once economically viable and profitable in spite of the rudimentary agricultural techniques practised become uneconomical to operate and less attractive to their owners when faced with higher labour costs. This is not at all surprising since labour has been the major factor-input, or cost of production, in the 'hacienda' system. Once the main source of profit – cheap labour – disappears from the system, the big landowners tend to become less opposed to some measures of agrarian reform, especially if the compensations paid for loss of land are sufficiently attractive. This causal chain of events probably explains why big land and estate-owners in Latin America have, with very few exceptions, initially been strongly opposed to improvements in wages and working conditions for their workers.

There are, however, cases where the effective organisation of peasants has stemmed from direct land demands as, for example, when landowners attempt to evict peasants from smallholdings or 'minifundios', which they have possessed and worked for years, for the purpose of expanding their estates. Faced with the threat of landlessness, peasants may react strongly, especially if they perceive such claims to *their* land to be illegal. In this context, it should be noted that well co-ordinated actions by strong peasant organisations against 'land grabbing' have played a more important role in precipitating measures of agrarian reform in Latin American countries than that which may be attributed to purely progressive policies on the part of governments. This is true, for example, in the case of the peasant organisation in the Convención Valley in Peru, already mentioned.

In several Latin American countries agrarian reform and land redistribution are now recognised and guaranteed by legislation, thereby giving legitimacy to some of the land demands of peasant organisations. Increasingly such demands are becoming a priority issue in the action programmes of peasant groups and they dominate discussions in meetings and assemblies at the local level, as well as congresses, rallies or conventions held at the regional or national level. Such visible manifestations of peasant solidarity and strength have been instrumental in swinging public opinion in favour of demands for the effective implementation of agrarian reform and land distribution programmes, thus bringing pressure to bear on government. In a similar vein, organised peaceful marches and demonstrations in urban centres by peasants which attract much public attention have in some cases served to strengthen the political bargaining power of their representative organisations.[20] One of the most important and immediate effects of this type of organised action by peasant organisations is the confidence which it bestows on the peasants themselves, stemming from the realisation that their cause is considered legitimate and just even by 'higher' socio-economic groups outside their own humble environment. This sympathy and even respect for their action by those whom they consider to be their superiors can have a considerable psychological effect on peasants, encouraging them to defend their rights and interests more solidly.

Peaceful and symbolic occupation and subsequent cultivation of under- or unutilised land by peasants is another means by which peasant organisations have effectively asserted their demands. The effectiveness of this method of protest could be seen from the fact that a number of official agrarian reform measures in Peru, Mexico, Colombia, Venezuela and Bolivia were put into operation following symbolic land invasion by local peasant groups.

For several reasons it seems important that long standing agrarian conflicts should now be subjected to new forms of conflict-resolution strategies. The continued suppression of legitimate demands of peasant groups, especially those pertaining to strongly felt acts of injustice, can lead to violent explosion, as has happened in the past, if the oppressed groups believe that redress and justice cannot be achieved through peaceful means. Therefore efforts should be directed towards the legitimisation and institutionalisation of peaceful forms of organised peasant protest action aimed at changing an unjust social system. Similar efforts have made the strike a peaceful but effective bargaining weapon in urban labour disputes. This is particularly important since it is precisely the lack of such institutionalised means of protest and bargaining that had led, in the past, to prolonged class conflicts, repression and consequent violent actions in the rural areas of Latin America. It is worth noting that, in the initial stages of the trade union movement in Europe, certain activities undertaken in support of legitimate demands of workers, which were then branded as 'illegal' or 'subversive', are now today legally recognised features of collective bargaining and industrial relations. There is thus a great need to analyse and appraise realistically the various tactics used by peasant organisations in conflict situations, with a view to giving legal recognition to the more effective but peaceful ones in much the same way as collective action by trade unions in urban and industrial settings. In particular, the legal and practical implications of peaceful and orderly occupations by peasants of idle land (which is sometimes held merely for speculative reasons while the mass of the rural population is landless), or land that they can legally claim according to existing agrarian reform laws, should be carefully examined.

It is often claimed, mainly by interest groups that stand to lose from agrarian reforms, that if protest is not suppressed it could lead to disorder and violence, and even disruption of economic life. But the forces involved in a conflict can be channelled and effectively directed towards a non-violent solution before they become disruptive. The orderly negotiation of peasant demands, within a framework of adequate legislation, could in fact become the basis for implementing requisite structural changes in a system without disruptive violence, as the recent experience of Peru (1968–75) has shown.[21]

Peasant Participation in Agrarian Reform

For Latin America as a whole a useful and relevant general indicator of peasants' participation in the development process is the extent and effectiveness of peasant organisations in instigating the official adoption and thorough implementation of appropriate agrarian reform measures, given that the main interests of these organisations revolve around land demands. Such an approach in fact constitutes a broad enough analytical framework that extends as well to the critical political activities of peasant organisations, in so far as agrarian reform in Latin America can be regarded as an important part of the overall political process with various socio-economic groups competing for power and control.

The Mexican agrarian reform process, which has been going on for over fifty years, illustrates the close correlation between the political power of peasant organisations and progress in agrarian reform. At those times when the peasants had political power or 'power capability' (threat of power) through organised action, land distribution proceeded at considerable speed and significant gains were made. This was clearly so in the case of the peasant groups led by Zapata in the initial stage of the Mexican Agrarian Reform Programme (1910–19) and again more recently in the late 1950s when the peasant movement headed by Jacinto López in the north-western development areas was a force to be reckoned with in national politics. During the period of the Cardenas administration (1934–40) the peasants gained influence because the Government needed their political support, and as a consequence they were able successfully to demand certain agrarian changes. But at other times when the peasant movement, for one reason or another, was politically weak and ineffective, progress with respect to the implementation of agrarian reform measures was virtually at a standstill. The fact that landlords remained in effective possession of land which was the subject of reform measures can be explained largely by their relatively greater share in political power which was grossly out of proportion to their numbers in society.

The trend showed a similar pattern of fluctuation in the other Latin American countries which had adopted large-scale agrarian reform programmes, namely Venezuela, Bolivia and Peru. In Bolivia, after years of strong opposition from vested interests, the peasant organisations in some areas became highly organised and politically strong, and succeeded in forcing a new reformist government to implement what could be

210

regarded as a radical agrarian reform programme. This consisted of *de facto* distribution of most of the available land within a period of less than a year. Eventually, this led to a fundamental change in the rural power structure and provided the reformist government with a reliable base of popular support needed to withstand pressure from the traditional rural elites.

In Venezuela a similar development took place after 1958, though the gains by peasants were relatively smaller. There the Government initially adopted an effective land reform programme mainly as a way of appealing to the peasants whose support was considered crucial for election purposes. Thus, the participation of the peasants in the agrarian reform process was institutionalised, and they were to play an important role in the execution of the programme. First, legal provisions were established which closely linked the agrarian reform process with the activities of the peasant organisations. In a given locality where land was available for distribution among the peasants, their representative organisation was required to file a petition for land after which land was legally transferred to the group as a whole. Individual peasants could not directly petition for land as this may have further complicated the process. Once land had been assigned to a peasant group, it was left with the group to decide on how it was to be distributed among the individual peasants. In some cases the distribution was decided in advance of the transfer of ownership to peasant groups. But on the whole the existence of an organised peasant group and a few elected persons who could deal with the authorities as representatives of the entire community greatly facilitated the actual implementation of the programme.

As already noted, some peasant organisations have been very successful in bringing pressure to bear on the government agency responsible for executing an agrarian reform programme. Such pressure may, however, not be necessary where the responsible authority undertakes its task efficiently and vigorously, as in the above-cited example. Peasant organisations can then direct their attention and efforts towards neutralising opposition at the local level from landowners who might try, through legal and even illegal means, to slow down or halt the process of land reform.[22]

Thus peasant organisations should not only aim at securing from government favourable land reform legislation but, perhaps more important, they should also seek to influence the implementation process, which itself might require certain structural changes simultaneously. Experience from Bolivia and elsewhere in the region indicates that it is possible to bring about a rapid and drastic transformation of the rural social structure in a non-violent manner through a conflict-resolution strategy. The participation of peasants as an organised interest group in decision making, minimises the risk of government adopting well-intentioned but, from a local point of view, inappropriate policies and projects aimed at consolidating peasants' rights to land. In Bolivia, in particular, peasant organisations became a major implementing partner of the Government in the planning and execution of agricultural projects that were introduced after land had been legally transferred to the peasants. Local peasant organisations in some cases took over collective management functions on large estates which were being farmed by individual peasants on a sort of co-operative basis. Their involvement in the day-to-day running of such estates also made it easier for the peasants to accept and adopt new production techniques and other new ideas necessary for increasing agricultural production. Similarly, the actual involvement of peasant groups in the implementation of agrarian reform in Venezuela was instrumental in ensuring the peaceful but effective execution of the programme and a number of related post-reform development projects. For example, local peasant groups actively collaborated with officials of CORDIPLAN, the Venezuelan National Community Development Programme, in the planning and implementation of two pilot agricultural projects in areas where peasant organisations had recently gained access to land within the framework of the land reform programme.

However, with reference to the participation of peasant organisations in agrarian reform, it is important that government officials who deal with peasants at the local level adopt an appropriate approach suitable to local conditions. Since most officials may have urban middle-class backgrounds, they would require relevant training in order to be able to deal with peasants in other than the paternalistic manner which often causes resentment on the part of peasants and, hence, makes a dialogue impossible.[23] On the other hand, peasants and their leaders could themselves benefit considerably from direct contacts with administrative and technical officials who are working with them – an important consideration with respect to their new roles as landowners, commercial producers and suppliers. In general, the willingness of peasants to collaborate in post-reform efforts is to a large extent determined by the extent of their participation in the reform programme itself right from the beginning: where, through their representative organisation, peasants have been consulted on major decisions, they tend to be more enthusiastic in co-operating with the government on issues of rural development. Besides, the peasants have the advantage of local knowledge which can facilitate the implementation of local development projects. In a number of cases in Bolivia peasants' knowledge of their local environment was found to be indispensable by government officials involved in field surveys and expropriation work as part of the agrarian reform process.

At the regional and national levels, the participation of peasant representatives in decision-making bodies responsible for executing agrarian reform measures can be most useful. It is perhaps no coincidence that land distribution has progressed rapidly and with less violence in Venezuela, where there are two representatives of the peasant federation on the five-man board of directors of the Instituto Agrario Nacional, than in some other countries in the region where noticeably genuine and direct peasant representation at such a high level of policy making is virtually absent. One can see a definite role for peasants' participation in the making of decisions pertaining to the definition and priorities of social needs as distinct from the purely technical or economic criteria for distribution of land in an agrarian reform programme. The planning of a land reform programme at the national level requires the making of difficult choices between economic criteria and social needs, and it is only through involving those whose livelihood is at stake in the making of key decisions that popular and widely acceptable choices can be made. Yet it is important to stress again in this context that the leaders of peasant organisations who represent their members in higher-level policy-making bodies must be truly representative of the peasantry and reflect their views. There is, as already observed, a grave danger of peasant representation falling into the hands of aspirant politicians who could use their new positions more to further their own personal ambitions than adequately to promote the interests of peasants in the context of national decision making.

CONCLUSIONS

The various experiences of peasant participation in Latin America touched upon in this chapter suggest that economic development and modernisation have not always served the interests of peasant communities. As a consequence, peasants have often organised themselves into specific interest groups and taken organised action in defence of their interests, particularly those relating to land demands and conditions of work. In this they need, and in some cases have obtained, the support of national or local government agencies to counteract fierce opposition to desirable changes and social progress from both traditional and modern economic elites, through the implementation of appropriate conflict-resolution strategies. The climate of violence which has sometimes characterised peasants' efforts to defend their interests through organised action has, to a large extent, been the spontaneous reaction of a disadvantaged group to repressive measures utilised by vested interests in rural areas – often in defiance of the law. When organised peasant action is confronted by various 'anti-participation structures',[24] peasant organis-ations tend to react strongly or even violently especially if they are faced or threatened with armed repression and denied adequate protection by the responsible authorities. Furthermore, experience has shown that when governments openly or covertly support 'structures of anti-participation' they gradually lose their credibility and legitimacy among the peasant population. The combination of loss of confidence in the ability of government to resolve rural conflicts in a just manner and the growing consciousness of peasants about their situation of relative deprivation and deteriorating standards of living, ironically as a result of modernisation, has indeed led to the adaptation of more radical forms of peasant actions to the detriment of all those concerned.

We have strongly argued, and provided much supporting evidence in this chapter that effective peasants' participation in the development process can be achieved by peaceful and orderly forms of collective action within the framework of a conflict-resolution type of development strategy. In the absence of an appropriate conflict-resolution strategy, not only can the efforts by peasant organisations to further the interests of their members easily and quickly change from peaceful to violent action but overall development itself may be adversely affected by the non-participation of the majority of the population. The basic-needs approach to development has identified popular participation as an important and indispensable requirement for alleviating poverty alongside economic growth and social progress. In the specific context of Latin America, there can be no denying the tremendous potential of the large mass of peasant population in several countries for raising output in agriculture and related sectors, once access to productive land and other requisite inputs is guaranteed. The adoption of labour-intensive techniques in agro-business, wherever this is feasible, could effectively serve both employment and income objectives of development in the rural areas. The participation of peasant organisations in decision making could contribute to a more balanced pattern of national development. Yet all of these gains would hardly be realised if the political and socio-economic structures and public institutions that are conducive to popular participation in the development process are absent within the system. The adoption and implementation of appropriate conflict-resolution strategies, as an alternative approach to development, in Latin America would go a long way towards bringing about necessary structural and institutional changes for effective peasants' participation in development in a non-violent manner.

NOTES

1 For example, see Erich Jacoby: *Agrarian unrest in south-east Asia* (Bombay/London, Asia Publishing House, 1961); Gunnar Myrdal: *Asian drama, an inquiry into the poverty of nations* (New York, The Twentieth Century Fund, 1968), vol. 1, part 2: Political Problems.

2 Irving Louis Horowitz: *Three worlds of development: The theory and practice of international stratification* (Oxford, Oxford University Press, 1966), p. 379.

3 The 'view from below' approach, as well as the illusion of 'objective' cherished by most social scientists, and the considerable misunderstanding about peasant life which results from it, have been amply dealt with in Gerrit Huizer and Bruce Mannheim

(eds): *The politics of anthropology* (The Hague/Paris, Mouton, 1984).

4 Lewis Coser: *The functions of social conflict* (New York, The Free Press, 1963).

5 Conflict-resolution development strategies as used here refer to strategies which seek to promote development through the adoption of measures aimed at correcting structural and institutional distortions and imbalances which are usually the basis of existing societal conflicts.

6 This evidence is derived mainly from action-research carried out by the author, mostly for the ILO, between 1966–1971. The main sources of evidence are Huizer: *The revolution potential of peasants in Latin America* (Lexington, Heath-Lexington Books, 1972); idem, *Peasant rebellion in Latin America* (Harmondsworth, Penguin Books, 1973); and idem, 'How peasants become revolutionaries', in *Development and Change*, Institute of Social Studies, The Hague, vol. VI, no. 3, July 1975.

7 United Nations, *Report of the world land reform conference*, 1966, Doc.E/4298/rev.1, New York, 1968, 15.

8 In Mexico, land reform legislation had existed since the time of the Mexican Revolution (1910–19), yet a dynamic land reform implementation did not take place until during the Cárdenas administration, 1934–40, which came to power through massive peasant support. During that period foreign interests in agriculture, as well as the oil industry, were mostly nationalised, and peasants were encouraged to organise in defence of their interests, as part of an overall conflict resolution strategy. Thus, acute conflicts of interest between large landowners and landless agricultural workers were made a point of departure for overall regional development efforts. In the Laguna area of Mexico, for example, after a major strike by agricultural workers in 1938 because of extremely low wages, the Government decided to implement the prevailing land reform laws in the area. Landowners were left with what the legal ceiling allowed them (150 hectares) and the rest of the immense estates were distributed among the 30 000 workers who formed a collective enterprise in each village for the continued production of cotton (the main product of the area). For details, see Clarence Senior: *Land reform and democracy* (Gainsville, University of Florida Press, 1958) and Gerrit Huizer: 'Community development, land reform and peasant organisation' in T. Shanin (ed.): *Peasants and peasant societies: Selected Readings* (Harmondsworth, Penguin Books, 1971).

9 In Cuba peasant organisations had been formed from the early 1920s to defend themselves against usurpation of their lands by – mainly foreign – plantation companies and other owners of large estates. Although the existence of peasant organisations was legally recognised for the purpose of defending existing rights, they were increasingly opposed by the companies and landlords and even by the authorities, and in particular violently oppressed during the Batista regime. This led them to turn their non-violent struggle into an outright revolutionary effort when oppression came to a climax and an alternative of armed resistance was offered by Fidel Castro and his guerilla group. The peasants joined this movement and land reform was introduced progressively in the liberated areas. Upon its accession to power, the new regime extended agrarian reform throughout the country. The author has benefited from relevant data and information provided to him by the Asociación Nacional de Agricultores Pequeños, Havana, during a field trip; see also, Antero Regalado: *Las luchas campesinas en Cuba* (Havana, 1973).

10 For further evidence, see Ernest Feder: *Strawberry imperialism* (The Hague, Institute of Social Studies, 1976).

11 See, for example, Charles Erasmus: *Man takes control: Cultural development and American aid* (Minneapolis, University of Minnesota Press, 1961).

12 Cynthia Hewitt de Alcántara: *Modernizing Mexican agriculture* (Geneva, UNRISD, 1976).

13 See Paolo Freire: *Pedagogy of the oppressed* (New York, Herder and Herder, 1972).
14 The whole problem of 'development' versus 'liberation' is well explained in Gustavo Gutiérrez: *Theology of liberation* (New York, Orbis, 1973).
15 A good account of this can be found in a collection of newspaper articles from that period in Hugo Neira: *Cuzco: Tierra y muerte* (Lima, Popuplibros Peruanos, 1964).
16 Over the last few years, Amnesty International has amply documented, with respect to Latin America, serious cases of infractions of basic human rights related to repression by powerful elites opposed to the formation of rural workers' organisations. See Amnesty International: *Yearbook of political prisoners, 1976–1979; The Republic of Nicaragua, An Amnesty International Report* (London, 1978); also Roger Plant: *Guatemala, unnatural disaster* (London, Latin America Bureau, 1978).
17 See the various Amnesty International reports mentioned above.
18 Judith Adler Hellman: *Mexico in crisis* (New York, Holmes and Meier, 1978), particularly chapter 4, p. 95 ff.
19 For details on the early years of the Peruvian land reform programme see Howard Handelman: *Struggle in the Andes. Peasant political mobilization in Peru* (Austin, University of Texas Press, 1975); and for an evaluation of the entire programme see José Matos Mar and José Manuel Mejia: *Reforma agraria y cooperativismo en al Perú*, Marzo (Instituto de Estudios Peruanos, mimeographed, 1978).
20 For some spectacular examples of this form of activity see James L. Payne: *Labour and politics in Peru. The system of political bargaining* (New Haven, Yale University Press, 1965). This tactic to win public support and sympathy for their cause has also been successfully used on several occasions by peasant organisations in the Laguna area of Mexico and in Colombia in recent times.
21 See Mario A. Malpica: *Biografia de la revolución* (Lima, Ediciones Ensayos Sociales, 1967), p. 527–32. For details about peasant mobilisation in Peru see also Howard Handelman: *Struggle in the Andes. Peasant political mobilization in Peru*, op. cit.
22 For example, it is not unknown for landlords to intimidate peasant groups which have sponsored petitions for land reform or to corrupt government officials who are responsible for implementing reform measures.
23 See Gerrit Huizer: *Rural extension and peasant motivation in Latin America and the Caribbean*, Food and Agricultural Organisation, Occasional Paper no. 2, Rome, July 1973.
24 This term came into use at the *Second UNRISD Dialogue on Participation*, Geneva, 6–7 Feb. 1978, document UNRISD/78/C.11, p. 3 ff. For specific country examples see Hugo Cabieses and Carlos Otero: *Economia Peruana: Un ensayo de interpretación*, DESCO (Lima Centro de Estudios y Promoción del Desarrollo, 1978); Antero Regalado op. cit; Thomas and Marjorie Melville: *Guatemala – another Vietnam?* (Harmondsworth, Pelican Latin American Library, Penguin Books, 1971).

8 Popular Participation: The Role and Activities of Women's Organisations in China

Elisabeth J. Croll

Over the past few decades the Government of the People's Republic of China has been explicit in its commitment to the principle of popularising political processes and creating opportunities to involve a number of traditionally oppressed groups of low social status in both local and national arenas of political and economic decision making. Women, alongside peasants and labourers, were recognised as one of the groups which, as a result of the traditional division of labour, had been deprived of the authority, skills and experience necessary for effective popular participation. Policy statements have constantly reiterated that women constitute half the population and, therefore, their participation in socio-economic development is essential to the effective mobilisation and fuller utilisation of the country's resources.[1] Besides the potential contribution of women to the development process through their involvement in political and economic decision making, Government policy has also emphasised the importance of women in decision making as a prerequisite for improving their own position in society. On numerous occasions it has been stressed that women would not derive their full share of the benefits of development as long as they were under-represented in the membership and leadership of political institutions, and occupational and community associations.

An important component of the strategy to redefine the sexual division of labour and improve the position and welfare of women has been the establishment of separate women's organisations. Since its founding in 1921 the Chinese Communist Party has maintained that women's organisations, devoted to protecting and furthering women's interests, are necessary for involving women in the political process and in a wider range of economic activities as well as for facilitating their access to productive assets and share in the control over the allocation of resources. The Chinese experience of women's organisations with reference to participation in the making and implementation of decisions which affect the satisfaction of women's own and their families' basic needs is significant and relevant. Indeed, evidence from various socio-economic spheres suggests that there may be a direct correlation between the existence of separate women's organisations devoted to female economic and political interests and the attainment of a high degree of female participation in political and economic activities.[2]

This chapter sets out to examine the premises on which the formation of women's organisations have been encouraged in China and the mechanisms, both general and gender-specific, by which the participation of women in decision making has been facilitated. It attempts to evaluate the degree to which women's organisations in China have effectively defined and expressed the needs of women, compelled attention to their demands and influenced the choice and implementation of policy alternatives. Finally, with the aim of assessing the prospects for replicating the Chinese experience in other societies, it suggests some of the factors which may have inhibited the full and effective involvement of women and their organisations in both participatory institutions and practices.

PARTICIPATORY INSTITUTIONS: THE DEVELOPMENT OF WOMEN'S ORGANISATIONS

Women's organisations form one of a number of mass organisations in China which have been established to create and reach specific constituencies such as peasants, labourers, youth or women. These mass organisations have as one of their aims the alteration of the traditional division of labour which had historically deprived certain disadvantaged groups of opportunities to influence the decision-making process and to have a share in political and economic power. Since the early 1920s the Communist Party had strongly supported and nurtured the separate organisation of women on account of their special experience of oppression and from the need to establish an independent power base for women. The oppression of women as a group – which was identified as different from the political, clan or religious oppression that they shared in common with men of their own social class – distinguished them as a special case and, indeed, a separate social category. This distinctive form of oppression was derived from the customary sexual division of labour and the inheritance of an ideology of male supremacy. These two factors, it was argued, were responsible for the low jural status assigned to women, their economic dependence, and their exclusion from 'public affairs'.

Yet, the Communist Party held the view that while a government could provide the legal basis and the material conditions favourable to improvements in the position of women, it was the women themselves who must recognise their common needs and interests and negotiate a new role for themselves within the family, the enterprise, the local community and the nation. In consonance with this view, one of the early leaders of the national women's organisation pointed out that, 'it is important to recognise that the full realisation of [women's] rights must depend upon their own struggle and cannot be bestowed upon them by others.'[3] Similarly, one local leader later made the following observation: 'It's easy enough to talk about the freeing of women, but it isn't a thing that happens of itself; even when we have a government that makes laws to give women equality with men, we have to make an effort ourselves.'[4] Women's organisations from the beginning were thus assigned a major role in encouraging women to define their interests and to intervene in the political process in defence of these interests. To this end, the Chinese Government has sponsored the establishment of local women's organisations as part of the country-wide structure of the National Federation of Women.

Local women's organisations grew out of the informal women's groups characteristic of rural and urban neighbourhoods. Although the domestic and public spheres in China were highly differentiated on a sexual basis with authority largely in the hands of the male members of the household and the local community, women's groups could, and did, influence the affairs of individual households and the village. At the local level the women's community, often made up of loose and overlapping groups, was at its most visible when women of neighbouring households gathered together at the village well or at the local market to perform their domestic chores and talk and exchange information about their situation.[5] Margery Wolf, in her study of the politics of village neighbourhoods, concluded that through such informal exchange of views the local women's group actually exercised a certain degree of influence on decision making and that the women who had most influence on village affairs were those who worked through the women's community.[6] Yet the formal establishment of local women's organisations needed more than the institutionalisation of the local women's community. Their establishment required, in addition, that women perceive of themselves as a separate social category of political importance whose interests were not always coincidental with those of their menfolk; that they speak out in defence of these interests; and that they openly and directly participate in village affairs. It was this significant step which often posed difficulties in the early years of Communist rule in China.

Women's groups were first established in the villages of rural China, or in factories and urban neighbourhoods following the arrival of specially-trained women leaders or cadres in the locality in the wake of the Communist revolution. Between the late 1930s and early 1950s these cadres covered numerous localities throughout the country, initially making contacts with individual women known to be influential in the women's community as well as with specially oppressed women such as adopted-in daughters-in-law recruited into their husband's household in early childhood or deviant women who earned a living in one of the few occupations open to women like midwifery or sorcery. Over time the cadres were able to persuade members of the women's community to organise themselves formally in defence of their common interests.[7]

Attempting to organise the women in this manner, however, was never an easy task. In some cases the very sight of the young uniformed and free-striding urban-educated girl cadres was enough to frighten the local peasant women indoors.[8] Sometimes it was only after the cadres had discarded their uniforms, donned peasant clothing and begun to help with washing and babysitting that the peasant women could be encouraged to talk about their lives and openly admit their suffering and subordination.[9] Then came the task of persuading them that only through recognition of their common grievances and the formation of separate women's groups to redress those grievances would they be able to identify effectively, claim and defend new rights. In many cases, when meetings were first held, the women often responded with a certain degree of scepticism to the idea of making women the equals of men and thereby changing the traditional role of women in relation to their menfolk in the society: 'Of course it would be wonderful if women were the equals of men, but what chance did they have if from ancient times till now men had been the Heaven and women the Earth'. One of the leaders of the Women's Federation noted that in those early days the fight to eradicate the idea that women knew nothing but household affairs was particularly difficult, nor was it easy to give women a sense of collective purpose and importance.[10] Thus, women cadres were constantly exhorted by the Communist Party to adopt a 'practical and factual approach' based on the specific needs of the women in the local community or factory, and they were repeatedly warned against adopting slogans for the women's movement, mapping out plans in the abstract and setting up women's meetings needlessly when women were already beset by many family responsibilities and problems of earning a livelihood.[11]

Difficulties pertaining to attempts at organising women in China also arose from the fact that rural and urban women were divided by social class and generation gap. Thus, initially, women's groups were often identified with one category of women to the disadvantage of other women. For example, poor peasant women, such as adopted-in daughters-in-law, found their interests to be neglected relative to those of women from richer households,[12] or richer women boycotted meetings of women's groups and sent their menfolk or servants instead implying that such meetings were attended by women of ill-repute or a low social order.[13] There was also a tendency for women's groups to become the monopoly of the younger generation or daughters-in-law who had no support or power base of even the most informal kind within the household. Not surprisingly the older generation – for example mothers-in-law who had at last gained a position of relative respect and authority within the household – felt threatened by women's organisations to whom defiant daughters-in-law and servant girls could turn for protection.

In the early days of women's organisations in China, housewives (individually and collectively) found it difficult to counter the opposition of their menfolk to the extension of their activities beyond the domestic sphere. Husbands, fearing that their wives might go astray, objected to their attending public meetings. Individually, women usually encountered much difficulty and found the path to emancipation as 'rough as stones' if their elders did not approve.[14] Collectively, as women organised themselves into a separate association, attended public meetings and entered political life, they frequently encountered increased opposition which sometimes took quite virulent forms.[15]

A major contributing factor to the widespread acceptance and eventual establishment of women's organisations as a form of participatory institution was the absence of men in local communities during the anti-Japanese war (1941–45) and the Civil War (1946–49). This necessitated and led to the appropriation of new political and economic roles by women. Also the acceptance of women's organisations by rural women was noticeably easier when these were linked to such practical endeavours as agricultural work teams, co-operative handicraft ventures or literacy groups.[16] These occupation-related women's groups were later to play an important supporting role in solving practical and emotional problems of their members. This itself could be regarded as a condition for raising consciousness and awareness of grievances and particular needs among a hitherto oppressed social group.

Once established local women's organisations, centred on enterprises and other places of work or in the urban and rural neighbourhoods, take on a variety of forms such as practical work teams, study groups or 'exchange of experience' groups. The main aim has been to pursue activities and interests that meet the immediate needs of members in a particular context. Each group elects delegates to attend and represent its opinions at local women's conferences where issues pertaining to conditions of work and life of women are discussed and decisions are taken on the ways and means of influencing policy in the right direction.[17] Throughout the country women's representative conferences are held periodically at various administrative levels, ranging from the production brigade, commune or urban enterprise and neighbourhood to the county, city, municipality, province and finally the national level. The main functions of these conferences are to discuss policies and systematically review past performance of the women's organisations in their respective localities; to formulate and adopt new programmes of work; and to elect delegates to higher-level women's conferences and political leadership committees at equivalent administrative levels.

PARTICIPATORY PRACTICES: WOMEN IN THE POLITICAL AND PRODUCTION PROCESSES

Women's organisations in China have been specifically charged with initiating, legitimising and institutionalising women's participation in decision making through formal channels. The appropriation of new political roles demanded both that women secure access to non-gender-specific participatory institutions and that they acquire the necessary skills and experience required for effective intervention in the political process. Since 1949, the recommendation by Mao Zedong that women should 'unite and take part in production and political activity to improve their economic and political status'[18] has been the major underlying principle for the establishment of the women's organisations and the basis of their links with practical activities. Furthermore, the authorities have always maintained that there is a direct correlation between the entry of women into productive employment, on the one hand, and the degree of their access to productive assets and control over the allocation of resources, on the other. It was also assumed that entry into the labour force and consequent improvement in material well-being would enable women to acquire a new independence, confidence and political power which would allow them to share in the benefits of socio-economic development. Women's organisations have played a major role in the implementation of successive government policies designed to increase production and substitute individualised peasant and handicraft production with collectivised agriculture and industrial enterprises. Their members were encouraged to take advantage of the new opportunities made available to them for a full and wide-ranging participation in the production process. Indeed, the pursuance of practical activities by women's organisations is based on the assumption that:

> . . . the mobilisation of women to participate in production is the most important link in the chain that protects women's own vital interests. . . it is necessary to begin with production for both economic prosperity and economic independence, promote the political status of women, their cultural level and improve their livelihood, thereby leading the way to emancipation.[19]

To facilitate the participation of local women in the political process, women's groups were urged to study Marxist writings and government policies in order to acquire the requisite knowledge and information and to familiarise themselves with the language of political debate. In their own local meetings women often discussed the implications of policy alternatives for women and in the process learnt how to speak out confidently and collectively when in the company of men both at home and in their work places. The National Women's Federation also arranged area training courses for leaders of women's groups and production units and circulated materials and teaching aids for instruction. Women's groups were exhorted to mediate between their own members and other equivalent organisations and political organs and to act as an external pressure group responsible for ensuring that the interests of women are not ignored or neglected by decision-making bodies. Institutional channels of communication were established by the Government to facilitate co-operation between the gender-specific and mixed organisations. For example, city branches of the National Women's Federation were expected to liaise with workers' organisations and 'to concern themselves with the establishment, improvement and progress of women workers in conjunction with these departments'.[20] To fulfil this obligation the National Women's Federation set up committees to encourage regular liaison with other organisations and to facilitate the exchange of information and opinions.

In carrying out its campaign to encourage women to participate and intervene in political decision making, the Women's Federation called upon the Communist Party and other political bodies to give women the opportunities to acquire the relevant experience that tradition has so far denied them. At the Eighth Party Congress in 1956, the Vice Chairperson of the Women's Federation spoke out against the discriminatory practices which still operated within the Communist Party itself and the inadequacy of the measures taken to counter this prejudice against women. She reprimanded the Party leaders for not having put into practice the Party's commitment to the principle of equality of representation, outlining in some detail the specific practices which invited criticism, and at the same time putting forward proposals to rectify these anomalies.[21]

The degree to which women's organisations in China have facilitated the incorporation of women into participatory institutions and their involvement in participatory practices can be evaluated on the basis of certain important criteria, as presented below.

WOMEN'S ORGANISATIONS AND THE PROMOTION OF WOMEN'S PARTICIPATION IN DECISION MAKING: AN EVALUATION

Degree of Participation and Representation

The initial value of women's organisations in instilling confidence in their members and providing them with the training and experience in political affairs necessary for full participation and equal representation in decision-making bodies became evident from certain observations reported in a document published in 1948. It was found that in areas where there were no separate women's organisations women continued to feel uncomfortable in the presence of men and few felt confident enough to speak at any of the village meetings. Women themselves had admitted that when speaking in the company of men 'those who ought to say a lot say very little'. In contrast, it was found that in other areas where women's organisations have been established, more women attended village meetings; they displayed a higher degree of enthusiasm; they participated in political affairs; and in general they had no reservations about speaking in public.[22] Other commentators have confirmed that the establishment of women's organisations did initially encourage women to speak out for themselves and to openly and directly participate in political affairs. One resident in a village in the north of China in the late 1940s observed that within the women's associations, wives and daughters-in-law 'untrammelled by the presence of their menfolk could raise their own bitterness and encourage their sisters to do likewise' and at the same time work to bring to the village-wide gatherings the strength of 'half of China'.[23] Fellow workers of the Vice Chairperson of the Peking No. 2 Cotton Mill's Revolutionary Committee could remember back to the days when she was a shy and timid girl who would blush even when learning to speak out in their small group discussions.[24]

The national magazine of the Women's Federation acted as a medium of communication for informing women of current political developments and reporting on the programmes, activities and achievement of individual women and groups. In addition, the Federation held leadership courses for women and circulated materials for study and training in political skills.[25] In one village the committee members of the women's association, none of whom had had any previous experience of leadership, were sent on a fifteen-day course run by the county for training women leaders; they returned to their village greatly impressed by the course, for not only were they encouraged to discuss their past sufferings but they were also urged to express their opinions and even offer their criticisms of the course and of those who ran it. Apparently it was the fact that their opinions were solicited that impressed them most.[26] The Women's Federation also aided local women's organisations by recommending and providing them with suitable materials for study in small discussion groups. In Peking, for example, the Municipal Women's Federation helped a local neighbourhood women's committee to establish a political study group made up of housewives, mostly 'middle-aged and grey-haired grandmothers', and it was observed that as the women read widely they became more interested and concerned with affairs beyond their own doorsteps.[27]

Although women's organisations have been instrumental in promoting and increasing the level of participation by women in political decision making, there is impressionistic and quantifiable evidence to suggest that women have not as yet attained equal representation and influence in non-gender-specific participatory institutions. The experience of the past quarter-century indicates that although major changes in the structure of the economy have resulted in a significant increase in the proportion of women in wage employment as well as the creation of new participatory institutions, these have not necessarily resulted in the elimination of traditional discriminatory practices operating against women acquiring a share in political power. Remnants of the dominant traditional ideology which had advocated that women should have no say in public decision making or knowledge of political affairs and which had predicted disorder and disarray should women be allowed to break this taboo still remain to discourage and inhibit participation by women. Although today it is no longer the common practice for women to have the ethical codes in their classical forms quoted to them, yet numerous folk-sayings and proverbs – such as 'just as a mare can't go into battle, a woman can't go into politics'; 'the horse is a leader and the donkey runs between the traces'; or 'when a woman rules the roost everything is in a mess' – have been used in recent years to disparage women and belittle their contribution to social and public affairs. One women's group in Henan province reported that while it was accepted that women should enter wage employment the idea that 'politics is certainly not for them' still prevailed.[28] Another group from Guangxi reported that many women there still were in the state of 'carrying the hoe outdoors, handling the pot indoors and taking a back seat in a meeting or in study.'[29] Those women who were elected or appointed to public office often narrated personal experiences of long struggles to overcome traditional and social constraints and to gain acceptance and recognition as the equals of men in similar positions.

Ideological constraints have been identified as major obstacles to the full and effective participation of women in political affairs in China. In 1973, on the eve of the campaign to criticise Confucius and Lin Biao, a national newspaper noted that so far in China it has been impossible to eliminate totally the Confucian ideology underlying the sexual division of labour between the domestic and public spheres and the discrimination against women in the public sphere.[30] Similarly, it was observed that although new opportunities in Chinese society had made it possible for women to participate in public affairs, the training, selecting and promoting of female cadres still remained a problem. One commentator observed that this problem stemmed from the widespread belief among male cadres that women possess low cultural standards, and that also because of their 'family complications' and disabilities inherent in them it would be difficult for women to assume and effectively discharge the additional duties and responsibilities of public office. The same commentator concluded that this kind of thinking greatly lowered women's status at the local and national levels.[31] Although the campaign to criticise Confucius and Lin Biao sought to refute such ideological-based beliefs and assumptions,[32] as recently as 1975 there were reports of women workers in agriculture and industry being the object of folk sayings disparaging their contribution; according to the women concerned, this affected their morale and shaped their expectations of themselves. Although they were often offended by such sayings, they nevertheless did not know how to respond, and it took some time before individual women could overcome their inferiority complexes and defend themselves publicly or participate in political discussions.[33]

One quantifiable measure of women's participation and representation in political decision making is the number of women who are in positions of responsibility in the Communist Party, government organs and production units. It had been assumed that one of the benefits accruing to women as a result of their entry into wage employment would be access to productive assets and a share in the control or allocation of socio-economic resources. Yet an analysis of available relevant statistics indicates that the numbers of women voted into public offices, admitted to Party membership or selected for positions of decision making in government organs were not commensurate with the expansion in the total number of women workers entering employment. Taking the membership of the Communist Party and the Youth League as examples, women made up only some 10 per cent of the Party membership[34] and about 30 per cent of the membership of the Young Communist League in the 1950s.[35] At the basic level, the proportion of women among people's deputies elected in all parts of the country increased from 17.3 per cent in 1953[36] to only 22.4 per cent in 1963.[37]

The situation improved only slightly in the 1970s. Of the six million new members admitted to the Communist Party between 1966 and 1973, just over 27 per cent were reported to be women.[38] However, in the provincial congresses of the newly reconstituted Young Communist League an average of 40 to 60 per cent of the delegates in 1973 were women.[39] In 1972 women were said to account for 16 to 20 per cent of all Party and revolutionary committees at the district, xian and bureau levels in Peking.[40] In Shanghai in the same year, women cadres accounted for 17 and 22 per cent respectively of the city's Party and revolutionary committees,[41] while in Henan province they accounted for 30 per cent of cadres of the Rural Production Brigades.[42]

With one notable exception – that is the urban neighbourhood residents' committees where women usually form a large majority of the membership – the degree of women's participation and involvement in the political process at both local and national levels – as measured in both relative and absolute terms – was often far from consistent with the ideal of equality of representation up to the 1970s. Furthermore, the anomaly has not been only with respect to the numbers of women participating in formal political institutions, but also in terms of the quality of their representation in decision-making bodies at all levels, which is, perhaps, more crucial to the effective participation and intervention of women in the political process. The disproportionate representation of women in decision-making bodies has been the source of disappointment and dissatisfaction as was candidly reported in a leading newspaper.[43]

Effectiveness of Participation and Intervention

From their early days the very presence of women's organisations began to alter the balance of power within households and in rural and urban neighbourhoods or enterprises. An anthropologist working in a south China village in the early 1950s noted that the novel presence of an independent organisation of women concerned with public affairs 'was itself a new phenomenon of considerable importance; something entirely out of context in the social order based on the sexual division of labour and the seclusion of women from public affairs'.[44] The existence of an alternative source of power was a potential threat to that of the household head and village elders, and for the first time women were able to seriously challenge their traditional authority. Reports exist of many instances when individual women turned to newly formed women's groups for support in resolving a difficult or oppressive domestic situation. It was not unknown for chauvinistic fathers-in-law or husbands to be publicly called on by women's associations to explain their conduct.[45]

These associations also enabled women to initiate action and to intervene collectively to defend their newly won political rights to participate in neighbourhood and enterprise forums of discussion and decision making. In one area the attempt by men to redistribute land according to the provisions of the Agrarian Reform Law without involving the women of the village was halted by women's collective criticism and action. Originally the women's organisation had not been invited to attend a meeting of the peasants' association, and the all-male meeting had ruled that girls under a certain age should not be eligible for a share in land that was to be distributed. The local women's organisations drew attention to the law, and successfully demanded another meeting at which they were represented and had the original decision rescinded.[46] In another village where women had been excluded from the first village elections, the women's association refused to recognise the newly elected head of the village. The association reinforced its intervention by collective action which took the form of its members withdrawing their labour at home. This action led to the recognition of the right of women to participate in village elections and in a re-run of the elections the association had one of its members elected deputy head of the village.[47]

At the national level the Women's Federation has also intervened and apparently influenced the choice of the policy measures in certain instances. In the early 1950s it was the Women's Federation which brought to public notice the increasing resistance to and abuse of the new Marriage Law. The Federation drew attention and gave wide publicity to cases involving forceful and even violent opposition of the older generation to changes advocated in the law, genuine misunderstanding of the law, and examples where its abuse was clearly due to the chauvinistic attitude of local Party leaders and cadres. One report identified the cadres' ignorance and suppression of the new legal rights of women and how they abused their new positions of authority as the greatest obstacle to the implementation of the law.[48] It was mainly as a result of reports by the Federation on the difficulties of implementing the new law that the government decided to investigate the situation towards the end of 1952, and consequently launched a new campaign to popularise and enforce the provisions of the Marriage Law in March 1953. Again during the heated debates of the early 1950s over whether birth control should be made widely available, the Women's Federation organised a campaign to show its opponents that there was indeed a demand for birth control. At a time when the large population of China was considered to be its greatest strength and birth control was viewed as either unnecessary or immoral, the women's organisations published articles arguing strongly that the need to plan and space families was in the interests of women. They argued that the age of marriage was so low that many women still in their early twenties had 4 or 5 children, and 7 or 8 by the time they reached thirty: 'This is a heavy burden on them and it was from such considerations that the question of birth control arises'. In support of their position the Women's Federation published a survey carried out in Peking which showed that the majority of women wanted information on birth control.[49] Eventually the government responded to these and other pressures and subsequently began to popularise and promote the practices of birth control in 1955.

Despite the few examples of success cited above, there is also evidence that overall women's organisations have found it increasingly difficult to intervene to protect or further their members' interests. Indeed, activists in women's organisations have often found themselves pushed to the defensive and arguing for the existence of their own separate organisations that have been established specifically to draw attention to the needs and interests of women. Even several years after its establishment, the Vice Chairperson of the National Women's Federation found it necessary at

228

the Eighth Party Congress in 1956 to argue that the discrimination against women was still such that it was necessary to sustain their separate organisations which would collectively 'give expression to their aspirations, protect their rights and interests as well as those of their children, and supervise the implementation of the policy and decrees regarding the equality of men and women'.[50]

As a matter of fact, local groups often lacked vitality or purpose and as a consequence were allowed to lie dormant or abolished because they were thought to be no longer necessary.[51] The popular and limited definition of 'emancipation' or 'liberation', taken to mean mere entry into social production, had itself caused some groups to conclude that their goals had been achieved once most of their members became engaged in wage employment. Moreover, the women leaders and activists themselves often felt that as long as the construction of a socialist society proceeded apace, improvements in the position of women would automatically follow. In these circumstances, women's organisations were assumed to be at best a temporary and secondary phenomenon, and many women preferred to participate actively in class associations or general leadership bodies rather than in gender-specific organisations. The Women's Federation criticised this tendency to neglect the female constituency and to regard the work of women's organisations as a subsidiary and less urgent task lying outside the mainstream of economic and political activities.[52] A document published by the Women's Federation in the early 1960s criticised those who could not be bothered by the apparently 'petty needs' of women as well as the narrow outlook of so many women themselves. It re-emphasised the importance of women's organisations as a necessary component of socialist development and one that demanded as much attention as any other form of political activity:

> It must be realised first of all that every kind of work is part of the revolutionary work, and that the work among women is an indispensable part of the work of socialist revolution and socialist construction... and is something which women cadres should do wholeheartedly and energetically... It is certainly not something of no importance or something which it is entirely up to oneself to do or not to do. The view that work among women is tedious and troublesome, does not involve any policy, and does not have any political significance is wrong.[53]

The preoccupation of the Women's Federation with arguments to defend the very existence of a specifically female constituency and the continuing discrepancy in the distribution of the benefits of production between the sexes suggest that women's organisations have not intervened sufficiently to bring about an equitable distribution of the benefits of a socialist society. It has been assumed that once women entered social production they would acquire an equitable share of the fruits of production. Women have indeed entered the labour force in large numbers and they have acquired a new measure of economic independence, but despite constant campaigns to institute 'equal pay for equal work', their levels of remuneration are consistently lower in both agriculture and industry. Women still tend to be allocated to certain gender-specific occupations which often receive a lower evaluation and remuneration, and even where they perform the same jobs as men they are not consistently equally rewarded.[54]

Furthermore, in cases where women's interests may be seen to conflict simultaneously with overall priorities of development, women's organisations have not intervened sufficiently to effect a reallocation of socio-economic resources in their favour. In the late 1950s policies to socialise as many domestic tasks as possible by taking them out of individual households and establishing the relevant community services were implemented on a wide scale. But in actual fact, the experimental collectivisation of household chores within the rural commune, or urban neighbourhood, that was intended to either substitute or at least supplement individual household tasks such as child care, processing of foods, cooking of meals, laundry and sewing, was short lived. Although policies aimed at the collectivisation of domestic chores were apparently popular among women, they failed mainly as a result of the considerable expenses that would be involved in replacing the formerly unpaid domestic labour of women by paid labour in the public sector.[55] The institutionalisation of the policy decision to reduce household chores undertaken by women required large-scale (re-)allocation of socio-economic resources to the service and consumer sectors of the economy, and it seems that without the backing of a specifically committed and powerful female constituency advocating the requisite changes, individual women committee members of local production units may not on their own have been able to press for the required allocation of resources. Some women representatives, on their own admission, were not conscious of their responsibilities and were 'sleeping partners' on enterprise management committees. One woman member recalled how she had sat silent at her brigade management committee meetings, more preoccupied by thoughts of her own household and children than with the collective interests of women and the affairs of the community or state.[56]

In making an evaluation of the extent to which women's organisations have effected a redistribution of political and economic power and authority in their favour, the tremendous changes in the conditions under which women now live and work must also be recognised. Almost without exception, women now enjoy a higher standard of living with respect to consumption of the basic necessities of food, clothing, housing, health care and education than before the revolution. Most women have entered employment at some time and have acquired a measure of economic independence. The elevation of women to positions of responsibility and

230

management marks a new and significant phase in Chinese politics. Women's organisations have, with varying degrees of success, drawn attention to the particular needs of women and effectively intervened in favour of their constituency in the political and production processes. However, evidence also exists to suggest that their existence has not automatically resulted in the active defence of specifically female interests in all cases. Despite the presence of women's organisations in participatory institutions at all levels and their crucial role in creating and utilising favourable opportunities for women to participate in political and economic decision making, the extent and effects of their intervention in the making and implementation of policies have not always been what may be considered commensurate with the numeral strength of their constituency. The inablility of women's organisations to intervene sufficiently at all times may not be due so much to their failure to perceive the anomalies of the existing situation as well as the sources of prejudice and discrimination (although at times this may be so) but, perhaps, more so to the pressures on the time and energy of women and the conflicting demands on their loyalty arising out of the specific socio-political structure operating in contemporary China.

Obstacles to Participation

Policies introduced to encourage women to participate in politics and collective decision making have been jeopardised by the dual demands of production and domestic labour on the time and energy of women once they had entered employment on a wide scale. Thus, it has been pointed out in numerous newspaper articles over the years that every effort should be made to avoid making the entry of women into new political and economic activities an additional burden of work and strain, implying that the traditional division of labour assigning domestic labour to women prevents them from acquiring the new decision-making positions in society. Despite policies to socialise domestic tasks and equally distribute these between men and women within the household, women still largely perform domestic chores in both the rural and urban areas.[57] In the rural areas especially, domestic tasks are quite substantial because the household is still a unit of production, albeit on a smaller scale, and this combined with the persistence of the traditional division of labour means that women have to engage themselves in the provision and processing of food as well as the general servicing of the household. At the local level the competition for the time and energy of women by domestic and public duties has been particularly acute, given that many of the political leadership positions, apart from being unpaid, are part-time and often coincide with the times of peak demands on women's domestic labour such as lunch times and the evenings. In those circumstances women themselves have had to be persuaded of the benefits of participation in gender-specific and general class forums and management committees, in addition to the struggle to convince their menfolk that women are capable of holding responsible positions in public affairs and as such should be encouraged to acquire political skills and aspire to public positions.

Popular prejudices and sex stereotyping in the rural areas for example are reinforced by the fact that a peasant woman faces structural constraints at every stage of her life cycle. Young women who are unmarried and therefore often have fewer domestic responsibilities and more time and energy for other activities are often considered as only 'temporary' members of the villages of their birth since they are expected to leave on marriage; for this reason it is not considered worthwhile to train them for positions of responsibility in the community. Women who are already married and have children are more likely to concern themselves with motherhood and servicing of their households. Moreover, if, as is usual, they move to their husband's village, they are considered as 'outsiders' and it might take some time before they become familiar with a new political arena and build up their own networks of support and communication. Women may also find it difficult to participate fully in decision-making bodies, such as production units, which have permanent male members related to them through kinship ties. Further, it was expected of older women to retire from public life and devote their time to meeting the demands of domestic labour; hence, older women often withdrew from collective production units upon the marriage of their sons and, therefore, in effect also withdrew from the arena of decision making. Their withdrawal coincides with the period in their life cycle when their experience and knowledge of local affairs might have enabled them to take full advantage of the opportunities for participation.

The second factor which may have increasingly inhibited the effective participation and intervention of women's organisations, as well as pushed them on the defensive once they had initiated substantial changes in the position of women, is the apparent conflicting role of women as members of gender-specific organisations within the Chinese political structure. The existence of separate social groups has been viewed as a tendency towards stratification of the society on class basis and, therefore, one that should be discouraged in the struggle to promote the requisite social changes in China. Although the historical subordination of women was sufficient justification for the establishment of their own organisations, the functions and activities of these organisations were acceptable only in so far as these were not based on the premise that there existed an abstract 'class-less' group, namely women. Rather, each sex was perceived to be inherently divided into classes, the nature of which primarily determined their social attitudes and priorities, and the government expected that women's organisations should play a key role in arousing consciousness of existing class interests and to participate fully in the continuous struggle to eradicate class divisions within their ranks.

Moreover, in cases of conflict between the interests of class and those of gender, the interests of the former were to take priority.[58] While in theory the fulfilment of the goals of class and women's organisations were seen to be mutually compatible and interdependent, in practice there has been an uneasy relationship between the two.[59] Indeed, the conflict of the dual objectives has caused some controversy within the government regarding the definition of the scope of activities and methods of work of women's organisations; and concomitantly this has resulted in competing claims on the loyalty of women within the women's organisations.

In general, opinion has been divided on the question of whether women should primarily identify with their sex or with their class. Should women exclusively join women's organisations or, alternatively, class assoc-iations, or should they assume a dual political role and join both which would entail doubling their duties and responsibilities? One article, published in the Party magazine in 1964 under the title 'How the Problem of Women Should be Viewed?', analysed the present state of the women's movement and revealed that there was some controversy between the view that solidarity among women was paramount, and the other that priority should be accorded to class solidarity. The controversy, it noted, was centred around whether the divisions between the sexes or those between classes were the primary divisions in society. 'Was it possible to distinguish a single female, as opposed to male, conception of life, and if so, how far were the widely disparate social attitudes of different classes of women sufficient to divide women one from another and cancel out the basis for their separate organisations?'[60] It seems likely that this and similar controversies affected the types of demands, the orientation and priority of policies and the abilities of the female constituency to intervene in the political and production processes and to further women's interests.[61] Certainly, the controversies within the government and the women's movement over these issues and the increasing tendency to think that perhaps women's organisations had outlived their usefulness led to their demise as national and local functioning organisations on the eve of the Cultural Revolution in the mid-1960s.

The Overall Contribution of Women's Organisations

An important test of the value of separate women's organisations within the context of the political process occurred during the Cultural Revolution when Chinese women experienced a period without the support and intervention of their own organisations. The Government had often been tempted to incorporate women directly into non-gender-specific (i.e. mixed) class and government bodies on the assumption that once general social consciousness about the nature and causes of the subordination of women was sufficiently high, these bodies would themselves take the initiative and responsibility for introducing and adopting policies that seek to improve the situation of women. During the Cultural Revolution the Government, accordingly, proceeded to incorporate women directly into the same political and vocational groups as men. In the absence of their own separate organisations, there were special efforts to include women in the class struggle that characterised the Cultural Revolution, and the very definitions of class terminologies were deliberately broadened to include attitudes to and of women. Indeed, there is some evidence to suggest that women did take a significant part in the event of the Cultural Revolution both at the national and, in particular, the local levels.[62] For instance, when the Swedish writer Jan Myrdal returned to Liuling village in 1969, seven years after his previous visit, he found that one of the greatest changes in the village was the attendance of women at political meetings. Women had acquired this right during the Cultural Revolution when, as a reaction to the endless stream of excuses made to deny them participation, they had directly put the question to the local brigade: 'Are we, or are we not, to participate in political work?'. This question gave rise to much discussion about the role of women, and in the end the brigade accepted and adopted the principle that women should have the same right as men to go to meetings. Practical measures to facilitate the participation of women – for example arrangements for babysitting – were also adopted to support this principle, so that 'it wouldn't only be the men who spoke at meetings and decided things'.

There is, nevertheless, evidence to suggest that women lost their ability to intervene and to call attention to, and further their special interests during the Cultural Revolution. Certainly at both the national and local levels there was little attention given in the media to the position of women in society after the suspension of the National Women's Federation and its magazine. Articles published in newspapers after the Cultural Revolution and this author's own interviews conducted in China in 1973 substantiate the impression that many individuals, associations and enterprises gave little attention to furthering women's interests. When members of the revolutionary committee assumed responsibility for the political affairs of Lochang xian, for example, it was stressed that since women would be involved in all aspects of its work, it was therefore unnecessary to have a woman cadre specially representing women's interests. Yet the absence of separate women's organisations to further the interests and representation of the female constituency resulted in the neglect of its interests; the revolutionary committee had much more work to do than it could cope with to the extent that it was not possible for it to devote time and attention specifically to the gender-specific concerns and needs of women.[63] Similarly, in Henan province it was reported that during the Cultural Revolution the local revolutionary committees either thought that anything they could do would have little bearing on the general position of women or tended to assume that 'since work in every field included women' there was no need to concern themselves with their interests as a separate group.[64] In 1968 an article in a Shanghai newspaper had generally warned revolutionary committees against the new tendency to operate a facade by 'showing concern for women without involving the women themselves'.[65] This author's own interviews with municipal and local leaders of women's groups in the summer of 1973 also suggested that revolutionary committees had tended to ignore women's interests. Many of those interviewed said that, as a result of the experience of the Cultural Revolution, they had learned that it was not only enough to include women generally in political work in various fields, but more important, in their view, is the need for collective representation of women on decision-making bodies and the ability to intervene actively in support of the special needs and interests of the female constituency.[66] It would appear then that it was mainly as a result of the experience of women at the hands of the revolutionary committees during the Cultural Revolution that the need for separate women's organisations was once again given wide recognition, thereby leading to their re-establishment in the late 1960s and early 1970s.

CONCLUSIONS: LESSONS AND PROSPECTS

The recent revival of separate organisations for women in China is itself a manifestation of their value in representing women's interests; during the Cultural Revolution when they were inactive, the women themselves had felt this to be a disadvantage. At the same time as there has been a renewed emphasis on the value of separate women's participatory institutions, there has also been a reiteration of the principle of the interdependence of women's and other class and general government organisations.[67] The main function of women's organisations is once again perceived to be dual: (a) to further the gender-specific interests of women, and (b) to raise the class consciousness of women in the overall class struggle. The competing claims on the time and loyalty of women have once again been theoretically resolved by giving priority to the class struggle on the grounds that without the establishment of a socialist (classless) society there can be few benefits to be derived by the masses from the development process. How the dual demands and competing claims that have characterised the history of women's organisations (sometimes affecting their ability to define independently the needs of women and represent their interests) can be juxtaposed in practice, when their interests seem to conflict, remains as yet to be seen.

In China one of the aims of the separate women's organisations has been to facilitate women's participation in political and socio-economic decision making. This chapter has attempted to evaluate the degree to which women's organisations have been successful in defining and expressing the needs of women, compelling attention to their demands and influencing policies within the political process. The analysis undertaken suggests that although these organisations may have been more effective in soliciting women's support for government policies than in influencing the adoption of policies to serve women's needs, they have nevertheless fulfilled a very important function in providing the female constituency with the skills and experience necessary for effective participation in the political and production processes. In China the tensions produced by the sexual division of labour and the inherent difficulty of combining class interests with the special interests of women within the same political process have affected the ability of women to intervene effectively on their own behalf. At the same time, the experience of women in China during the absence of their own separate organisations suggests a direct correlation between the presence of women's organisations devoted to the promotion of female participation in political and socio-economic decision making, on the one hand, and the furtherance of women's interests in society, on the other.

Against a background of increasing interest in the position of women in international circles and given the rising consciousness among women in China in particular and the Third World in general, the potential of women's organisations globally may now be even greater. In the meantime, an examination of the experience of China over the past few decades provides an opportunity to observe the mechanisms and conditions required for establishing and operating women's organis-ations, including structures and activities and the often ambiguous relationship between gender-specific and mixed national and local organisations. The Chinese experience itself cannot be regarded as applicable and relevant to each of the wide variety of socio-political systems that exist globally, but its lessons should be particularly useful and of much interest to all those concerned with and intent on redefining the position of women in favour of their greater and more effective participation in the political process and in socio-economic development wherever they may be.

NOTES

1 'Resolution of the Communist Party, 1939' in Brandt, et al.: A documentary history of Chinese communism (Cambridge, Harvard University Press, 1962), p. 326.
2 P. Sanday: 'Towards a theory of the status of women' American Anthropologist, New Hampshire, American Anthropologist Association, 1973, pp. 1682–1700; C. Hoffer: 'Bundu: Political implications of female solidarity' in D. Raphael (ed.): Being female (The Hague, 1975).
3 Deng Yingzhao: Renmin Ribao (People's Daily), 26 May 1950.
4 Shen Jilan: 'How we become equal' in China Reconstructs, March 1955.
5 M. Yang: A Chinese village, Taitou, Shantung Province (New York, Columbia University Press, 1945), p. 153.

6 M. Wolf: 'Chinese women: Old skills in a new context' in M. Rosaldo and C. Lamphere (eds): *Women in culture and society* (Stanford, Stanford University Press, 1974).

7 D. Cusack: *Chinese women speak* (London, 1959), p. 198; M. Selden: *The Yanan way in revolutionary China* (Cambridge, Mass., Harvard, 1971), p. 116.

8 I. Epstein: *The people's war* (London, 1939), p. 249.

9 Xu Guang: 'Women's liberation through struggle' in *China Reconstructs*, 1 March 1973.

10 D. Cusack, op. cit., p. 198.

11 Cai Chang: 'Welcome the new policy in women work', Mar. 1943, in All China Democratic Women's Federation (ACDWF): *Documents of the women's movement* (Peking, 1949).

12 I. and D. Crooks: *Revolution in a Chinese village* (London, 1959), pp. 100–104.

13 A. Smedley: *Battle hymn for China* (London, 1944), p. 190.

14 Yang Yu: 'The story of Dong Yulan' in *People's China*, 16 Dec. 1954.

15 W. Hinton: *Fanshen* (New Yoprk, Pantheon Books 1966), p. 157.

16 Yang Yu, op. cit.; J. Myrdal: *Report from a Chinese village* (London, 1967), pp. 285–6.

17 'Women work in the rural districts of the liberated areas', 20 Dec. 1948, in *Documents of the Women's Movement*, op. cit.

18 Mao Zedong: *Women of new China*, 20 July 1949.

19 Cai Chang, op. cit.

20 Report of Women's Federation: *Survey of World Broadcasts*, no. 217, 11 Jan. 1953, p. 24.

21 Deng Yingzhao, Speech in *Report of the Eighth Party Congress* (Peking, FLP, 1956).

22 D. Davin: 'Women in the liberated areas', in M. Young (ed.): *Women in China: Studies in social change and feminism*, Michigan Papers in Chinese Studies (University of Michigan, Centre for Chinese Studies), no. 15, 1973, pp. 80–81.

23 Hinton, op. cit., p. 157.

24 E. Croll: 'Women in the trade unions' in *China Now*, Mar. 1975.

25 'Teaching materials on duties relating to work with rural women', in *Zhongguo Funu (Women of China)*, 1 Feb. 1962.

26 I. and D. Crooks, op. cit., p. 45.

27 *Women of China*, no. 3, Mar. 1965.

28 'Report of the writing group, Henan Provincial Revolutionary Committee' *Honggi (Red Flag)*, no. 10, 1 Sept. 1971.

29 'Investigation and report on the Tungchin, Guarangxi' *Honggi* (Red Flag), no. 2, 1 Feb. 1971.

30 *Renmin Ribao* (People's Daily), 8 March 1973.

31 Xia Ping: 'Make energetic efforts to train women cadres' in *Honggi* (Red Flag), 1 Dec. 1973.

32 *Honggi* (Red Flag), 1 July 1974: E. Croll: 'The anti-Lin Biao and Confucian campaign: A new stage in the ideological revolution of women' *Australian and New Zealand Journal of Sociology*, Feb. 1976.

33 *New China News Analysis*, 7 Mar. 1975; *China Reconstructs*, Mar. 1975.

34 J. Lewis: *Leadership in Communist China* (New York, 1963), p. 109.

35 *Renmin Ribao*, 3 May 1959.

36 *New China News Analysis*, 22 Sept. 1959.

37 *Peking Review*, 8 Jan. 1965.

38 *Renmin Ribao*, 1 July 1973.

39 J. Maloney: *Current Scene*, vol. XII, no. 3–4, 1976.

40 *New China News Analysis*, 11 Mar. 1972.

41 ibid., 16 Mar. 1973.

42 *Renmin Ribao*, 6 Mar. 1972.
43 ibid., 8 Mar. 1973.
44 D.K.A. Yang: *A Chinese village in early communist tradition* (Boston, 1959), p. 157.
45 Hinton, op. cit., p. 158; J. Beldon: *China shakes the world* (London, 1951), pp. 289–310.
46 ACDWF: *Women of new China* (Peking, FLP), p. 36.
47 Beldon, op. cit., p. 316.
48 Report in *Renmin Ribao*, 29 Sept. 1951.
49 Chou Ngo-fan: 'Birth control in China' *People's China*, 1 June 1957.
50 Deng Yingzhao: 1956 speech, op. cit.
51 I. and D. Crooks: *The first years of Yangyi commune* (London, 1966), p. 251; Myrdal, op. cit., p. 239.
52 Editorial, *Renmin Ribao*, 8 Mar. 1978.
53 'Reference materials for training basic-level women cadres' *Zhongguo Funu*, Feb. 1962.
54 E. Croll: *Women in rural development: The People's Republic of China* (Geneva, ILO, 1979).
55 I. and D. Crooks, op. cit., 1966, pp. 68–71, 157–158.
56 J. Myrdal and G. Kessle: *China: The revolution continued* (London/New York, Pantheon Books, 1973), p. 116.
57 Xia Ping, op. cit.
58 Xu Guang, op. cit.; 'Interview with Ding Ling' in G. Stein: *The challenge of Red China* (London, 1945), p. 206.
59 See E. Croll: *Feminism and socialism in China* (London, Routledge and Kegan Paul, 1978).
60 Wan Mujan: 'How the problem of women should be viewed' in *Honggi*, 28 Oct. 1964.
61 *Zhongguo Funu* (Women of China), July 1966; ibid., Aug. 1966; ibid., Sept. 1966.
62 'Cadres in Henon' in *Renmin Ribao*, 15 Nov. 1969; 'Training women cadres in Dazhai' *Peking Review*, 30 Mar. 1973.
63 'Report of the Revolutionary Committee, Lochang Xian, Guangdong Province' *Honggi*, no. 2, 1 Feb. 1971.
64 'Report of the Writing Group, Henan Provincial Revolutionary Committee', op. cit.
65 'Role of women on Revolutionary Committees' in *Wenhuibao* (Shanghai Newspaper), 14 June 1968.
66 E. Croll, op. cit., 1978, pp. 319–23.
67 Wang Ze: *Peking Review*, 8 Mar. 1973; Su Guang, ibid., 8 Mar. 1974.

9 Participatory Development at the Local Level in Bangladesh: A Case Study of the Ulashi-Jadunathpur Self-Help Canal-Digging Project

Muhiuddin Khan Alamgir

When Bangladesh became independent from Pakistan at the end of 1971, the economy was almost totally dependent on low-productivity agriculture characterised by an extremely unfavourable man/land ratio.[1] The damages of war compounded the already fragile state of the economy to increase the extent and magnitude of poverty.[2] Being poorly endowed with natural resources and served by essential services and basic infrastructure that were in a poor state of repair and at any rate grossly inadequate in relation to actual demand and needs, the basis for reconstruction and sustained growth was extremely tenuous. At the same time, the country was experiencing a very high rate of population growth – estimated at about 2.8 per cent in 1972 – which effectively posed a threat to development prospects in terms of significantly raising the standard of living of the mass of the population. Right from its birth, Bangladesh was therefore a real test case of development.[3]

In the rural areas where the majority of the country's population live and work, the nature and extent of poverty was closely linked to the serious under-utilisation of labour due mainly to lack of access to productive assets, especially land. In the context of the post-war reconstruction programme, the immediate task confronting the new Government then was to create sufficient productive employment opportunities for the country's teeming millions. These people now had high hopes and rising expectations concerning their material well-being in what they regarded as a new socio-political order and apparently just society compared to the one from which they had just won their liberation.

The Government, in full awareness of the development problems it had inherited and the limitations on its own resources, assigned a key role to popular participation in the development process as an important means of reducing poverty and spreading the benefits of development more widely than hitherto had been the case. Thus the first Five-Year Development Plan, 1973–78, which similarly had poverty alleviation and equitable growth among its main objectives, identified local self-help projects as an integral part of the development path to be pursued by the nation.[4] Although such projects had existed in the former East Pakistan, they were essentially devoid of any meaningful degree of genuine popular participation in the decision-making process. Local-level development planning has historically been characterised by non-participation of the people in the making and implementation of decisions which affected their livelihood.[5]

In the pre-independence period, the best known attempt to involve local population groups in the development process was made through the *Works Programme* (WP) which was launched in the early 1960s within the framework of Pakistan's 'Basic Democracies'.[6] The WP, which was later expanded and modified to become the Thana Irrigation Plan (TIP), was launched as an instrument for channelling increased levels of public investment into infrastructural and irrigation projects in the rural areas under the joint co-ordination of the central Government and formal local government authorities – that is, Union, Thana and District Councils, or *Parishads* as these authorities became known later.[7] While the WP was fairly effective in terms of redirecting public investment to the rural areas, at least in the initial period, the programme was not successful in promoting popular participation at the grass-roots level for a number of reasons.

First, the centralised organisational structure of the WP made it impossible effectively to decentralise decision-making powers and resources to the village level; accordingly, decisions on choice of projects and mode of implementation often did not reflect popular local needs and aspiration. In many cases, the WP at the local level led to an alliance between local rural elites and the administrators which often worked against the interests of the masses. Second, and as a consequence, the types of projects undertaken within the WP benefited mainly the land-endowed and land-rich – a factor which led to the erosion of popular support and confidence and effectively militated against the enthusiastic participation of the landless and the poor in such projects. Finally, the use of the formal institutional structure of the 'Basic Democracies' to implement the WP served essentially a political motive which was incompatible with economic welfare. Apart from monopolising decision-making powers, the local bureaucracy and elites were able to claim official support for their actions and activities which often served to maintain existing privileges for the rich and thereby accentuate inequalities. At best, the WP turned out to be paternalistic and 'pro-patronage' rather than genuinely participatory. Neither did it provide a basis for self-reliance at the local level. Its contribution to local-level development was, therefore, not significant from the standpoint of equity.

The experience of the WP indicates, in general, that where the institutional and administrative structures are not amenable to broad-based participation in the decision-making process it becomes extremely difficult to create and sustain popular interest in local-level development. More specifically, lack of popular influence on decision making within the framework of the WP eventually resulted in the situation wherein the benefits of development projects and activities based on community participation were unevenly and inequitably distributed. As a con-sequence, the broad mass of the local population became disillusioned and less inclined to contribute their efforts to community development projects of the WP type. As already mentioned, the administrative structure of the 'Basic Democracies' did not allow for the effective decentralisation of planning responsibilities to the village level where WP projects were actually being implemented. This in fact was the situation well after independence despite the new Government's commitment to the promotion of popular participation in the development process: it was not until 1976 that local government authorities below the district level were officially recognised as basic units for local-level development planning and, thus, given some responsibilities for planning and implementing publicly-funded development projects in their own areas.[8]

The experience reported in this case study is based on the personal involvement of the author, who as Deputy Commissioner and head of the civil administration in Jessore district, was responsible for co-ordinating the planning and implementation of the specific self-help project which is the subject of the study. The introduction of the new local government structure in 1976 provided an institutional framework that was more conducive to the promotion of popular participation in local-level development than in the past. The launching of the project in 1976 could be considered as timely in the sense that it provided an opportunity to test the relevance of the new structure for translating into action the policy of government as regards the promotion of popular participation in the development process at the grass-roots level.

The Ulashi–Jadunathpur (UJ) Self-help Canal Digging Project came into existence as a result of collaboration between the local authorities in the Sarsha Thana of Sadar sub-division in Jessore district and the Deputy Commissariat. The original project included both drainage and irrigation works and involved the digging of some 16.5 million cubic feet of earth almost entirely by the local people themselves. The project was launched at the beginning of November 1976 and was completed six months later on schedule. At the time, it was the largest self-help project to be undertaken in the country, and its successful implementation demonstrated the potential for mobilising and utilising the country's most abundant and often under-utilised resource – labour – to meet the basic needs of people at the local level.

While it would be somewhat misleading to present self-help development projects as an ideal solution to the problems of poverty and underdevelopment at the local level – the UJ project itself was not without its shortcomings – the experiences reported in this case study nevertheless have lessons that are relevant for the mobilisation of local resources to support employment and poverty alleviation objectives of development. But, as is now widely realised, the idea of self-help development itself is not to be regarded always as a suitable strategy for improving living conditions at the local level, in view of the scope that exists for abuses of the concept in its various practical forms. This implies that the planning and implementation of local self- help projects require in particular certain conditions for success. It is therefore the aim of this study to draw attention to those conditions and illustrate the extent to which they may have contributed to the success of the UJ project. At the same time, the study will also highlight possible dangers of which organisers of local self-help projects should be aware and will attempt to suggest how to avoid these or minimise their impact.

THE ULASHI–JADUNATHPUR SELF-HELP CANAL-DIGGING PROJECT

Location and Main Features

The project involved the construction of a relatively short man-made canal – 2.6 miles in length – between the villages of Ulashi and Jadunathpur. The actual course of the canal was determined by the location of the River Betna,[9] which flows through the northern part of Ulashi village: the proposed canal would effectively divert water from the river to provide irrigation for an estimated 18 000 acres of 'one-crop' land around both villages. However, for reasons related to the topography of the area, the project involved extensive civil construction work for which a massive input of labour was required. For example, the delineated course of the canal had to pass through 30 square miles of water-logged terrain, which includes the four main 'beels'[10] of the project area, and it was therefore necessary first to drain the land of excess water in order to reclaim about 110 acres that would be affected by the construction of the canal. The topography of the land also necessitated the digging of a relatively wide and adequately deep canal – ranging from 65 to 120 feet in width, with an average depth of 13 feet – and the building of permanent

.

drainage facilities to regulate the flow of water.

Limitation on financial resources also affected the technical specification and the mode of implementation of the project. The initial contribution of government was for purchasing land through which the canal would pass at a total cost of Tarka (Tk) 629 000[11] – the amount paid out as compensation for land compulsorily expropriated by government in the interest of the public. [12] Since the actual cost of construction was to be met by the local communities themselves, this effectively placed a limitation on the type of canal and irrigation system to be constructed. From an engineering point of view, the ideal solution to the problem of retaining sufficient water during the dry season for irrigation – given the sloping nature of the surrounding land and the meandering course of the river – would be to build a number of sluices, ranging from 1 to 3 vents, at an estimated average cost of Tk900 000 each. However, the cost involved was found to be enormous and much in excess of financial resources that conceivably could be mobilised locally. It was, therefore, decided to dig a single linear canal between Ulashi and Jadunathpur and at the same time devise a practical way of discharging the excess water upstream over a length of nearly 10 miles – in this case by using low-lift pumps. Financial constraints meant that the project had to rely almost exclusively on labour-intensive methods of construction, even for the most physically demanding and arduous tasks. Furthermore, not only was a labour-intensive alternative an obvious choice for the project, but it was also clear that the required inputs of labour had to be provided mainly on a voluntary basis. Hence, the concept of 'self-help' came to be adopted as the main strategy for implementing the project.

The major task in this regard then was how to motivate the local people to provide the requisite labour inputs voluntarily. The participation of people on such a basis – even where the opportunity cost for this labour is negligible – would require certain incentives. In the case of the poor peasants in the project area, who have been the victims of varying degrees of exploitation as far back as they can remember, their perception of benefits to be derived from the project was a critical factor in the decision of whether or not to participate. To overcome this obstacle, right from the beginning the possible benefits from the project were spelt out clearly and publicised widely among the potential participants. As we shall see later, a genuine attempt was also made to relate labour inputs to estimated benefits on an individual household basis. Summarised in concrete terms the global benefits of the project were identified as follows:

1 the reclamation of about 180 000 acres of hitherto uncultivatable land upstream;
2 the settlement of the land- poor and the landless in the community on the reclaimed land;
3 the use of excess water discharged from upstream beels to irrigate

land downstream on both sides of the Betna and the UJ canal by using electrified low-lift power pumps;[13]

4 the cultivation of three crops a year, based on a well-designed cropping pattern, in a hitherto one-crop area and subsequent increase in per acre yield as a result of irrigation and the adoption of improved seed–fertiliser technology;[14]

5 the introduction of pisciculture and duckery in the ox-bow lake that will be formed in the loop of the old course of the Betna river and also in the newly-dug canal, mainly for the benefit of the land-poor and the landless; and

6 the afforestation of embankments of the canal with future prospect for the development of a forestry industry on a small-scale basis.

In terms of increased production, the completion of the canal was expected to result in an estimated additional output of at least 360 000 maunds[15] of foodgrains and 50 000 maunds of other crops[16] (mainly vegetables) annually, at a total estimated value of Tk25.5 million; and 4955 maunds of fish valued at Tk1.44 million a year. Assuming costs of production of 40 per cent and 30 per cent for crops and fish respectively, the estimated additional net income from increased production was therefore estimated at about Tk16.3 million per annum. Furthermore, the income thus gained could have a significant impact on overall economic activities in the surrounding localities in terms of stimulating new investments in local trade, cottage crafts and transportation. Finally, and perhaps most significant, if the project turned out to be a success, in terms of the realisation of the benefits outlined above, it would contribute immensely to the creation of confidence among the villagers themselves in their own ability to initiate and support similar community development projects in the future. This was particularly important in the context of a society wherein people had in the past depended mainly on 'outside' assistance to satisfy their most elemental needs.

Planning and Organisation of Work Tasks

The initial planning and organisation of the project embraced a number of institutions, both formal and informal. Although the initial planning and co-ordination of the project was the responsibility of the Office of the Deputy Commissariat for Jessore District in association with the Water Development Board (WDB), there were usually prior consultations with representatives of the local people on important matters such as the preparation of the physical plan for the construction of the canal. Hence, in delineating the actual course of the canal, it was decided that whenever possible the project should bypass homesteads in deference to people's attachment to their homes; such a decision was necessary for obtaining popular support for the implementation of the project. Throughout the planning phase the views of the local people were sought and often adhered to in the making of key decisions.

As regards the contribution of labour to the project, it was decided that this should somehow be related to expected benefits. Apart from local communities in the two unions through which the canal would actually be located, the project was expected to benefit directly villagers in some of the neighbouring unions in the form of drainage facilities and reclaimed land to be provided. In addition, it was envisaged that as many as 27 Unions in the two Thanas within the Sadar sub-division of Jessore district would derive indirect benefits from the canal through the impact of the project on economic activities. Thus, participation of labour was sought from villages outside the two unions where the canal would be located. However, it was stipulated, at least in principle, that labour inputs from the various groups of participants should be somewhat proportionate to their respective potential benefits.

The mobilisation of labour from among the people in all of the Unions that stood to benefit from the project called for a vertical extension of existing informal organisations down to the village level. Yet it was important that such organisations should not, at least in the initial period, form a parallel structure to that of the existing formal local government system, since past experience has shown that this could be counter-productive due to possible rivalry over spheres of responsibility and related functions. The aim of the organisers was to obtain the requisite local support from the people at the village level, without at the same time arousing the suspicion of those who held positions of authority and power within the formal local government structure. By operating directly at the village level, where the presence and influence of formal local government authorities was less conspicuous, it might be possible to develop and strengthen grass-roots mobilisation capacity for self-reliant development. Thus, much attention was paid to the identification and organisation of the different socio-economic groups at the village level during the planning phase.

The physical work to be undertaken in connection with the construction of the canal was first roughly divided between the different socio-economic/occupational groups within the Sadar sub-division. Then for each identified group, as far as possible, individual or household work quotas – in terms of cubic feet of earth to be dug and moved – were assigned according to some rough assessment of potential benefits to be derived from the project when completed, for example, land area that will be irrigated. However, the programme of work was made flexible so as to accommodate additional labour inputs from new as well as irregular participants and to allow for possible shortfalls arising from unforeseen circumstances. As far as the organisation of work tasks was concerned, the emphasis was on consensus, rather than on coercion, and implementation was to be based more on expediency and convenience than on a rigid schedule.

It was also decided that individual contributions to the project could take the form mainly of either labour inputs or cash contributions. However, each participant, irrespective of class or status, was expected to contribute a minimum quota of physical labour in addition to cash contributions: such token contribution of labour by all was seen as necessary for motivating the broad mass of the population. Whereas the poorer segments of the population were expected to contribute their labour, it was felt that other members of the community who are gainfully employed on a regular basis or otherwise occupied – for example, big landowners, businessmen, traders, transport operators and civil servants – might find it more convenient to fulfil part of their assigned work tasks by employing paid labour to work on their behalf. Thus, the project would also provide opportunities for paid employment among the unemployed and seasonally under-employed groups who, in addition to fulfilling their own assigned work task, could also take on paid employment on the project. In addition, the Food for Work Programme was to be incorporated into some phases of the project to provide further opportunities for remunerative employment. Additional direct labour inputs were envisaged to come from a variety of irregular volunteers, such as local students, *ansars* (youths serving their para-military national service), the army and the police.

In order to minimise costs as well as to maintain effective local control over the project, it was decided right from the beginning that no additional state personnel would be recruited specifically to work on the project. Instead, with the co-operation of relevant government departments, the services of government officials based in the district would be requested on an *ad hoc* basis as and when necessary. In this regard, such officials, including the army and police, would be expected to work in close liaison with the villagers as well as to put in a certain amount of physical labour as a visible demonstration of official support for the project. As far as the supervision of the work was concerned, each group was supposed to be responsible for accomplishing its assigned task in a manner acceptable to its members. However, in the absence of an appropriate local government body at the village level, the role of co-ordinating state and local efforts was assumed overall by the Deputy Commissariat.

It was also decided that full compensation would be paid to landowners for land needed for the construction of the canal before the start of work in each union. This was thought necessary in order to secure broad-based local support for the implementation of the project.[17] Given the linearity of the planned course of the canal, the possibility of deliberately diverting the canal to traverse the land of 'favoured' individual landowners for the purpose of obtaining compensation was somewhat reduced. Furthermore, the avoidance of homesteads in plotting the course of the canal meant that all land expropriated was of a more or less uniform type, and, as such, the

246

rate of compensation to be paid out would be the same for each affected landowner.

Above all, it was consciously felt that the planning and implementations of the project should not be completely isolated from the existing institutional structures and legal framework. It was not the aim of the organisers, or presumably of the local people, to change radically the socio-economic system overnight: the underlying philosophy was more reformist than revolutionary. In the specific context of Bangladesh then, and even now, any attempt to completely bypass the formal system would have been detrimental to the successful outcome of the project. As will be seen later, the Government took a keen interest in the project right from the start and until its completion. The more than passive role of government in this regard should, however, be viewed in the light of the more positive attitude of the people to a regime that was considered to be more sympathetic to their problems than was the case before independence.

Finally, to enhance self-reliance among the local people, it was decided that financial assistance and other material contributions from outside the Sadar sub-division should be restricted to necessary supplementary inputs required for effective implementation, and that these should be accepted only on the condition that the donors would not interfere in the making and implementation of project decisions. On this basis Tk629 000 was provided by the Water Development Board (WDB) for payment of compensation for land that was compulsorily acquired; the Khulna Division Development Board[18] donated Tk200 000 for the purchase of spades, baskets and the costs of transportation.

Also, the WDB spent about Tk20 000 on the inaugural day to cover the cost of midday meals provided for the participants.[19] Overall, the planning of the project was carefully undertaken to ensure that implementation would be carried out on a truly self-help basis. The labour of the people was regarded as the most important locally available resource which, if properly mobilised, could effectively be transformed into productive capital. This thinking in fact underlies the dominant slogan of the entire operation: 'Our hands are but millions of tons of equipment'.[20]

Implementation

Actual implementation of the project started on 1 November 1976 with a formal launching ceremony performed by the then Head of State, General Ziaur Rahman. The presence of the Head of State at the launching of the project was symbolic of the support from the national leadership for local self-help projects. A project committee comprising local leaders and a few local-level government officials – chairmen of the 27 Union Parishads in the Sadar sub-division and civil servants from government departments at the district level concerned with public works and water development and the Deputy Commissariat – was established for the purpose of co-ordinating and reviewing work tasks on a daily basis.

Implementation was characterised by a variety of experiences. Initially, there was a seemingly unending flow of apparently enthusiastic volunteers: on the first day over 10 000 volunteers (drawn from local farmers, students, government officials, the army and the police) gathered on the site for work, but only 4 000 could be provided with spades and baskets. However, by the second week the number of volunteers available for work on the project had dropped significantly to the extent of causing a fall in the scheduled daily aggregate work rate. While a decline in the initial enthusiasm of local volunteers was to be expected, the situation of labour shortage which actually threatened progress so soon after the project was launched was partly due to frictions which had arisen within the project committee. Although local interests were represented by the chairmen of the Union Parishads, many villagers felt that this formal local government structure was not sufficiently decentralised to cater for their needs. More specifically, there were scepticisms at the village level about the role of government officials on the project committee as regards decision making, especially as in the past government had usually exerted strong influence on the functioning of local authorities. But as it turned out the representatives of the Union Parishads were more than keen to protect the interests of local people on the committee and this led to conflicts with government officials. Thus when faced with a range of different views the organisers found it difficult to agree on a compromise solution, indicating clearly the inherent conflicts between purely local and wider interests.

These initial difficulties were soon overcome by the introduction of a more decentralised institutional arrangement which allowed for greater local control over different sections of the construction work at village level. In each of the 27 Unions involved, a local project committee was formed. Each local committee, which was made up of elected members of the Union Parishads and natural leaders of the villages, was responsible for mobilising and organising the local people for work on the project in its area. It was also responsible for distributing the total work tasks assigned to the Union amongst the constituent villages. Furthermore, in most of the 27 Unions concerned organising sub-committees were formed at the village level to establish and strengthen contacts with villagers. This was found necessary for sustaining popular interest in the project through the dissemination of relevant information. Decentralisation of the organis-ational structure right down to the village level also made it possible somehow to involve the landless and the land-poor in decision making through their own representatives on the village sub-committees. In addition to the establishment of sub-committees at the village level, the higher district-level project committee was empowered to co-opt representatives from village-level popular organisations on an *ad hoc* basis. With these changes and the determination of all concerned to

248

achieve success, the project gained widespread support and attracted new participants who became very committed to the task ahead.

To facilitate the implementation of the project, the office of the Deputy Commissariat in consultation with the local Union committees and the village sub-committees established a special project office at Ulashi to deal with the provision of transportation for participants who lived outside a three-mile radius from the work site and the distribution of midday meals. This office was also responsible for assessing and recording the progress of work done by each group on a daily basis. Acting as a sort of liaison bétween local village leaders and the Deputy Commissariat, the Project Office was to play a major role in ensuring the success of the project, particularly with respect to the provision of outside technical personnel such as surveyors and engineers who were redeployed from the district level to work on the project on an *ad hoc* basis.

The provision of transportation was regarded as an important incentive for encouraging participants from distant villages to work on the project. According to the distribution of weekly work tasks, a transportation timetable was worked out with respect to the requirements of each Union; trucks were sent out each morning to collect participants and, similarly, to take them home at the end of the working day. It was later found to be uneconomic, in terms of transport costs, to attract participants living outside a radius of 7 miles from the work site, and these were excluded from further participation in the project.

Participants were organised into groups of 10 to 30 workers, under the supervision of a local or traditional leader, and each group was assigned to a different work site along the course of the canal. This arrangement made for a more orderly pattern of implementation in contrast to the rather disorganised work methods that had characterised the start of the project. In order to motivate the villagers to greater efforts, leaders and supervisors were not exempted from physical work; they were required to work alongside volunteers in their respective groups.

After the first few weeks, implementation on the basis of individual work task was changed from a 'time rate' (hours worked) to a 'piece rate' (cubic feet of earth dug and moved), and the minimum quota was fixed at 35 cubic feet per person per day. This was found to be a more efficient way of achieving the target work rate, as participants were on the whole keen to finish their daily task as early as possible so as to be free for other activities in their daily lives. In addition, a system of daily reporting on work done (both in aggregate and per capita figures) by the different groups was introduced in order to monitor progress as well as to identify weaknesses in the implementation process. Reports on the performance of the different groups were sent to the Deputy Commissariat each evening, thereby enabling the central project committee to take appropriate steps to improve the overall efficiency of the project.

Throughout the implementation of the project, the organisers at the district level maintained regular contacts with the sub-committees at the village level. In addition, senior officials on the Deputy Commissariat often visited local villages to review progress and to have open discussions with the villagers on all aspects of the project, including potential benefits. The reliance on this form of consultation at the grass-roots level for decision making was found to be indispensable for sustaining popular interest in the project. Overall, the direct involvement of local people in the decision-making process turned out to be the single most important factor behind the successful implementation of the project on a self-help basis.

For example, in the distribution of work tasks the central project committee was influenced by popular views to adopt a formula that relates labour inputs to potential benefits. According to this formula the size of individual/household land holdings determined the volume of earth to be dug and moved by an individual or household within a group. This worked out roughly as shown in Table 9.1 for all land-owning participants.

Table 9.1

Size of Land Holding	Cubic Feet of Earth to be Dug and Moved
5 – 7 bighas[21]	1 000
8 – 10 bighas	3 000
11 – 15 bighas	5 000
16 – 20 bighas	10 000
20 + bighas	15 000

The landless and land-poor peasants in theory had proportionately smaller work tasks, although they were expected to contribute most of the manual labour since they were mainly underemployed or unemployed. However, since many of the relatively big landowners, traders, transport operators, and so on, found it convenient to employ paid labour to fulfil part of their quotas for them, the project provided part-time employment for the landless and the land-poor. Thus in addition to fulfilling their own work tasks as unpaid volunteers for, say, two days, they were also gainfully employed as paid labourers on the project for the rest of the week.

Table 9.2 shows the monthly progress of work, in terms of cubic feet of earth dug, for the duration of the project. Overall, the work progressed more or less on schedule and the digging of the canal was completed in about six months. Fluctuations in the monthly implementation rate were due to both external and internal factors. External factors included the demand for labour during harvesting and sowing time, adverse weather conditions, and local Union Parishad elections, all of which contributed to

Table 9.2 Monthly Distribution of Earth Work on UJ Canal

Month	Earth Work (in cubic feet)	Percentage of Total Work
November 1976	442 347	3.07
December 1976	1 377 207	9.56
January 1977	2 073 225	14.40
February 1977	3 174 288	22.04
March 1977	4 210 215	29.24
April 1977	2 222 718	15.44
May 1977	900 000	6.25
Total	14 400 000	100.00

a fall in the aggregate work rate. Internal problems which affected implementation were mainly limited supervisory capacity and poor logistic support. In general, supervisory capacity was contingent on the amount of time and attention that senior officers of the Deputy Commissariat could give to the project in addition to their routine administrative duties, the capability and attitude of the officials redeployed to the project office, as well as the organisational ability of union/village/group leaders on the work site.

A significant discernible fact about these fluctuations is that the rate of work was generally higher when paid workers were predominant on the project site – with the exception of the initial period of high enthusiasm. The conclusion then is that the landless and land-poor who do not stand to gain immediately and directly from the project naturally found cash payment[22] to be a very strong incentive for motivating them to work on the project, rather than prospects of indirect benefits in the future. Furthermore, most of this category of participants were seriously deficient in terms of current consumption requirements and needed the additional income to make up for the deficit in their basic needs.

The implementation of the project produced evidence to support the claim that popular participation could facilitate development at the local level. First it became obvious that by associating local leaders and ordinary people in the decision-making process, especially relating to the organisation of work task at the village level, it was possible to achieve higher implementation rates and better work performance than when such projects were undertaken exclusively by the central or local government. The authority given to the local organising committees and village sub-committees to mobilise labour and supervise on-site activities not only contributed much to progress in the implementation of the project, but also resulted in the creation of confidence among local people to initiate action aimed at improvements in their well-being. This later turned out to be crucial for further development activities in the project area. Secondly, the experience from the project clearly demonstrated that popular influence on decision making helps to overcome obstacles to development, as opposed to more centralised forms of decision making which often result in conflicts and contradictions. This implies that local people themselves are in a better position than officials from outside the community to understand local problems and, therefore, to resolve such problems in ways that are widely acceptable among all concerned. The decentralisation of planning and organisational responsibility to the village level also made it possible for villagers to be better informed about their contributions in relation to individual and collective benefits from the project, and thereby, become less suspicious about the motives of the authorities for involving them in the project.

It is significant that the initial obstacles and problems encountered in the implementation of the project were related to certain weaknesses in the institutional framework. The fact that formal local government bodies did not exist at the village level made it difficult to organise outside the traditional land-based power structure. The initial task of mobilising and organising labour at the village level could have been easier had representative local government bodies existed at the village level. This not being the case, it was necessary to create an appropriate participatory institution in the form of the village sub-committees to fill the gap. Also local custom and beliefs contributed to the initial difficulties. The participation of women at the beginning was exceptionally low because of the practice on religious grounds of keeping women away from outdoor life and activity, as well as the shortage of women organisers. Similarly, the rather misguided view of some school teachers that participation of students in self-help projects was not in any way linked to their educational development led initially to a low turnout of students for work on the project. However, the popularity of the project helped to influence change of attitudes: the more determined and enlightened among women organisers and student leaders took the bold step to volunteer for work on the project and this had a demonstration effect on some of their numbers.

Finally, the part played by the Office of the Deputy Commissariat in the implementation of the project provides a useful insight into the controversy surrounding the role of the State in local self-help projects. While one cannot generalise on this issue, since in a given context the existing political structure and socio-economic circumstances will influence the nature and extent of government involvement, there are nevertheless certain salient features of the UJ project which should be noted in terms of their wider relevance.

First, undoubtedly, the open support and encouragement from the national leadership went a long way in creating and sustaining enthusiasm among the local people. In particular, the official recognition given to the project as a worthy example of local-level contribution to national development provided the necessary inspiration for sustained local interest and support. The participation of local-level officials in actual physical work, albeit token in some cases, proved useful for motivating the masses to give their best to the project; official recognition from the highest level was also instrumental in obtaining the necessary co-operation from relevant government departments and agencies. In the specific context of Bangladesh this is an important condition for the successful implementation of self-help projects in view of the usual bureaucratic obstacles that so often impinge on the planning and implementation of local-level development projects. Furthermore, official support for the project from the highest level produced an active interest amongst 'urban middle-class' groups such as academics, businessmen and administrators who are usually indifferent to the conditions and problems of the rural poor.

Second, the prompt payment of compensation by the authorities for land acquired, together with widespread publicity initiated by the Deputy Commissariat about the nature and distribution of potential benefits, helped to increase the confidence of local people in the role of the State. If the issue of compensation for land had not been satisfactorily resolved right from the start it is very doubtful that the project would have had the level of popular support required for its successful implementation. The administrative and technical support provided by the authorities helped to convince the people about the seriousness of the pledge of the Government 'to help them help themselves'.

EVALUATION OF THE PROJECT

In this section an attempt is made to evaluate the UJ self-help canal project in terms of its contribution to overall development at the local level and the realisation of benefits relating to improvement in living standards for the mass of the population. For the purpose of this evaluation, the analysis is focused on the following broad categories of benefits which are considered relevant to the fulfilment of basic needs-oriented development objectives.

1 Mobilisation of unemployed and under-utilised resources at the local level;
2 Increase in output;
3 Employment creation;
4 Equitable distribution of benefits;
5 Self-reliance.

Mobilisation of Local Resources

An important aspect of the self-help approach to local-level development is the opportunity provided for mobilising locally available human and material resources – often otherwise under-utilised – for development-related activities that have an impact on living conditions. The project which is the subject of this case study was undertaken in a context wherein labour existed in abundant supply at the local level, although most of this was either unemployed or under-utilised. The project, therefore, provided an opportunity for mobilising and channelling under-utilised labour into the provision of a vital infrastructure as required for bringing about some improvement in the living standards of the local people. However, the successful implementation of the project itself depended critically on the stimulation and sustenance of popular interest during the construction phase. The key factors in this connection were identified as the scope for popular influence on decision making at the local level; people's perceptions and understanding of equity in relation to tangible benefits to be derived from their participation in the implementation of the project; and the opportunity cost of labour throughout the implementation of the project.

The decision that the implementation of the project should be based on labour-intensive methods was based on the realisation that labour was about the only required factor input that was readily available and in abundant supply in the project area. But even to regard labour as unemployed in the sense of being idle is somewhat misleading since most of those who were expected to contribute their labour to the project were extremely poor and, therefore, could not afford to remain idle – they somehow had to scratch a living, based on low productivity activities, in order to survive. In this sense then the opportunity cost of labour cannot strictly be regarded as zero. At the same time, in the context of the socio-economic situation in rural Bangladesh it is highly doubtful whether for the vast majority of the landless or the land-poor there was an opportunity cost of labour of any economic significance. There was little or no hope for them to find alternative employment opportunities that were productive and adequately remunerative. Thus the mobilisation of labour within the project area to work on the canal represented a more efficient use of available labour for the benefit of the local community, as well as a saving on scarce capital investment resource which is the only alternative factor input for embarking on such a project.

To appreciate fully the element of saving, implied in the implementation of the project as a self-help activity based mainly on voluntary labour, one should look at the alternative cost to government of building the canal by the conventional method involving the use of machinery and wage labour. It has been estimated that the total capital costs to government, including the cost of the land, for constructing a similar canal by conventional methods would have been approximately Tk2.28 million.[23] This amount in fact relates only to the costs of wage labour and materials and, as such, does not include additional costs attributable to the use of machinery and equipment and salaries of supervisory and technical personnel. Alternatively, by implementing the project as a self-help activity based on labour-intensive methods the total capital outlay, including the costs of land and implements used for manual work, has been estimated at roughly Tk1.41 million – representing a net saving in total capital investment of Tk870 000. Furthermore, it should be noted that the total amount of Tk1.41 million includes as well the cost of paid labour employed on the project which amounted to about Tk560 000. This amount was raised locally through cash contributions made by richer members of the community who had opted to fulfil part of their assigned work quotas by employing paid labour to work on their behalf.

From the stand-point of national economic development, the mobilisation of local resources to build the canal may be regarded as an attractive and profitable investment option for government, which, as a result, economised on the use of high opportunity cost scarce resources. In addition, local resource mobilisation meant that the foreign-exchange requirement of the project (mainly machinery) was negligible – an important consideration in the case of Bangladesh which further enhances the value of local resources mobilised. The effective mobilisation of low opportunity cost labour to undertake the project on a self-help basis has clearly resulted in substantial saving for the government, which was hardly in a position to afford the capital cost of such a development project.

Overall, the experience of the UJ self-help canal project strongly supports the view that, given the right type of organisational structures and institutional arrangements, local resource mobilisation can represent an extremely profitable investment opportunity in the context of national development. This assumes even greater importance especially in circumstances where investment capital by government is the most limiting factor in economic development.

Increase in Output

The completion of the canal undoubtedly contributed to an increase in agricultural production in the project area. Before the project was implemented there was hardly any mechanised form of irrigation in the area; the construction and operation of the canal immediately made possible the irrigation of nearly 60 per cent of the existing cultivatable land area. The completion of the canal also led to improvement in the drainage system of the Betna river and, as a consequence, the reclamation of some 1 800 acres of hitherto submerged, uncultivatable land in the upstream area. In addition, the provision of flood protection facilities covering an area of nearly 15 300 acres of crop land now made it possible to grow staple crops throughout the year without the uncertainty posed by the vagaries of the weather.

The provision of irrigation facilities in the project area, as in most other parts of Bangladesh, represents a critical factor for agricultural production. Before the construction of the canal, irrigation was very limited in the project area, restricted mainly to a few larger landholdings; in general, the efficiency of operation was low, given the enormous physical task of transporting water mainly by manpower and draft animals. The mechanised system of irrigation, introduced with the construction of the canal (diesel and electrically-operated low lift pumps), had a much wider coverage which benefited smaller farmers who could not afford their own individual system. As a result of the much greater land area covered by the communal irrigation system, it was possible not only to increase and stabilise crop yields for small farmers but also to facilitate the widespread diffusion of high-yielding varieties.[24] Widespread introduction of irrigation technology and the improved drainage system in the project area now made it possible to cultivate up to three crops a year on hitherto one-crop land. Most important, the project made it possible for some of the land-poor and the landless in the project area to become self-employed as small farmers following their resettlement on reclaimed land.

In concrete terms, the increase in agricultural output in the project area as a direct result of the construction of the canal was significant. The expansion of cultivation on account of reclaimed and irrigated land was expected to result in an additional yield of 179 000 maunds of paddy rice, valued at about Tk15 million,[25] for each of the two rice-crop seasons, the *Aus* and the *Aman*.[26] Actual total production in the first year following the completion of the canal exceeded this estimate by nearly 40 000 maunds due to higher levels of paddy yield per acre on both reclaimed and irrigated lands. In the next cropping period between the *Aman* and the *Aus* seasons (i.e. from November to February), also known as the *Boro* season, when wheat is traditionally grown by local farmers, a local survey revealed that total ouput of the crop increased on the previous year's by about 45 060 maunds, officially valued at Tk3.78 million. This increase in output was largely on account of an additional 3000 acres of land that was brought under cultivation during this dry period as a result of irrigation.

Thus, in an area where previously only one rice crop was a certainty, i.e. during the wet *Aman* season, the construction of the canal has now made possible the certainty of a second rice crop during the *Aus* season as well as a stable wheat crop during the dry *Boro* season; before the construction of the canal a substantial portion of cultivatable area was left idle during the dry season due to lack of irrigation. Furthermore, increased yields per acre were recorded for all of the main crops in the project area as a result of irrigation and improved drainage system. In monetary terms, the increased crop output during the first year after the completion of the canal was estimated at a gross value of Tk33.86 million. Assuming that 40 per cent of this amount was accounted for by production costs, the net value of additional output during the year was about Tk20.32 million. Set against the total cost to the community of constructing the canal (even including the value of paid communal labour according to the market wage rate), benefit in terms of annual net increase in output in monetary terms was nearly nine times the original investment in the first year. This indeed is a highly significant incremental output/investment ratio. In the future the prospect is that the increase in output will be even greater as the local variety of paddy is progressively replaced by higher-yielding varieties which can now be adopted successfully – partly as a result of irrigation and improved drainage.

Employment Creation

As already mentioned, the construction of the UJ canal involved the use of voluntary as well as paid labour. The employment of labour on a wage basis was confined to the landless and land-poor peasants who, in addition to fulfilling their own assigned work quotas, were available and willing to hire their labour for paid employment on the project. According to the formula adopted for assigning work quotas, the big landowners, Jotdars, and local businessmen who are expected to benefit more from the project were assigned higher work quotas than the landless and land-poor, although most of the former found it more convenient to make cash contributions in lieu of their labour to fulfil part of their individual quotas. Such contributions were used to engage labour on a wage basis for work on the project. In all, it was recorded that about 50 per cent of the total work on the canal, involving the digging and moving of some 7 million cubic feet of earth, was accomplished by paid labour. This is in addition to another 10 per cent of total work estimated to have been undertaken by communal labour in return for food (rice and wheat) within the framework of the on-going Food for Work Programme (FWP) in Jessore District. Total paid employment (both money and food) thus accounted for about 60 per cent of the total man-days worked on the project.

Although benefit in the form of paid employment was temporary in nature, being limited to the six-month duration of the project, its importance can be deduced from the fact that about 30 per cent of the labour force in the project area were landless people who did not have any income during the slack period in the agricultural cycle. The provision of part-time paid employment on the project therefore benefited mainly this category of landless labour who seized the opportunity for remunerative employment thus accorded. Hence, it was observed that many of the landless often worked on the project for two days a week as unpaid volunteers and for the remaining five days as paid employees at a piece rate of Tk70–100 per thousand cubic feet of earth dug and moved. The total income earned from part-time employment on the project was estimated at about Tk560 000, in addition to an estimated Tk112 000 worth of staple food that was earned by the landless and the land-poor who participated in the FWP component of the project.

Employment benefits from the project of a more long-term nature may be more difficult to quantify. However, there are certain indications that suggest longer-term employment gains emanating from the construction of the UJ canal. First, as already noted, improvements in irrigation and drainage resulted in expansion in total cultivatable land area for major crops; this in turn led to an increase in demand for farm labour, thereby contributing to employment creation in agriculture, albeit subjected to seasonal fluctuations. Second, some of the reclaimed land was used to resettle the hitherto landless and land-poor who, with the aid of irrigation and other inputs such as improved varieties of paddy and fertilisers, were able to launch out on their own as individual self-employed farmers. It could well be that the expectation of increased employment opportunities on the part of the landless and land-poor was instrumental in motivating them to contribute their labour voluntarily towards the implementation of the project.

Another indication of indirect employment benefit from the project relates to the expansion in overall economic activities in the project area following the completion of the canal. Apart from the introduction of pisciculture and duckery on the ox-bow lake which was formed by the diversion of the Betna river, there was a noted expansion in local cottage and craft industries as well as retail trade. What seems to have happened is that several small farmers invested their windfall profits on non-farm activities since the opportunity for them to plough back profits into agriculture did not exist as in most cases available land was already intensively cultivated. In addition, there was significant and continuous increase in the general level of effective demand for consumer goods in the area as a result of higher farm incomes and wages earned by farm workers: the average daily wages (in money terms) for agricultural labourers in the area increased from Tk4.51 in 1976 to TK6.86 in 1977 and to Tk 11.36 in 1978. The unprecedented expansion in economic activities, in the period immediately following the completion of the canal, provided further impetus for higher levels of both wage and self-employment.

Equitable Distribution of Benefits

In attempting to evaluate (a) the extent to which specific benefits from the project were equitably distributed among the various socio-economic groups in the community and (b) the impact of the project on poverty alleviation through equalisation of socio-economic opportunities and access to productive resources, certain considerations should be taken into account. First, for a project concerned with the provision of communal irrigation and drainage facilities it is obvious that the distribution of benefits will be somewhat skewed. More specifically, the landless, by definition, will be excluded from sharing directly in benefits arising from improvement to land; the major beneficiaries are likely to be large owner-farmers and landlords, followed by, say, leasehold tenants, small farmers, and then sharecroppers. Thus, the prevailing land tenure system will be an important determinant of the distribution of direct benefits accruing from improved irrigation and drainage facilities. Second, and related, the distribution of benefits from a communal project among various groups in society will depend on the nature of decision-making institutions. If these institutions are not based on effective popular participation, it is likely that decisions regarding the distribution of benefits will be biased in favour of those who dominate the decision-making process. On the other hand, greater popular influence on decision making could lead to a more equitable distribution of benefits from communal projects. Third, given that people would normally volunteer their labour for self-help projects only if they perceive some benefits, individually or collectively, in return for their contributions, the successful implementation of a project such as the UJ canal will depend to some extent on the possibility that the poorer segments of the population will also benefit from the project.

One of the potential benefits from the project, that must have certainly appealed to the landless and the land-poor, was the prospect of access to land. The importance of land in rural Bangladesh is not only limited to its intrinsic value as a productive asset and, hence, a principal determinant of income and wealth distribution, but it is also the basis of socio-economic stratification and the power structure in society. Thus in a situation in which well over half of the population in the project area were landless or land-poor, it would be reasonable to conclude that the majority of the participants had hitherto been excluded from effective participation in the development process on account of their non-land owning status; this also significantly reduced their chances to benefit from development in the past. The fact that the project resulted in the resettlement of some of the landless on reclaimed land could therefore be regarded as a move towards equalisation of socio-economic opportunities. Furthermore, given that production in the project area is land-based, access to land for the hitherto landless members of the community should have some favourable impact on the distribution of income.

While there can be no doubt about the need for a more equitable distribution of land in rural Bangladesh as a whole, the outcome of this project in terms of providing some of the landless with cultivatable plots, should not be regarded as insignificant to the more complex and wider issue of agrarian reform on a national scale. Instead, the experience from the project should realistically be viewed as a move in the right direction that could contribute to the resolution of more controversial issues underlying agrarian reform policies. If the achievement of the project in this regard can be replicated in several other areas in rural Bangladesh, the total impact on poverty and inequality nationwide would certainly be significant.

Although the project, as it is, stands to benefit the big landowners more than other groups, it should also be stressed that the allocation of work quotas among the different socio-economic groups was somehow related to potential benefits according to size of land-holding. Thus, for example, big landowners with holdings in excess of 20 *bighas* were assigned individual quotas of 15 000 cubic feet of earth to be dug and moved, whereas small farmers with landholdings of 5–7 *bighas* were assigned a work quota of only 1000 cubic feet. As a result of this pattern of distribution of work load, the big landowners who were identified as major beneficiaries were made responsible for about a third of the total work load on the project (through their own labour and paid labour) even though they represent only a very small fraction of the total population. On the other hand, the landless and the land-poor peasants who make up about two-thirds of the total population were expected to contribute only about a third of the total physical work. The other one-third of the total work load was to be covered from inputs by the armed forces, the police, students and other irregular volunteers and the FWP.

Self-Reliance

The successful implementation of the project helped to create greater confidence among the local people in their own ability to plan and execute local development projects on a self-help basis. Even before the canal project was completed the local people on their initiative had prepared a 9-point 'agenda' for development and *swanivorisation*[27] that was presented to the authorities at the formal opening of the canal. This took the form of a comprehensive local-level development programme consisting of proposals for a number of government-aided self-help projects aimed at expansion in agricultural production, eradication of illiteracy, improvement in health and sanitation facilities, and popularisation and expansion of family planning practices.

The programme which soon received official approval and support[28] provided a basis for local people to participate in the decision-making process on matters pertaining to their well-being. As part of the planning process with reference to the expanded programme, the views of villagers were obtained through base-line socio-economic surveys of all villages in the area. The purpose of this exercise was to identify specific needs, and to assess available and potential resources for implementing proposed projects according to priorities as indicated by the villages themselves. Next the representatives of villages at the Union level came together for the purpose of consolidating their individual 'plans' into an area development plan, involving a total planned investment of nearly Tk110 million to be shared more or less equally between the government and the local communities as shown in Table 9.3. The *UJ Pilot Area Development Plan*, covering eight Unions in two Thanas with 132 villages and a total population of about 140 000, was thus formulated and launched.

The projects included in the plan ranged from the provision of deep tube wells, schools and health centres to family planning facilities and fertilisers. These are all needs identified by the villagers themselves as fundamental to their livelihood. Thus, the successful implementation of the plan should therefore contribute to the reduction of poverty in the area.

The implementation of the plan was based essentially on the active participation of all groups in the community. To ensure that villagers participated in the decision-making process, the authorities decided simultaneously to decentralise formally planning responsibilities right down to the village level by giving decision-making powers to the *Gram Parishad* which is the village assembly open to all adult villagers. In order to sustain popular interest in the plan at the local level, particular attention was paid to the creation of conditions that would ensure that especially disadvantaged groups such as the landless, the land-poor and women also benefit from the implementation of the plan. For example, the locations of tube wells and water channels with power pumps were in some cases determined by the need to provide water supply to plots owned by poorer farmers who had recently formed co-operatives for production and marketing purposes. Steps were also taken to ensure that women benefited from adult literacy programmes by organising special classes for them in the evenings when they were free from their usual domestic duties.

Furthermore, it was also decided that the village assembly would have full responsibility for the running of communal facilities such as schools and health centres. To cover recurrent expenditures the plan provided for the establishment of a development fund for each village to which government would make an annual grant in addition to local contributions coming mainly from a progressive levy on landowners according to size of landholdings. This in effect constitutes a decentralisation of tax-raising and spending powers to the village level which further supports the objective of local self-reliance. For example, in some villages it was decided that any surplus amount in the development fund at the end of the year would be used to provide credits to villagers who wish to pursue self-employed activities such as local crafts, pisciculture and rickshaw transport.

In terms of concrete achievements, by the end of the first year the implementation of the plan had resulted in the installation of 111 power pumps, the sinking of 15 deep tube wells, the construction and operation of 19 primary schools, the provision of adult-literacy courses for over 1400 adults who can now be considered as literate, the construction of

Table 9.3

Financial Requirements of UJ Pilot Area Development Plan
(July 1977 – June 1979)

| Purpose/Sector | Source of Investment | | | Percentage of Self-Help in Total |
	Self-Help (in Taka)	Government Investment (in Taka)	Total (in Taka)	
1. Law and Order	2 005 750	142 200	2 147 950	93.00
2. Food Production	13 541 924	18 630 592	32 172 516	42.10
3. Other Productions	3 108 760	32 500	3 161 260	98.34
4. Population Control	483 200	494 200	977 400	49.50
5. Primary Education	4 028 000	6 065 400	10 093 400	39.90
6. Adult Education	3 221 922	2 383 460	5 605 382	57.47
7. Employment Measures	16 276 216	17 652 558	33 928 774	48.03
8. Health Measures	13 943 415	7 764 200	21 707 615	64.23
Total	56 609 187	53 185 110	109 794 297	51.65

12 000 feet of irrigation channels, and the reclamation and settlement of the landless on 210 acres of previously submerged land. In terms of benefits to individual families, higher levels of output and income and the extension of credit and hire-purchase facilities to smallholders have led to the sinking of 150 privately-owned shallow tube wells, the operation of 10 rice/wheat huskers and the expansion of organised village crafts with an estimated annual turnover of Tk250 000. Overall economic expansion resulting in an increase in demand for wage labour not only contributed to more employment opportunities but also helped to bring about a two-thirds increase in the average agricultural wage rate in the area between 1977 and 1978.

CONCLUSION

It may be useful to recapitulate the salient features of the UJ canal project as a self-help activity undertaken in response to a felt need of the local people. In theory, the self-help approach to development is a cost-effective means of meeting local demands for essential public services and facilities in so far as it emphasises the mobilisation and use of available local resources which otherwise might remain idle or under-utilised. In this case labour was the most important local resource input. Another aspect of the approach, that makes it attractive as an alternative strategy for local-level development, concerns the possibility of a saving to government through implementing vital development projects on a cost-sharing basis with local communities. However, the involvement of the state in self-help development is itself a highly controversial issue because of the risk that state intervention, if not properly monitored, might lead to distortions in prioritisation and resource allocation to the detriment of the well-being of the mass of the population.

In the case of the UJ canal project, this risk was minimised by the adoption of an institutional framework that allowed for popular participation in the decision-making process right down to the village level. Thus, although the state was actively involved in the planning and implementation of the project, its role was essentially limited to that of a catalyst working in close contact with local people and on the basis of adequate consultation with their leaders and representatives. This experience in fact demonstrates that, given the right conditions and institutional arrangements, the state could make an important contribution to self-help development at the local level. The successful implementation of the UJ canal project as a state-supported self-help activity may have strongly influenced the decision of the government to recommend that similar schemes should be encouraged by civil servants and local leaders in each Thana in the country.[29] This recommendation was later officially endorsed by the Government in its national development plan, wherein it was explicitly stated that state-supported self-help projects will be a major instrument for optimising local development efforts in a manner that is complementary to the national development efforts and objectives.[30]

The UJ canal project also provided evidence to support the claim that the self-help approach to development enhances self-reliance that may be necessary for meeting basic needs at the local level. As already stated, the successful implementation of the project provided the impetus for the formulation of the more comprehensive UJ Area Development Plan which evolved from mainly local initiatives. Although the plan was partly to be financed by government, the efforts by the local people themselves to initiate action and make a substantial contribution to the implementation of the plan underlines the growth of self-reliance in the project area. Some may argue that self-reliance, in the strict sense of the concept, should exclude 'outside' assistance which could make local people even more dependent on the machinery and institutions of government. While one cannot overlook this possibility, it can also be argued that the critical issue is not external assistance *per se*, but the manner in which it is provided. Where existing institutional arrangements permit effective popular participation in the making and implementation of key decisions at the local levels, government or bureaucratic involvement in local-level development planning will pose less of a threat to self-reliance. As long as government participation in local-level development activities does not lead or contribute to an erosion of confidence among local people in their own ability to take initiatives – and this has not been the experience from the UJ canal project – it should be possible to bring about a shift in the pattern of development towards greater self-reliance through state-supported self-help projects.

It is also useful in the context of this study to reflect on the potential of self-help activities to promote effective popular participation in the development process in support of basic needs satisfaction. The experience from the project suggests that certain conditions may be necessary for promoting broad-based participation in the development process. The most important is the need to decentralise planning responsibilities, including decision-making power right down to the grass-roots level. This condition was fulfilled in the project by the creation of organising sub-committees in each of the villages concerned. More importantly, perhaps, was the attempt made to ensure representation of diverse interests on those sub-committees where local-level decisions on project implementation were taken. At the same time the organisers at the district level found it necessary to maintain a strong link with the village sub-committees, on the one hand, and the central government, on the other. This was necessary to secure popular support for the mobilisation of resources at the local level and to influence higher-level authorities to take appropriate decisions pertaining to the provision of requisite technical and administrative inputs by the civil service machinery.

It also became evident from the experience of the project, that broad-based participation in local-level development activities is more likely to be fulfilled when such participation is seen to result in significant improvements in the living conditions of the mass of the population. The prospect of access to reclaimed land for the landless was a major factor in sustaining the interests of the poor in the project; this also proved to be crucial to the implementation of the UJ Area Development Plan on a self-help basis. The spread of development benefits to the poor in a form that contributes to some improvement in well-being is certainly a first step in the right direction even if the immediate impact on the longer-term goal of equalisation of socio-economic opportunities within the community may not be that substantial. Clearly, poverty alleviation in the project area would require more deliberate policies to reduce existing inequalities including major structural changes within the economy as a whole. But given the magnitude of the problem of poverty in Bangladesh and taking into account that desirable structural changes might not be realised in the short term, the promotion of popular participation in a manner that ensures a wider spread in the benefits of development assumes an even greater importance.

Finally, while the project as planned and implemented was not without its shortcomings and weaknesses as already noted, the experience demonstrates overall the possibility for improving living conditions at the local level through self-help participatory-oriented development pro-grammes. More specifically, the project has shown that it is possible to:

1 undertake self-help activities with the active involvement of the state apparatus without sacrificing popular control or influence over decision making as required for the fulfilment of poverty alleviation and basic-needs objectives;
2 mobilise local resources, often under-utilised, to support the satisfaction of basic needs without reducing present consumption levels of the economically deprived groups or the vast majority of the people; and
3 meet the basic needs of the poor at a faster rate than thought possible otherwise, through people's participation in communal projects that relate cost/sacrifice to income/benefit for all participants irrespective of social status.

In a test case of development such as Bangladesh, these possibilities constitute critical components of a strategy by which the majority of the population who are deficient in basic needs can break through the poverty–unemployment–low productivity syndrome. The challenge that has to be faced lies not only in adopting new ideas and policies but also in breaking away from the old development-inhibiting ones. Judging from the experience and outcome of the UJ canal project, self-help development seems to represent a viable means for meeting this challenge.

NOTES

1 See A.R. Khan: *The economy of Bangladesh* (Delhi, Macmillan, 1972); and S. Bose: 'The strategy of agricultural development in Bangladesh' *Development Dialogue*, vol. 1, 1973.

2 A.R. Khan: 'Poverty and inequality in rural Bangladesh' in ILO: *Poverty and landlessness in rural Asia* (Geneva, 1977).

3 J. Faaland and J.R. Parkinson: *Bangladesh: The test case of development* (London, C. Hurst and Co., 1976).

4 Government of Bangladesh: *The First Five-Year Development Plan*, 1973–78, esp. ch. 1 and 6.

5 For an illuminating description of this situation, see G.W. Chowdhury: *The last days of united Pakistan* (Bloomington, Indiana University Press, 1974).

6 For details, see R. Sobhan: *Basic democracies, works programmes and rural development in East Pakistan* (Dhaka, Bureau of Economic Research, Dhaka University, 1968).

7 *Union Parishad* is the lowest formal local government body comprising on average about 15 villages with about 1000 people in each village. The next tier is the *Thana Parishad* which comprises several Union Parishads; at present, on average, a Thana comprises an area of about 130 square miles with about 180 000 people. Above the Thana Parishad is the District or *Zilla Parishad* which is made up of a number of Thana Parishads. The entire country is administratively divided into 19 districts or Zilla, which are administered jointly by the central government and the respective Zilla Parishad.

8 Following the enactment of the Local Government Ordinance of 20 Nov., 1976.

9 'Betna' is a colloquial form of the original name 'Betrabati' which means a river following a meandering course.

10 'Beel' is the local name for a saucer-shaped submerged and, invariably, marshy area in the deltaic formation of the river.

11 One US Dollar was equal about Taka 16 at the time.

12 Under the provision of the Emergency Requisition of Property Act of 1948 which is still in force in Bangladesh.

13 The use of electricity from existing power supply to operate the low-lift pumps was estimated to cost about half that of diesel fuel which had hitherto been used for similar operations in the country.

14 See M. Muqtada: 'The seed-fertiliser technology and surplus labour in Bangladesh agriculture' *Bangladesh Development Studies*, Dhaka, Oct. 1975.

15 A 'maund' is a local weight measurement: approximately 27 maunds (mds.) is equal to 1 ton.

16 These estimates are based on a minimum output of one crop a year, but with adequate irrigation two crops a year should be possible.

17 In this connection one may recall the Chinese experience from *Tachai* where it was found necessary, in the initial period, to pay compensation to original owners of land, cattle and pigs that were taken into collective ownership by the commune – see W. Yin and L. Hua: *Tachai: The red banner* (Peking, Foreign Language Press, 1977).

18 One of six statutory bodies set up by the government in 1976 to promote regional development.

19 This was a simple meal served on the leaves of the water lily plant – the national flower

266

– to all, irrespective of rank or status to symbolise equality.

20 This was later inscribed on the commemorative plaque which was unveiled at the formal opening of the canal.

21 One 'bigha' is equal to approximately ⅓ acre. The average size of landholding in the project area was no more than the national average of 2.65 acres (i.e. about seven bighas) including homesteads.

22 The rate was between Tk70 and 100 per 1000 cubic feet of earth dug and moved. In the case of the Food for Work Programme, participants received a maund of wheat or paddy, valued at about Tk70 per 1000 cubic feet of earth dug and moved.

23 See M.K. Alamgir: 'Development through self-help – Ulashi-Jadunathpur: A review' in Q.K. Ahmad and M. Hossain (eds): *Development through self-help: Lessons from Ulashi* (Dhaka, Bangladesh Institute of Development Studies, 1978).

24 See M. Muqtada: 'The seed-fertiliser technology and surplus labour in Bangladesh agriculture', op. cit.

25 This value is based on the controlled producer price of Tk84 per *maund* at which the Government bought paddy from local farmers.

26 *Aus* and *Aman* are the two rice-crop seasons in Bangladesh, each with a duration of about 4 months; *Aus* lasts from about Mar. to June (i.e. the winter crop) and *Aman* from roughly July to Oct. (Monsoon crop).

27 'Swanivor' which means self-reliance, is the name given to a government-supported programme established in 1975 with the aim of making the country self-reliant. Focusing on the rural sector, the objective is to create an awareness among the rural population about the possibilities of local development through their own initiatives and resources. For details of the programme see M.A. Chashi: *Self-reliant rural Bangladesh: Problems and prospects* (Dhaka, Bangladesh Economic Association, 1976).

28 President's Address to the Nation, *The Bangladesh Observer*, 1 May 1977; and Ministry of Finance, *The Budget Speech of the President*, 1977, p.10.

29 This directive was initially issued in the form of a Ministry of Cabinet Affairs Circular to all 419 *Thanas* in May 1977.

30 Government of Bangladesh, Planning Commission: *The Two-Year Plan, 1978–80*, p. 139; and Ministry of Finance: *Bangladesh Economic Survey*, 1977–78, p. 234.

Index

generation of resources 24-6, 53
identifying basic needs 22-4,
 52-3
improved access to goods and
 services 26-7, 28
need for efficient distribution
 27-8, 53
psychological satisfaction and
 motivation 28, 53
Bolivia
 agrarian reform 210-11, 212
 land invasion and 209
 Confederación de Trabajadores
  Campesinos de Bolivia 200
 effect of modernisation on peasants
  193
 Ministry of Peasant Affairs 199
 peasant federation 199
 peasant organisations
  in mining areas 201
  repression of 204
 peasant protest in 195
 peasant union of Ucureña 198
 trade union support for peasant
  groups 199
Brazil
 effect of modernisation on peasants
  193
 opposition to peasant organisations
  203
 peasant leagues (Ligas Camponesas)
  198, 200, 202, 205
 Serviço de Asistença Rural peasant
  organisation programme 197

Camara, Dom Helder, Archbishop of
 Recife 197
Castro, Fidel 205
Chaco War, Latin America 195-6
Chile
 opposition to peasant organisations
  203
 peasants' organisations in mining
  areas 201
 workers' control in, 1970-3 81
China
 agrarian changes 99
  collectivisation 101-2
  confiscation of land 99
  involvement of rural masses
   100-1, 102, 103, 104, 107
  redistribution of land 99
 Agrarian Reform Law 99, 227
 'Ankang Charter' 117

anti-Japanese War, 1941-5 221
birth control 228
Civil War, 1946-9 221
Communist Party (CPC) 99, 100,
 101, 103
 decentralisation of planning 111
 discrimination against women
  223, 229
 official support for women's
  organisations 217-18, 219
 percentage of women in 226
 training of local leaders 116, 117
co-operative enterprises 70
Cultural Revolution 122, 233
 women in 234, 235
decline in birth rate 106
domestic technological capacity
 106-8
 diffusion of information and
  knowledge 107-8
 mass participation in industry
  106-7
failures and weaknesses in system
 121-2
family planning 103
 mass participation in 105-6
gains for women in 71
institutional requirements for mass
 participation 110-20, 121
 decentralised planning 110-13,
  121
 local leadership and administrative capability 114-18, 121
 'May 7 Cadre Schools' 116
Marriage Law 228
mass participation in 97-9, 100
 incentives for sustaining 118-20
 socialism and 122
National Federation of Women 219,
 220, 223, 229
 influence on marriage law and
  birth control 228
 magazine 224
 suspension during Cultural
  Revolution 234
people's communes 101, 113-14
 financial management 118
People's Liberation Army 116
policy implementation in agriculture
 103-6
 agricultural planning 112
 control of foodgrain market 104
 direction of labour into
  agriculture 103, 104-5

Guatemala
opposition to peasant organisations 203
Guinea
political influence of women in 71
youth groups in 72

Hughes, Arnold 52
resumé of chapter by 4
Huizer, Gerrit 189
resumé of chapter by 6

ICFTU 74, 75
India
co-operative ventures among peasantry 26
communal violence 66
joint industrial councils in 81-2
traditional communal organisations 65
Industrial democracy 77
context of 79
defined 77
experiences of 79
European 79-81
Third World 81-2
objectives
of 'democratic theory' approach 79
of 'humanistic psychology' school 79
of 'management' school 79
of 'participatory left' 79
popular participation levels and scope 78
relation to BNA 82-3
Institutional approach to popular participation 31-3, 48-50
alternative forms of institutions 53, 85-91
evaluation of 55
performance re definition of needs 86
performance re distribution 87
performance re growth in resources 86-7
performance re psychic satisfaction 87-8
basic community as framework for 38-9, 48
central government budgetary transfers 45-6
external technical support 46-7, 49

local public works 42-4
local taxation and levies 44-5
representative local-level decision making 39-42
craft guild and small business unions 83
institutional development and popular participation 33-8
evaluating public institutions in planning system 34-6
increasing popular participation 36-7
political dimension 33-4
institutional opposition 31-2
local government and administration 55-60
agencies permitting limited participation 59
characteristics of local authorities 56
examples of mal-administration 58
process of consultation or information 59-60
question of ability or desire to perform role 58-9
question of ability to allocate resources 57-8
question of discretion enjoyed by 58
question of representation of needy 57
See also Agrarian associations, Employers'/professional organisations,'Self-Help' associations, Trade unions, Women's organisations and Youth organisations
International Labour Organisation 83, 90
Comprehensive Employment Mission to Kenya, 1972 160
examines local-level planning 129
fights for union rights in Latin America 203
recognises plight of women in Third World 70
road programme in Kenya 25-6, 160
World Employment Conference 1, 52
Ivory Coast
distribution of nutritional and medical facilities 27
women's organisations 71

274

Venezuela 199, 200
Instituto Agrario Nacional 213
National Community Development
  Programme (CORDIPLAN) 212

WCL 74, 75
Wolf, Margery 219
Women's organisations 70-2
Women's position
  participation in decision making
    71-2
  plight in Third World 70
  women and BNA 70-1
World Bank

road programme in Kenya 25-6
World Federation of Trade Unions
  (WFTU) 74, 75

Youth organisations 72-3
  autonomous modern-sector type 73
  government/ruling party sponsored
    type 72-3
  traditional age-grade type 73
Yugoslavia
  industrial democracy in 80

Zapata, Emiliano 210